America's Role as a...
Covenant Nation

To Senator Bruce Thompson.

Donald S. Conkey
3/15

Donald S. Conkey

Published by Yawn's Publishing
198 North Street
Canton, GA 30114
www.yawnsbooks.com

Library of Congress Control Number: 2015933173

ISBN: 978-1-940395-80-7   paperback
        978-1-940395-81-4   eBook

Printed in the United States

Front and Back Covers by Adam Ellington

This Book was written to help America reconnect to its God, Jefferson's Creator and Supreme Judge of the World, and to its Spiritual roots.

Author's Note

The fundamental theme of this book – that the United States of America is a Covenant Nation and is subject to the same blessings and curses as was ancient Israel – came from nearly sixty years of persistent study of the Holy Bible and nearly forty years of comprehensive study of America's Declaration of Independence and Constitution. The belief that America's Founding Fathers were inspired men of God raised up to establish the United States of America as a Special Land of freedom and liberty is a common American belief – but associating biblical scriptures to America's Foundational Documents is less common and is the primary focus of this book. These scriptural associations reflect my personal belief that the United States of America was and is a 'Special Nation' that entered into a covenant relationship with God in 1776 - and is still subject to those same blessings and curses that both blessed and cursed ancient Israel.

Contents

Dedication

This book, *Covenant Nation*, is dedicated to the Bible's Old Testament God of Abraham, Isaac and Jacob – Thomas Jefferson's Creator and Supreme Judge of the World – and to helping America's God-fearing citizens help the United States of America achieve and fulfill its role as a **COVENANT NATION** to:

> *Reestablish God's basic principles of freedom in the world;*
> *Assist in the gathering of God's scattered people;*
> *Be an example of a free people led by God!*

John P. Foote provided the author with two poems he wrote in November 1988, one titled *BOOKS*, the other titled *TIME*, and agreed to their use in this book, one as an introductory poem, the other as a closing poem.

Donald S. Conkey

BOOKS

Have you ever thought when you saw a book
And picked it up and its challenge took
And opened it up and read it through
That you would be a different you

That you would see the world no more
The way you did the day before
Armed with knowledge you now can see
The difference between truth and duplicity

Oh some books change us little still
While others take and bend our will
And make us cry or make us laugh
Then send us down a different path

The knowledge on each written page
Is distilled from life in exchange for age
Rare truths that took a life to find
In a few short hours can be in our minds

Oh I think books are magic stuff
They smooth the corners that once were rough
They polish the facets and make them shine
On a jewel in the rough that was our mind.

Acknowledgements

The following are the main motivators in my life. There would not be enough room in this book were I to name all those individuals who have touched and enriched my life for over 86 years. But the following, in touching my life, changed my life for the better. To them I owe much.

- To God the Father, to His Son Jesus Christ, and to the Holy Ghost, they who have preserved me through years of illnesses in order to write this final book.
- To my wife Joan and our ever growing family.
- To my parents, Hal and Christine Walker Conkey.
- To Dr. W. Cleon Skousen, my mentor via his many books on the history of the United States and on the religious history of America
- To Zeldon Nelson for his encouragement to become involved in the battle to preserve America's freedoms and liberties.

Suggested Books for Building a Personal Library of Freedom

Each of the books listed below are in my personal Freedom Library and I recommend them to anyone who wants to build a personal Freedom Library. It is in these books where I learned that America is a Covenant Nation, founded on the foundation of God's "perfect laws of liberty."

1. * The King James Bible, or the Bible of your choosing
2. * America's Declaration of Independence and Constitution
3. * The Federalist Papers
4. * Thomas Paine's Common Sense
5. * The Making of America by Dr. W. Cleon Skousen – Available at www.nccs.net
6. * The 5000 Year Leap by Dr. W. Cleon Skousen – Available at www.nccs.net
7. * William J. Federer's "America's God and Country – Encyclopedia of Quotations"
8. The Real George Washington - by Perry, Allison and Skousen
9. The Real Thomas Jefferson – by Allison, Maxfield, Cook and Skousen
10. The Real Benjamin Franklin – by Allison, Skousen and Maxfield
11. The Story of Civilization, the 11 volume set by Will and Ariel Durant
12. Stand Fast by Our Constitution – by J. Reuben Clark Jr.
13. The Majesty of God's Law by Dr. W. Cleon Skousen – Amazon books
14. Frank W. Fox's 2000 book, The American Founding – Brief Edition

Preface/Introduction

Introductory commentary: As an aged citizen of the United States of America, long retired, I am just one of millions of other aging Americans who have been privileged to have lived through what has been the most prosperous period in the world's history. But I am not too old to shed a tear or two when the American Flag passes by or when I recite the pledge of allegiance or sing America's National Anthem, "The Star Spangled Banner." My heart still skips a beat when I hear or sing America's moving patriotic songs: "God Bless America," America the Beautiful," or "My Country 'Tis of Thee."

My generation is called the "greatest generation" because it was the generation that gave their lives to defend the freedoms threatened by the Axis Nations, Germany, Italy and Japan, nations led by evil leaders, leaders who would have re-enslaved the world much as the world was enslaved at the time the United States was born on April 30, 1789, the day that George Washington took the Oath of Office as the first President of the United States of America.

Shortly after World War II ended this generation had to stand against a new evil nation - Russia, an ally during the Great War but then an avowed enemy creating the Cold War that emerged openly as the Korean War in 1950, a war that never ended. My generation fought wars to preserve America's freedoms.

But while most historians laud this generation as the "greatest generation," other historians have suggested it was this generation that opened the door for the coming decadent generations. They compare this generation with two other nations that rose to great economic and political power before self-destructing from within due to moral decadence and political corruption. Those nations, ancient Israel and the Roman Empire, both had their 'golden eras' before moral decadency and political corruption destroyed both nations from within.

5

This comparison of these three nations is plausible because it was from America's 'war generation' that the next two presidents of the United States would come: popular Five-Star Commanding General Dwight D. Eisenhower and Naval Hero John F. Kennedy.

It was during these two presidencies that America began to walk up those same five steps that Edward Gibbons described in 1787 as the steps that led to the self-destruction of the Roman Empire. Those five steps of self-destruction Rome walked up, according to Gibbons, were:

1. "The undermining of the dignity and sanctity of the home, which is the basis of [all] human society."

Commentary: Consider how the sanctity of the family has been trampled on recently in the United States with the advent of new definitions for marriage and with developing babies being murdered by the legalized abortion industry. The traditional family, one man married to one woman, usually with children, is still considered by God as the moral foundation of all civilized societies.

2. "Higher and higher taxes and the spending of public monies for bread and circuses for the populace."

Commentary: With a debt nearing $18 trillion what would Gibbons have to say about nearly a third of American families living on food stamps and/or living in public housing and receiving free cell phones?

3. "The mad craze for pleasure, sports becoming every year more and more exciting and brutal."

Commentary: I wonder what Gibbons would have to say if he saw America's craze for sports today. But this sports craze is not just in America, it's a craze all around the world, in every nation.

4. "The building of gigantic armaments when the real enemy was within the decadence of the people."

Commentary: Since World War II, when America became a world power, America has spent trillions on arming itself, and other nations, while ignoring the enemy within its own borders, the growing decadence and corruption of its people and its elected leaders.

5. "The decay of religion – faith fading into mere form, losing touch with life, and becoming impotent to warn and guide the people."

Commentary: Following World War II America's pride in itself began to override dependency on the 'protective hand of God.' America began to forget what God had done for them in helping the Founders establish a new nation of freedom and by helping those Founding Fathers win a Revolutionary War or in holding the nation together during a deadly Civil War. Allowing pride of self to replace their faith and dependence on God has caused many nations to self-destruct.

Today's generation of 2014 reminds me of the words found in Judges 2:10-14, words that read:

➢ "And also all that generation were gathered unto their fathers [died]: **and there arose another generation after them, which knew not the Lord, nor yet the works which he had done for Israel.** And the children of Israel **did evil in the sight of the Lord,** and served Baalim: And **they forsook the Lord God of their fathers**, which brought them out of the land of Egypt, and followed other gods, of the gods of the people that were round about them, and bowed themselves unto them, **and provoked the Lord to anger.** And they forsook the Lord, and served Baal and Ashtaroth. And the anger of the Lord was hot against Israel, and he delivered them into the hands of spoilers that spoiled them, **and he sold them into the hands of their enemies** round about, **so that they could not any longer stand before their enemies.**"

These verses also remind me of the words found in Jeremiah 6:17-19, words that read:

➢ "Also I set watchmen over you, saying, Hearken to the sound of the trumpet. But they said, **We will not hearken.** Therefore hear, ye nations, and know, O congregation, what is among them. Hear, O earth: behold, **I will bring**

7

evil upon this people, even the fruit of their thoughts, because they have not hearkened unto my words, nor to my law, but rejected it."

Jeremiah's words caused me to ask: "where are the watchmen today, who is warning America about the evils that befall a nation when they reject God's Word and God's laws?"

America has been blessed with 'watchmen' who have warned America about the coming calamities, but few heed the warnings. The scriptures are full of these warnings as are the words of those American leaders who looked ahead of their time. A few examples will suffice:

President Calvin Coolidge, during his watch in the 1920s, warned America with these words: "We do not need more material development, **we need more spiritual development**. We do not need more intellectual power, **we need more moral power.** We do not need more knowledge, **we need more character**. We do not need more government, **we need more culture**. We do not need more law, **we need more religion**. We do not need more of the things that are seen, **we need more of the things that are unseen.** It is on that side of life that it is desirable to put the emphasis at the present time. If that side is strengthened, the other side will take care of itself. **It is that side which is the foundation of all else. If the foundation be firm, the superstructure will stand."**

Roger Babson, 1875-1967, known as an investment guru and founder of Babson College in Massachusetts, is quoted as saying **"What this country needs more than anything else is old-fashioned family prayer."** Yes, our greatest need is a return to the old-fashioned, time-tested verities. In a talk given in 1973 Ezra Taft Benson, 1899-1994, who served as the United States Secretary of Agriculture under President Dwight D. Eisenhower from 1953 to 1960 and as the 13th President of The Church of Jesus Christ of Latter-day Saints, has provided America with the answer to its current moral dilemma with these words: **"The spectacle of**

a nation praying is more awe-inspiring, more powerful, than the explosion of an atomic bomb. The force of prayer is greater than any possible combination of man-controlled powers, because prayer is man's greatest means of tapping the resources of God." The Founding Fathers accepted this eternal verity. Do we? Will America today?

Question: Has the moral fiber of America improved during the past forty years?
Answer: No. There are two primary reasons for the continuing decline in the moral character of America. These two reasons are both addressed in this book.

The first reason: The rising generations in America today, as in the days of the Judges, "know not the works of the Founding Fathers, nor the work of God in creating America as a Covenant Nation." And I would also add that few even know God - both by cunning design.

The second reason: Today the Christian religion, the very foundation upon which America was founded, is badly fractured and does not speak with one voice to America's moral issues today. This is in part due to the growing efforts by our government to silence that once powerful moral voice of America – its churches. Those who are silencing America's religious voices have used the federal courts to ban the Bible, the Word of God, in America's educational class rooms and to totally ignore the fact that America grew into adulthood, **becoming a mighty nation on the breast milk of the Judeo/Christian Bible.**

Question: What does this book want to accomplish?
Answer: This book wants Americans to know: 1. that America is a covenant nation; 2. how America became a covenant nation; 3. why America became a covenant nation; and 4. that America, as a covenant nation is subject to those same blessings, curses and

9

wraths that befell ancient Israel. This book also tells who God covenanted with and explains why He covenanted with America's Founding Fathers. It also explains that the Bible was the Founding Fathers 'text-book' for restoring and implementing God's "perfect law of liberty" in America and it also shows how influential the Bible was in the creation of America and its Foundational Documents. This book also addresses that old truism that if you don't know where you came from it is difficult for you to chart a course for your future. It is also important for America's modern-day minutemen to understand that when they put on their 'whole armor of God' that they will be able to thwart and repel the fiery darts of the adversary, the one who would destroy America and its freedoms and liberties given it by the author of all liberty.

Question: What is the source of the material in this book?
Answer: This book is a brief review of many thousands of pages of history: American history, world history, religious history, plus those religious history books Ezekiel made mention of in Ezekiel 37:16-17:

> ➢ "Moreover, thou son of man, take thee one stick, and write upon it, For **Judah** (the Bible), and for the children of Israel his companions: then take another stick, and write upon it, For **Joseph**, the stick of Ephraim (Book of Mormon*), and for all the house of Israel his companions: And join them one to another into one stick; and they shall become one in thine hand."

I then read and pondered the writings of America's Founding Fathers, including America's Foundational Documents, its Declaration of Independence and Constitution - many, many times.
*****Commentary:** While it is universally accepted by the Christian community that the 'stick of Judah' is the Bible, this is not the case with the 'stick of Ephraim.' There continues to be disagreement over what the 'stick of Ephraim' is but for those millions who have read the Book of Mormon it is Another Testament of Jesus Christ, a book

written by the descendants of Lehi, that Lehi who was a contemporary to Jeremiah and Ezekiel at the time Judah was destroyed and the Jews were taken captive in 586 BC. Lehi and his family became one of those **remnant** families the Bible refers to from time to time, families God has used to preserve His Gospel following the destruction of Jerusalem and Judah. Lehi carried a copy of the Law (the Bible), through Isaiah, with them to the shores of America around 600 BC. Nineteen chapters of Isaiah are recorded in the first two chapters of the Book of Mormon. Regarding these **remnant** families we read in Isaiah and Jeremiah these words:

➤ "And it shall come to pass in that day, **that the remnant of Israel, and such as are escaped of the house of Jacob (Judah),** shall no more again stay upon him that smote them; but shall stay upon the Lord, the Holy One of Israel, in truth." (Isaiah 10:20)

➤ **"And I will gather the remnant of my flock out of all countries whither I have driven them**, and will bring them again to their folds; and they shall be fruitful and increase. And I will set up shepherds over them which shall feed them: and they shall fear no more, nor be dismayed, neither shall they be lacking, saith the Lord." (Jeremiah 23:3-4)

Question: Does this book associate America with ancient Israel's self-destruction?
Answer: Yes, very strongly. As one studies the Bible and the prophets and associates its words and the words of the prophets with the creation of America, one will see a strong correlation between what happened to ancient Israel after they rejected God as their lawgiver and then asked for a king **"to be like other nations."** (1 Samuel 8) One also sees a strong correlation between America's moral decline and the fall and self-destruction of the great Roman Empire.

Question: Is there a way for America to preserve its freedoms without first self-destructing from within – as did the ancient Israelites in their day, and the great Roman Empire in their day?
Answer: Yes. Both Babson and Benson provided America with the answer – prayer, getting America down on its knees and praying to God to help them to preserve America as a Covenant Nation. And as Benson noted: **"The United States of America has been great because it has been free.** It has been free because it has trusted in God and was founded upon the principles of freedom set forth in the Word of God. **This nation has a spiritual foundation.** To me, this land has a prophetic history."
Commentary: America's Founding Fathers may have seen their efforts in establishing America as a special land, even a Covenant Nation, as ancient Israel may have seen themselves anciently in these words that Isaiah spoke regarding **"the Lord setting his hand a second time to recover the remnant of his people"** in their new land. These are those revelatory words of Isaiah: "And it shall come to pass in that day, that the Lord shall set his hand again the second time to recover the remnant of his people, which shall be left, from Assyria, and from Egypt, and from Pathros, and from Cush, and from Elam, and from Shinar, and from Hamath, and from the islands of the sea. **And he shall set up an ensign for the nations**, and shall assemble the outcasts of Israel, and **gather together the dispersed of Judah** from the four corners of the earth. The envy also of Ephraim shall depart, and the adversaries of Judah shall be cut off: Ephraim shall not envy Judah, and Judah shall not vex Ephraim." (Isaiah 11:11-13)

Question: Will America's Constitution be completely destroyed?
Answer: No, but it will likely be badly battered before it becomes pristine again. But Americans of all faiths are beginning to come to its rescue and as more Americans come to the Constitution's defense it will survive, and become stronger than ever and America will survive

to fulfill all three of the goals that every covenant nation has been given throughout history. These goals being:

To establish God's principles of freedom back into the world;

To assist in the gathering of God's scattered people;

To be an example of a free people led by God!

Three worthy goals for a free people living in America, a Covenant Nation - established by God!

A Final Question: What inspired this book titled *Covenant Nation*? Answer: The impression to write this book came while reading three verses in the Book of James, verses 4 and 5 and verse 25. The words "If any of you lack wisdom…" in James 1:4-5 (I certainly lacked wisdom); and the words in James 1:25 that read "the perfect law of liberty" caused me to wonder what was causing America to reject the biblical foundation that America had been built upon and to cause the cracks in its foundation to begin to enlarge.

Then as I watched the small cracks enlarge and begin to endanger the entire structure I began to search the Bible for answers. I asked myself: had this happened in other nations before? I found my answer in 1 Samuel. The cracks greatly enlarged in ancient Israel's foundation when the elders of Israel went to Samuel and said to Samuel:

➢ "Behold, thou art old, and thy sons walk not in thy ways: **now make us a king to judge us like all the nations.**" (1 Samuel 8:5)

This chapter in Samuel triggered this book – two covenant nations, both raised up by God, both blessed beyond their wildest dreams, and now both turning their backs on the God who had blessed them for several centuries. It is a fascinating story to follow. Israel, after rejecting their God, after being led by kings into idolatry, were then scattered and/or destroyed; America, being raised up by God, now wanting to reject Him who greatly blessed America.

13

Closing commentary: From time to time the reader will note the author has used the same scripture in more than one location. This reuse of specific scriptures is on purpose because there are certain scriptures that need to be re-emphasized from time to time, along with those defining moments in the history of the United States that need to be strongly emphasized more than once - and are in this book.

Donald S. Conkey – November 2014

thus making America God's latest and newest nation, America, a "Covenant Nation" – the new nation that would soon win a Revolutionary War with his help and then begin to:

> ➤ "Proclaim liberty throughout all the land (world) unto all the (enslaved) inhabitants thereof." (Leviticus 25:10)

America was able to proclaim this liberty to the world because they were living and obeying God's foundational laws of freedom and liberty. They were living free as a nation led by God.

The Major Historical Events leading up to July 4, 1776
Event # 1

Question: What was the first of these major events in this time period?

Answer: The search for self-rule in the British Isles: 55 BC to 1300 AD, that period of time from 55 BC, the year the Romans invaded England, until about 1300 AD. This period is the longest period of the five historical events reviewed. It is included because it shows a stark contrast between several forms of governments. Event # 1 is divided into four smaller time periods and represents the evolvement of government over this time period. These four smaller time periods are:

Period # 1: That period between 55 BC and approximately 400 AD. This is the period when the Romans conquered, occupied, and ruled the "island tributary" the Romans called Britain. The people were subject to the **Roman Civil Law** and were ruled by delegated leaders sent by the Roman leaders in Rome. Roman Civil Law is not self-rule law.

Period # 2: That period between 400 AD and about 590 AD. After the Roman soldiers were pulled out of Britain to defend Rome against their new northern invaders, the native Celts were left to rule themselves. Soon the Celts were fighting amongst themselves, and one Celtic King named Kent, in Southern England, found his people being attacked by the Picks of Scotland. To protect his tribes Kent called for help from the Anglo-Saxons in Scandinavia, tribes then known for their ferocious fighting skills. The Anglo-Saxons were led by two brothers known as Hengist and Horsa. They brought their soldiers to Britain, beat back the Picks, but when Kent asked them to leave they refused. Eventually the Angle-Saxons ruled over most of Britain.

Commentary: The dominant tribe of the Anglo-Saxons was the Engels, or Yinglings. This name of Britain was changed to Yingling-land, or Engel-land, later to become known as England.

Period # 3: This was the period between 590 AD and 1066 AD. This is the period the English were converted to Christianity by missionaries sent by Gregory I from Rome. The Anglo-Saxons remained the ruling tribes and in the process of being taught Christianity they were taught Latin so they could read the Bible. As they read the Bible, especially the laws found in the books recorded by Moses, they realized their own traditional laws were recorded in the biblical books of Exodus, Leviticus, Numbers, and Deuteronomy. The Anglo-Saxon's King Alfred, who later recorded the biblical laws in the Anglo-Saxon language, wrote, "The law was first revealed in the Hebrew tongue." The student can read about the Anglo-Saxons in Turner's five volume set titled *History of the Anglo-Saxons*. During this time period the Anglo-Saxons perfected their "people's government" under King Alfred, 877 AD to 899 AD, and flourished as a free people. Their pattern of government followed the patterns established by Moses for the Israelites. The following eight items highlight this Anglo-Saxon period.

- Any powers granted by the people to their rulers were specifically described and strictly limited in scope.
- The English Anglo-Saxons considered themselves a commonwealth of freemen who had "inalienable rights" that could not be taken away by their rulers.
- Government was by freely elected representatives to their

general assembly. No law or assessment of taxes could be imposed upon the people unless they or their representatives had consented to it.

- The king was surrounded by a council of wise men called the Witenagemot (or Witen) who could remove the king if he was incompetent or did not abide the law. The ruler was not above the law.

- The people were divided into small manageable groups of one hundred families which constituted a community. They were further divided into groups of ten families under an elected "tithingman." Each group was held responsible for the good conduct of its members. Five of these groups constituted a "vil" or village of fifty families and the elected leader was called a vil-man. Two vils comprised a hundred families which then elected a "Hundredman" and this was the model unit for the Anglo-Saxon community. The elected leader of each group was both the judge and the administrator of the unit, and in time of war he served as the military commander over his group.

- Anglo-Saxon law also gave strong emphasis to local self-government with very strict limitations on the powers given to the elected leaders.

- The entire code of justice was based on "reparation to the victim" for any injury to his person or property. God's law was enforced with firmness and fairness. However, any person charged with a crime could demand a trial by a jury of his peers. Some historians believe the jury system can be traced back to King Alfred and the Anglo-Saxons.

- Under Alfred the Great there was freedom of religion which required separation of church and state and a spirit of tolerance between people of different faiths.

Period # 4: That period of time between 1066 AD, when the English were conquered by the Normans of France, and that period when the English people forced King John, with sword in hand, to sign the Magna Charta in 1215 AD. The English remembered their earlier traditions and longed for the freedom they had enjoyed under King Alfred, and when the Normans began to demand more and more they rebelled, a pattern later followed by the colonists in 1776. For a more in-depth reading of this interesting period of history read chapter 19 of Dr. W. Cleon Skousen's book, *The Majesty of God's Law*, pages 296 – 315.

Question: What was the second major event in this time period?
Answer: The Renaissance in Europe – 1300 to 1500 AD:
Beginning in the early 1300s the Europeans began to awaken from a long period of cultural darkness and religious stagnation. This led to that exciting period now known as the **Renaissance**. It spread throughout Europe beginning in the early 1300s, and continued through much of the 1500s.

The Renaissance helped develop a new spirit of individual thought and independence in Europe. It influenced political thinking and hastened the breakup of the religious monopoly that had dominated Europe for over a thousand years, a period some still refer to as the Dark Ages. And it encouraged Europeans to seek more freedom in all areas of their life, including more freedom of religious thought.

It was during this period, in the early 1400s, that Johannes Gutenberg invented the printing press. This invention would fuel the spirit of governmental and religious reform. This reform spirit spread across Western Europe like a prairie fire. The Renaissance opened up new avenues for educational pursuits as the number of universities more than tripled during this period of time.

Near the end of this period, in 1492, a man known as Columbus obtained permission, and funds, from King Ferdinand and Queen Isabella of Spain to find a shorter route to Asia. Columbus took his ships westward out across the Atlantic Ocean and eventually landed on an island he named San Salvador, an event that led to the discovery of what is known today as the western hemisphere.

Question: What was the third major event in this time period?
Answer: The 'Reformation:
The Bible was one of the first books published with Gutenberg's new printing press. The printing of the Bible played a major role in the **Reformation** that would begin with Martin Luther in Germany in 1517. As the number of people able to read the Bible in its original Hebrew and Greek text grew, so grew the Reformation movement. These new scholars searched the Bible and found what they believed to be major changes from the theology practiced in the days of Christ and his apostles.

The Reformation movement created the events that led to a vast migration of religiously persecuted Europeans to America, beginning at Plymouth Rock in 1620. (The landing at Jamestown in 1607 was an economic adventure, not a religious refuge.) This Reformation opened the people's eyes to a better way of life, both for them individually and for their families. It created a stronger desire to have their rulers more answerable to the people and that political power should be derived from the governed, as had been practiced by their Anglo-Saxon ancestors.

As the Reformation heated up more people joined in the demand for greater religious freedom. Political conflicts grew. Reprisals were common and the new faith groups were often forced to leave their home lands to protect themselves and their families.

The better known leaders of the Reformation were Martin Luther, John Calvin, John Knox, and John Wycliffe. It was an explosive period of time, often deadly, especially for the people with new religious beliefs as those who would not recant their beliefs were often burned at the stake.

It was also a time for strong-willed and determined people to prepare for their soon to begin migrations to America where they would find a land where they could worship God according to their own conscience, free from the harsh treatments of the ruling governments often controlled by the state religion in Europe. These were the people who would soon begin to populate the new land Columbus found in 1492. That migration would begin as a trickle, but would soon grow into a mighty flood that continues down to our day, with a not so **"silent invasion"** now taking place across the southern borders of the United States. And there are those who see this **"silent invasion"** of children from Central America as a fulfillment of a prophecy made by Isaiah that reads:

> ➢ "Thus saith the Lord God, Behold, I will lift up mine hand to the Gentiles, and set up my standard to the people: **and they shall bring thy sons in their arms, and thy daughters shall be carried upon their shoulders. And kings shall be thy nursing fathers, and their queens thy nursing mothers:** they shall bow down to thee with their face toward the earth, and lick up the dust of thy feet; and thou shalt know that I am the Lord: for they shall not be ashamed that wait for me." (Isaiah 49:22-23)

An example of a people persecuted during this period would be the Huguenots. In 1598 the King of France issued the Edict of Nante. It gave the Huguenots freedom to worship in 100 French communities. However when Louis XIV became king he repealed this Edict and 200,000 Huguenots fled France for their lives. Eventually many of these people migrated to America. The Huguenots, Puritans, Pilgrims, and others like them, were the better educated. They were also the craftsmen that would help build a new America a few years later.

And America, sparsely populated, with its fertile and heavily forested lands, was waiting. It was then a land inhabited by Native American tribes. Once the immigration began, and the immigrants became organized into colonies, with their own militia, these scattered tribes could not organize sufficiently to stop or prevent this mass inbound migration that would soon inundate their tribal lands, and change their nomadic way of life forever.

Question: What was the fourth major event in this time period?
Answer: The preparation of America for the influx of those religiously persecuted in Europe who wanted to find a place where they could worship God according to their own conscience.

America was inhabited by a tribal people. Prior to 1607 the western hemisphere was inhabited by a tribal people. Their descendants are known today as Native Americans. Archeologists continue to find evidence of their ancestors' more centralized governments, many now lost and long forgotten. Some of these civilizations existed for centuries while others simply vanished from the pages of history. The lost cities of one civilization, the Mayans, are now being excavated in the jungles of Central America and provide evidence of a high level centralized government and civilization.

This newly acquired evidence indicates these ancient people were well educated and well versed in the sciences, including the "science of good government." Recorded evidence show they studied astronomy and had created a perfect calendar. Other evidence indicates they were able to perform bloodless brain surgery, and were skilled builders, using a high level of technology to build numerous well designed and functioning cities over vast areas of the western hemisphere. Concrete roads even connected their cities.

But when those civilizations vanished, often due to civil wars, the survivors reorganized themselves into tribal governments, became nomadic and lived off the land. They lost their skills and the will to bring the tribes together under the rule of a larger more central government. These were the people who inhabited America when the first Europeans arrived in Jamestown in 1607.

Historical references to other civilizations that drifted from strong centralized governments to weaker tribal governments often include the Israelites. For many centuries, under the judges, the Israelites were organized under a centralized government governed by God's "perfect law of liberty" given them by Moses. But like many other civilizations, they began to self-destruct at the end of Israel's Golden Age under Saul, David and Solomon. These historical records strongly suggest several of these ancient governments had been created with divine assistance but then self-destructed, as had others, because of their failure to live the divine law their government had been founded on. In 721 BC, two hundred fifty-four (254) years after Israel divided in 975 BC, ten of the twelve tribes were taken into captivity, were scattered and soon lost from the pages of history. The books of 2 Kings and Lamentations provide a powerful story of how a once prosperous nation had self-destructed after being led into idolatry by their leaders.

America's Native Americans were well concealed from the people of Europe because, as some believe, the Lord was holding America in reserve as a place to re-establish, or restore, His **"perfect law of liberty"** first given to Moses on Mt. Sinai, and practiced by the Israelites for several centuries before demanding a king to rule over them as other nations had. (1 Samuel 8) American history often describes the 'cleansing of America's Native Americans' as tragic – and it was tragic, very tragic. The "Trail of Tears" of the Cherokee Nation was a tragic display of raw political power, not unlike that which God laid upon the Canaanite nations in ancient times.

In Deuteronomy 9:4-5 one learns why and how God intervenes when a nation becomes wicked. Moses, speaking to the Israelites prior to their crossing the River Jordan, led by Joshua, and destroying the nations in Canaan, said:

> ➤ "Speak not thou in thine heart, after that the Lord thy God hath cast them out from before thee saying, For my righteousness the Lord hath brought me in to possess this land: but for the wickedness of these nations the Lord doth drive them out from before thee.... but for the wickedness of these nations the Lord thy God doth drive them out from

24

before thee, and that he may perform the word which the Lord sware unto thy fathers, Abraham, Isaac, and Jacob."

Commentary: Many today wonder: could this be a reason the cleansing of America was so tragic for America's Native Americans?

Question: What was the fifth time period leading up to 1776 and today?

Answer: The four time periods between 1607 and today.

This time period spans 397 plus years. From our perspective in the 21st century, looking back nearly 400 years seems like an eternity. But from history's perspective 400 years is relatively short, similar to the 400-plus years the Israelites were held in bondage in Egypt.

However, this time period of American history is better understood when it is divided into four shorter but very distinct periods. Events in each of the shorter periods were prerequisites to the events that would shortly follow. These shorter time periods are:

- **The first time period:** those 156 years between 1607, Jamestown, and the signing of the Treaty of Paris in 1763 ending the French-Indian Wars.
- **The second time period:** those 13 explosive years between the signing of the Treaty of Paris and July 4, 1776, when the Declaration of Independence was signed by 56 determined and brave men.
- **The third time period:** the 11-year span between July 4, 1776, and September 17, 1787. These were the Revolutionary War and post-war years: adjustments and compromises had to be made by the 13 states if their experiment as a free nation was to survive.
- **The fourth time period:** the years between the signing of the Constitution in 1787 and 2014.

Question: What were the major events during the first 156 years after the arrival of the Pilgrims at Plymouth Rock in 1607?

Answer: The 156-year period, 1607 – 1763, was a period of preparing America for what lay ahead, and putting into place the necessary people and nations so that the new nation of America could be conceived and then born as a covenant nation. The significant events of this time period would be:

- The first two of these four time periods were the 169 years, 1607 – 1776, the time period America needed to prepare for that historic day of July 4, 1776, when the colonists declared and then celebrated their independence from Great Britain. There were no guidelines for creating a new untested form of government, but the Founding Fathers believed this was their destiny, and that God was their mentor. These were the years needed to bring together the right combination of people, the right political atmosphere, and the right leaders who had the skills and desire to separate from Great Britain. But when the separation came it was far from unanimous. The Colonial Loyalists, those who supported the English king, did not support the separation movement. Many Loyalists fought with the British, giving support to the British and after the war moved to Canada where they could maintain their loyalty to the king.

The major events between 1607 and 1763 include:
- The migration of thousands of Europeans to America, to a land located between the Atlantic coast and the mountains a few hundred miles to the west. These were the people that would provide the base population of nearly four million people (Israel had 3 million), from which they would draw their militia to wage their war of independence.
- Organizing four million people into thirteen colonies.
- Surveying the land and establishing land records.
- The consolidation of England, Wales, and Scotland into one united government: Great Britain in 1707 AD. This

consolidation was necessary for the colonists to be under the rule of only one government. Great Britain was the "mother-land" for most of the colonists. This created a strong bond between them, a bond that proved very hard to break.

- The four French-Indian Wars fought between 1689 and 1763 were major events in the formational history of America. The most important of these four wars was fought between 1754 and 1763. This war ended with the signing of the Treaty of Paris. Losing, France ceding all their Canadian lands, and all their lands east of the Mississippi River over to Great Britain. Britain also obtained the Territory of Florida from Spain via the Treaty of Paris. France had felt a need for an ally during this war, and to entice Spain to become that ally France gave Spain New Orleans and all French territory west of the Mississippi River. Now Britain controlled all of America east of the Mississippi River. This set the stage for the approaching conflicts between King George and British America. Those conflicts began almost immediately after this war ended.

- The first real attempt to bring the colonies together occurred in June of 1754 when leaders from seven colonies met in Albany, New York. These leaders from seven colonies met at the request of Benjamin Franklin who felt the colonies needed to unite for self-defense against the French and the Native Americans. Franklin had prepared a "Plan of Union" for the colonies to unite under. But neither the British nor the Iroquois Indians gave it much credence. This "Plan of Union" surfaced later as the foundation for the Articles of Confederation in 1776.

Donald S. Conkey

The Chronology of Events
Leading up to the signing of the Declaration of Independence

Commentary: This section describes the key events in America's struggle for independence and the key people leading the drive for separation from England that led to America's Declaration of Independence signed on July 4, 1776, the day America first became a **'spiritually and politically covenanted nation.'**

The chronology of this period is included because those fighting in our 21st century to preserve America's freedoms must realize that freedom, once gained, must be preserved and protected; that the freedom America has enjoyed for so many years did not come without major effort and challenges. Americans must also understand that their freedoms will not be preserved without similar challenges and without mighty effort on their part while utilizing all of the technology available to them in today's cyber world. Then, after doing all they can they must turn to Jefferson's 'Creator' and 'Supreme Judge of the World,' He whom Jefferson referred to in the Declaration of Independence as America's God, and the Founders God of Abraham, Isaac and Jacob, in mighty prayer and fasting.

Question: What were the major events that occurred between 1763 and 1776, the thirteen years of frustration and bitterness?
Answer: The events that shaped this time period began as soon as the Treaty of Paris was signed. King George III needed money, lots of money, to pay for his wars with France. His attempt to raise this needed money through new taxes from the colonists created so much resentment in the colonies that it ignited the Revolutionary War. The King was uncompromising and Parliament continued to pass tax laws that infuriated the colonists. Some laws even favored English companies, companies that members of Parliament had vested interests in. These laws fed the flames of resentment. The king's attitude

28

created a rebellious spirit among the colonists, and this rebellious spirit triggered the Revolutionary War.

The major events of this thirteen year period include:

- **1763:** The British stationed troops in the colonies.
- **March 1765:** The British Parliament passed its infamous Stamp Act. These were taxes on deeds, mortgages, liquor licenses, law licensees, playing cards, almanacs and newspapers to raise money to support the British army stationed in America.
- **October 1765:** The **Stamp Act Congress met in New York** and declared that Stamp Act taxes should not be collected without the people's consent.
- **1766:** Colonial resistance to these taxes forced the British Parliament to repeal the Stamp Act.
- **1767:** The **British Parliament** then placed import taxes on several items imported into the colonies.
- **1770:** Again, because the colonists considered such taxes illegal and refused to pay them, the British Parliament repealed all but one of those duties – the tax on imported tea.
- **March 5, 1770:** This was the date when five colonial patriots were killed by British soldiers. This event is known as the **Boston Massacre.** These five were the first casualties of America's Revolutionary War.
- **Early 1773:** the **British Parliament** passed the **Tea Act** to help the East India Company, a British trading company, out of its growing financial problems (Does this sound familiar today?). This act enabled the company to sell tea in America at a lower price and in effect it created a tea monopoly for this British company.
- **December 6, 1773:** This was the date of the famous **Boston Tea Party.** About 100 colonists, disguised as Indians, raided three British ships in the Boston Harbor and emptied 342 chests of tea into the Boston Harbor in order to avoid paying

29

the British tax on tea. The harsh British response unified the colonists and brought them together in their movement towards independence. Samuel Adams, known as the Father of the American Revolution, was heavily involved in this event.

- **1774:** The British Parliament passed a new set of laws and taxes that were dubbed the **Intolerable Acts.** These Acts closed the Boston Harbor and limited the authority of the Massachusetts legislature. These Acts solidified the colonists' opposition to British rule and led to the **First Continental Congress** which met between September 5 and October 26, 1774. Representatives from twelve colonies were involved in America's First Continental Congress. Rhode Island was not represented.

- **1774:** In response to the growing issues imposed on the colonists by the king, Thomas Jefferson wrote his accusatory pamphlet, *A Summary View of the Rights of British America.* This pamphlet spread quickly to all parts of the colonies, even across the Atlantic and into the hands of the king and the English Parliament. While this pamphlet infuriated the king it made Thomas Jefferson a prominent leader and household word in the independence movement. The issues he outlined in this pamphlet would later become a large segment of the Declaration of Independence he would write in June of 1776.

- **February 1775:** The English Parliament declared Massachusetts in open rebellion allowing British soldiers to shoot rebel colonists on sight.

- **April 18, 1775:** On this date 700 British soldiers began a march to Concord, Massachusetts, to capture the rebel leaders. This is the night Paul Revere took his legendary "the British are coming" ride.

- **April 19, 1775:** Seventy minutemen learned of the march and met the British Redcoats near Lexington, Massachusetts, where eight minutemen were killed and ten wounded. As the

Redcoats returned to Boston the minutemen fired on them and killed 250 British soldiers with 90 minutemen killed in the ensuing skirmish battles.

- **May 1775:** The Second Continental Congress met in Philadelphia, Pennsylvania.

- **June 14, 1775:** The Continental Congress established a Continental Army.

- **June 15, 1775:** George Washington was named Commander-in-Chief of the Continental Army by the Continental Congress.

- **June 17, 1775:** Breed's Hill, often referred to as Bunker's Hill, was the scene of the bloodiest battle of the Revolutionary War. A thousand British soldiers and 400 colonists were killed.

- **July 3, 1775:** George Washington took command of the Continental Army near Boston.

- **July 1775:** Most delegates to the Second Continental Congress wanted to maintain their loyalty to the king and in a last-ditch stand they had John Dickerson petition the king to hear their complaints as they reaffirmed their loyalty to him. The petition, known as the colonist's **"Olive Branch Petition"** was ignored by the king.

- **August 13, 1775:** King George III declared all the colonies in rebellion and soon after closed all British ports to overseas trade.

- **January 1776:** Thomas Paine wrote his sensational and famous pamphlet titled **"Common Sense,"** a pamphlet that stirred the passions of the colonists for separation.

- **March 17, 1776:** British troops abandoned Boston for safer ports in Canada.

- **June 7, 1776:** Richard Henry Lee of Virginia introduced a resolution of independence in the Second Continental Congress. It began with "that these United Colonies are, and of right ought to be, free and independent States…"

- **June 1776:** The Congress, in case Lee's resolution was adopted, appointed a committee composed of five men. This committee assigned Thomas Jefferson to draft a formal "Declaration of Independence."
- **June 1776:** Thomas Jefferson spent seventeen nights drafting his now famous Declaration of Independence, with fifteen of those nights devoted to drafting the first two paragraphs of that initial document. When he completed his draft Jefferson submitted it to the committee who made several changes. The committee then submitted the document to the full congress where it was debated for several days, with about a quarter of what Jefferson had submitted cut out with 86 total changes, most dealing with the slavery issue that Jefferson had wanted to address in this initial document. The southern states strongly opposed any language dealing with slavery be included in the Declaration of Independence.
- **July 2, 1776:** The Continental Congress adopted Richard Lee's resolution of independence.
- **July 4, 1776:** The Continental Congress adopted the Declaration of Independence. John Hancock signed it on July 4 along with the secretary but the final signing was in early August, 1776.

The United States of America had been conceived. America's turbulent pregnancy would last eleven long years with its birth on April 30, 1789, the day George Washington took his Oath of Office as the first President of the United States of America – born as a Covenant Nation.

Chapter Two

The Bible's Influence in Creating America

Opening commentary: Understanding the Bible's role in the lives of America's Founding Fathers and in the lives of America's patriots is key to understanding how and why the United States of America was established as a covenant nation and how it will be preserved, after being humbled, to continue its major role as a covenant nation, to proclaim liberty throughout the world and help prepare the world for the gathering of the scattered people of ancient Israel.

Question: What is the Judeo/Christian Bible?
Answer: The Judeo/Christian Bible is God's 'text book' for preparing man for mortal life and eternal salvation. It is the Bible that explains that God created the "heavens and the earth" and then explains why the earth was created. It is in the Bible where God has recorded the Ten Commandments, those foundational principles that all civilized nations are founded on. It is in the Bible where God explains about the good and the evil in the world and why man was given agency to make choices between the good and evil in the world. It is in the Bible where God had Moses record the blessings and the curses that individuals and nations are subject to when individuals and nations ignore and disobey His laws, statutes and commandments. This book also provides vivid examples of how the wrath of God has come down on individuals and nations when they ignore the laws of civility. And it's not usually a pretty picture.

The Bible also explains that there was a war in heaven led by Lucifer, also known as Satan and the Devil, on one side and how he lost that war and was then cast out of heaven down to this earth where he and his minions have continued their war on mortal men and women by enticing them to follow him even as he enticed Eve to partake of the forbidden fruit causing mankind's fall. (Revelation 12)

It is in the Bible where man learns of God's efforts to create a covenant people, a people who would be an example to the world of how a nation of free people, led by God and living His laws and commandments, prospered and were a happy people. It is in the Bible where it explains how God deals with Abraham's dysfunctional family, a family little different in many ways of all families in the world – by being patient with them as they/we struggle to find their/our way in a constantly changing world; in a world where Satan's role is to entice man to reject God's laws and those commandments that allow man to live free and become prosperous.

The Bible is the book that every human being should study and ponder on a daily basis; it is the book that Americans should better understand if they are going to preserve the freedoms that America implemented on June 30, 1789 when George Washington took the Oath of Office as the first President of these United States. Washington is believed to have opened his Bible to Chapter 28 in Deuteronomy, laid his left hand on those words, raised his right hand to the square and took the Oath of Office that is found in Article II, section 1, paragraph nine of the Constitution and then added four words: **"so help me God."** This act by Washington declared that America was indeed a politically covenanted nation – a nation willing to live according to "the Laws of Nature and of Nature's God" and become, as a nation, subject to the same blessings, curses and wraths of God as was ancient Israel.

These words uttered by Christ, as recorded in Matthew 25:34, strongly reinforce this belief:

> "… Then shall the King say unto them on his right hand, Come, ye blessed of my Father, inherit the kingdom prepared for you from the foundation of the world:"

Few know or remember that the Bible is the foundational scriptures for three of the world's great religions – Christianity, Islam and Judaism - each tracing their lineage back to Abraham and to the covenant God made with Abraham when he was ninety and nine years old. The connection between Christianity and Judaism is obvious to Bible students. However, the connection to Islam is less obvious to Christians unless they understand that Abraham's oldest son was Ishmael the son of Hagar. Hagar was Abraham's Egyptian concubine, Sarah his lawful wife. When Isaac was born to Sarah in her old age she became jealous of Ishmael and asked Abraham to ban Hagar and Ishmael. This was the beginning of a family feud that has continued to our day, all because of these two sons of Abraham. Abraham banned Hagar and Ishmael but not before receiving these powerful covenant words from God regarding both Isaac and Ishmael, words that read:

> "And God said unto Abraham, As for Sarai thy wife, thou shalt not call her name Sarai, but Sarah shall her name be. And I will bless her, and give thee a son also of her: yea, I will bless her, and **she shall be a mother of nations;** kings of people shall be of her. Then Abraham fell upon his face, and laughed, and said in his heart, Shall a child be born unto him that is an hundred years old? and shall Sarah, that is ninety years old, bear? **And Abraham said unto God, O that Ishmael might live before thee! And God said, Sarah thy wife shall bear thee a son indeed; and thou shalt call his name Isaac: and I will establish my covenant with him for an <u>everlasting covenant,</u>** and with his seed after him. **And as for Ishmael, I have heard thee: Behold, I have blessed him, and will make him fruitful,**

and will multiply him exceedingly; twelve princes shall he beget, and I will make him a great nation. But **my covenant will I establish with Isaac**, which Sarah shall bear unto thee at this set time in the next year. And he left off talking with him, and God went up from Abraham." (Genesis 17:15-22)

Commentary: This is a powerful action story often ignored by most world leaders, nor fully understood by most of the Christian and Jewish world. But in the minds of some this feud is the source of the continuing conflict between these two direct descendants of Abraham today.

This story continues in Genesis chapter 21 with these words:

➤ "And the child grew, and was weaned: and Abraham made a great feast the same day that Isaac was weaned. And Sarah saw the son of Hagar [Ishmael] the Egyptian, which she had born unto Abraham, mocking. Wherefore she said unto Abraham, Cast out this bondwoman and her son: for the son of this bondwoman shall not be heir with my son, even with Isaac. And the thing was very grievous in Abraham's sight because of his son. **And God said unto Abraham,** Let it not be grievous in thy sight because of the lad, and because of thy bondwoman; in all that Sarah hath said unto thee, hearken unto her voice; for in Isaac shall thy seed be called. **And also of the son of the bondwoman will I make a nation, because he is thy seed.** And Abraham rose up early in the morning, and took bread, and a bottle of water, and gave it unto Hagar, putting it on her shoulder, and the child, and sent her away: and she departed, and wandered in the wilderness of Beer-sheba." (Genesis 21:8-14)

Continuing, this story explains why the descendants of Ishmael have become the Islamic nations with lingering hatreds for those they perceive to have denied them their rightful inheritance as Abraham's oldest son. These words read:

> "And she [Hagar] went, and sat her down over against him [Ishmael] a good way off, as it were a bowshot: for she said, Let me not see the death of the child. And she sat over against him, and lift up her voice, and wept. And God heard the voice of the lad; **and the angel of God called to Hagar out of heaven,** and said unto her, What aileth thee, Hagar? fear not; for God hath heard the voice of the lad where he is. Arise, lift up the lad, and hold him in thine hand; **for I will make him a great nation**. And God opened her eyes, and she saw a well of water; and she went, and filled the bottle with water, and gave the lad drink. And God was with the lad; and he grew, and dwelt in the wilderness, and became an archer. And he dwelt in the wilderness of Paran: and his mother took him a wife out of the land of Egypt." (Genesis 21:16-21)

Question: Is the Bible more than these covenants made with Abraham and Isaac?

Answer: Yes, **much more** – it contains what James refers to in 1:25 as **"the perfect law of liberty."** It should be remembered that when James wrote these words the New Testament had yet to be assembled, so God's **"perfect law of liberty"** was to be found only in the Old Testament. America's Founders found that law and then patterned America's Foundational Documents after those laws and principles.

Many still profess that Christ came to destroy that law at his coming. Wrong. Here are his words regarding his "perfect law of liberty" that he embedded in the Old Testament:

> "Think not that I am come to destroy the law, or the prophets: **I am not come to destroy, but to fulfil. For verily I say unto you, Till heaven and earth pass, one jot or one tittle shall in no wise pass from the law, till all be**

fulfilled. Whosoever therefore shall break one of these least commandments, and shall teach men so, he shall be called the least in the kingdom of heaven: but whosoever shall do and teach them, the same shall be called great in the kingdom of heaven. For I say unto you, That except your righteousness shall exceed the righteousness of the scribes and Pharisees, ye shall in no case enter into the kingdom of heaven." (Matthew 5:17-20)

Other supportive scriptures include:

➤ **"Search the scriptures; for in them ye think ye have eternal life: and they are they which testify of me."** (John 5:39)

➤ "Then said Jesus to those Jews which believed on him, If ye continue in my word, then are ye my disciples indeed; **And ye shall know the truth, and the truth shall make you free.**" (John 8:31-32)

Commentary: Again it should be remembered the New Testament was yet to be assembled and Christ was referring to his law found in the Old Testament. Christ's words in Matthew should remind all American believers that all He, as Jehovah, declared in the Old Testament **"shall all be fulfilled."**

Question: Who were America's Founding Fathers?

Answer: These were men, as Jefferson declared in his declaration, who were 'endowed' by their Creator and Supreme Judge of the World with special gifts and talents to restore freedom and liberty to a world then enslaved by despots and dictators who were strongly influenced by the evil ways of Satan. The Founders were 'endowed' by God in the same manner as was Joseph of Egypt who was elevated to become the Prime Minister of Egypt under the Pharaoh, and Daniel who, as an enslaved Jew was raised up by a gentile king to rule over a vast nation that today would include Iran, Iraq and Syria. Both of these men, while relatively young, were 'endowed' by God with talents that would allow them to preserve that covenant God had made with Abraham, Isaac and Jacob, as these scriptures declare:

➤ "And Joseph was brought down to Egypt; and Potiphar, an officer of Pharaoh, captain of the guard, an Egyptian, bought him of the hands of the **Ishmaelites**, which had brought him down thither. **And the Lord was with Joseph**, and he was a prosperous man; and he was in the house of his master the Egyptian. And his master saw that the Lord was with him, and that the Lord made all that he did to prosper in his hand. And Joseph found grace in his sight, and he served him: and he made him overseer over his house, and all that he had he put into his hand. And it came to pass from the time that he had made him overseer in his house, and over all that he had, that the Lord blessed the Egyptian's house for Joseph's sake; **and the blessing of the Lord was upon all that he had in the house, and in the field.**" (Genesis 39:1-5)

➤ "As for these four children, **God gave them knowledge and skill in all learning and wisdom: and Daniel had understanding in all visions and dreams.** Now at the end of the days that the king had said he should bring them in, then the prince of the eunuchs brought them in before Nebuchadnezzar. And the king communed with them; and among them all was found none like Daniel, Hananiah, Mishael, and Azariah: therefore stood they before the king. **And in all matters of wisdom and understanding, that the king enquired of them, he found them <u>ten times better</u> than all the magicians and astrologers that were in all his realm.**" (Daniel 1:17-20)

In 1976 two university professors, Frank W. Fox and LaGrand L. Baker wrote a story for the June issue of the *Ensign Magazine*, a story titled "*Wise Men Raised Up.*" Their well-documented article made several observations regarding America's Founding Fathers, observations worth noting. While their observations are about the fifty-five men who crafted the Constitution, their conclusions could well be true for those fifty-six who signed the Declaration of Independence, especially for Thomas Jefferson who was given the assignment to draft the world-changing Declaration of Independence. Their observations would easily include George Washington who would be the one man who had been prepared with the leadership skills to lead a rag tag army to victory over the world's largest and best equipped army in the world at that time, especially if the Lord was with him, as many believe He was.

Baker and Fox begin their story by asking who those men that wrote the Constitution were. They then divided the fifty-five original delegates to the 1787 convention into three groups: group one favored a strong central government; group two feared the overpowering control of a strong national government; and group three, while favoring a strong central government also believed the states should play an important role in the affairs of its citizens.

Group one included such men as James Madison, James Wilson, Gouverneur Morris, Robert Morris (not related), and Alexander Hamilton. Group two included Elbridge Gerry, Roger Sherman, William Patterson, and Luther Martin and in group three they placed George Mason, John Dickerson, Oliver Ellsworth, and John Rutledge, all independent thinkers.

These three groups, with their distinct philosophies, played major roles in crafting the balanced structure of government America has today. The convention had its serious moments. A number of convention attendees, believing it was impossible to agree on anything, left the convention prior to its completion. Only thirty-nine of the fifty-five original delegates signed the final draft of the Constitution. Three delegates refused to sign the Constitution because they did not believe it sufficiently protected the individual freedoms they had fought for in the Revolutionary War. Those three men,

George Mason, Edmund Randolph and Elbridge Gerry, were responsible for the adoption of the first Ten Amendments – America's beloved Bill of Rights.

The two men who commanded the respect of all others were George Washington, elected president of the convention, and Benjamin Franklin whose role was to mold divergent opinions into workable compromises. Both men performed their roles well. Both had been "endowed by God" for the roles they were to play in restoring freedom to the earth.

There were, according to Fox and Baker, three men absent from the convention that played equally major roles in this defining event in history. These three men were John Adams, then ambassador to England, Thomas Jefferson, then ambassador to France, and Samuel Adams, now known as the Father of the American Revolution.

The Founding Fathers were well educated – thirty-one had been to college, two were college presidents, three college professors, two physicians, and four had studied law in England's best schools. And all were students of the Enlightenment: Rousseau, Montesquieu, Voltaire, Hume, Pope, Locke, Mandeville, Adam Smith, and the Bible. And all were conversant in the history and philosophy of the Greek democracies, the Roman Republic (Cicero's writings on the Laws of Nature and Nature's God), and the British constitutional system. Now they were prepared to test their theories against the whole history of mankind's struggle for freedom.

Timing played an important role in the creation of America

Fox and Baker pointed out that it was in the span of a single life time that these events had brought together America's best statesmen and her brightest thinkers – those we know as America's Founding Fathers. Fox and Baker pointed out that in 1740, a mere generation before the Revolution, the intellectual life in America was dominated by clergymen, but that by 1840, a generation after the Founders, scientists and inventors dominated the political scene.

As we study the lives of these Founders we learn they were leaders of their people more than they were representatives of their people. These were men **"endowed by God,"** as had others been endowed throughout history, with the vision and hope needed to formulate and implement such an unlikely undertaking.

Washington said:

- "In the first place it is a point conceded, that America, under an efficient government, will be the most favorable Country of any in the world for persons of industry and frugality..."

John Adams predicted,

- "Many hundred years must roll away before we shall be corrupted. Our pure, virtuous public spirited, federative republic will last forever, govern the globe and introduce the perfection of man."

The last paragraph of Fox and Baker's article is both powerful and insightful. It reads: "The writing of the Constitution was a miracle. But the miracle was not that the Lord found fifty-five men who understood so well the principles of a representative government. It is unlikely that any one of those men could have written the Constitution as it was in its finished form. The miracle lies in how that great document was produced: **The spirit of revelation is the spirit of peace,** and there was a prevailing spirit of peace among them. It was a miracle that these men – who represented extremely diverse political philosophies and who, in some instances, almost hated each other – sat during that sweltering summer to talk and compromise until they had written a document which is an expression of what the Lord called **'just and holy principles.'** They created a government so well balanced that it prevented anyone of its social or geographical factions from getting dominance over the other, a government so strong that it could protect the individual rights of all its citizens and yet so weak that it could not invade their private lives or infringe upon the exercise of their free agency."

This story does not mention the word *covenant* or *endowed* but it does use another phrase that strongly suggests the powers of God were involved in this equation, the phrase: **"The spirit of revelation …"** Except when God chooses to talk with man face to face, as he has done on numerous occasions, the Lord communicates and endows through the Holy Ghost – the "Spirit of Revelation" – as it was described in Acts 2, shortly after Christ's forty-day training visit with his disciples.

Question: What would have been those biblical scriptures that would have likely influenced America's Founding Fathers into believing they had been 'called of God' to create a new nation, a nation of freedom and liberty?

Answer: The following biblical scriptures would have likely been the more powerful scriptures that touched the spirits of America's Founding Fathers during that period of time.

> ➢ **"Search the scriptures**; for in them ye think ye have eternal life: and they are they which testify of me." (John 5:39)

> ➢ "Then said Jesus to those Jews which believed on him, If ye continue in my word, then are ye my disciples indeed; **And ye shall know the truth, and the truth shall make you free."** (John 8:31-32)

> ➢ "But whoso looketh into **the perfect law of liberty**, and continueth therein, he being not a forgetful hearer, but a doer of the work, this man shall be blessed in his deed." (James 1:25)

> ➢ "If ye **fulfil the royal law** according to the scripture, Thou shalt love thy neighbour as thyself, ye do well:" (James 2:8)

> ➢ "Think not that I am come to destroy the law, or the prophets: I am not come to destroy, **but to fulfil.** For verily I say unto you, Till heaven and earth pass, one jot or one

tittle shall in no wise pass from the law, **till all be fulfilled**." (Matthew 5:17-18)

➢ "**Proclaim liberty** throughout all the land unto all the inhabitants thereof:" (Leviticus 25:10)

➢ "And remember that thou wast a servant in the land of Egypt, and that the Lord thy God brought thee out thence through a mighty hand and by a stretched out arm: therefore **the Lord thy God commanded thee to keep the Sabbath day.**" (Deuteronomy 5:15)

➢ "Hear, O Israel: **Thou art to pass over Jordan this day, to go in to possess nations greater and mightier than thyself, cities great and fenced up to heaven, A people great and tall, the children of the Anakims, whom thou knowest, and of whom thou hast heard say,** Who can stand before the children of Anak! Understand therefore this day, that the Lord thy God is he which goeth over before thee; as a consuming fire he shall destroy them, and he shall bring them down before thy face: so shalt thou drive them out, and destroy them quickly, as the Lord hath said unto thee. Speak not thou in thine heart, after that the Lord thy God hath cast them out from before thee, saying, **For my righteousness the Lord hath brought me in to possess this land: but for the wickedness of these nations the Lord doth drive them out from before thee.** Not for thy righteousness, or for the uprightness of thine heart, dost thou go to possess their land: but for the wickedness of these nations the Lord thy God doth drive them out from before thee, and that he may perform the word which the Lord sware unto thy fathers, Abraham, Isaac, and Jacob. Understand therefore, that the Lord thy God giveth thee not this good land to possess it for thy righteousness; for thou art a stiffnecked people. Remember, and forget not, how thou provokedst the Lord thy God to wrath in the wilderness: from the day that thou didst depart out of the land of Egypt, until ye came unto this place, ye have been rebellious against the Lord." (Deuteronomy 9:1-7)

➤ "Now after the death of Moses the servant of the Lord it came to pass, that the Lord spake unto Joshua the son of Nun, Moses' minister, saying, Moses my servant is dead; now therefore arise, go over this Jordan, thou, and all this people, unto the land which I do give to them, even to the children of Israel. Every place that the sole of your foot shall tread upon, that have I given unto you, as I said unto Moses. From the wilderness and this Lebanon even unto the great river, the river Euphrates, all the land of the Hittites, and unto the great sea toward the going down of the sun, shall be your coast. There shall not any man be able to stand before thee all the days of thy life: **as I was with Moses, so I will be with thee: I will not fail thee, nor forsake thee. Be strong and of a good courage:** for unto this people shalt thou divide for an inheritance the land, which I sware unto their fathers to give them. Only be thou strong and very courageous, that thou mayest observe to do according to all the law, which Moses my servant commanded thee: turn not from it to the right hand or to the left, that thou mayest prosper whithersoever thou goest. This book of the law shall not depart out of thy mouth; but thou shalt meditate therein day and night, that thou mayest observe to do according to all that is written therein: for then thou shalt make thy way prosperous, and then thou shalt have good success. Have not I commanded thee? **Be strong and of a good courage; be not afraid, neither be thou dismayed: for the Lord thy God is with thee whithersoever thou goest."** (Joshua 1:1-9)

➤ "And it came to pass, when Joshua was by Jericho, that he lifted up his eyes and looked, and, behold, **there stood a man over against him with his sword drawn in his hand:** and Joshua went unto him, and said unto him, Art thou for us, or for our adversaries? And he said, Nay; **but as captain of the host of the Lord am I now come**. And Joshua fell on his face to the earth, and did worship, and said unto him, What saith my lord unto his servant? And the captain of the Lord's host said unto Joshua, Loose thy shoe from off thy foot; for the place where on thou standest is holy. And Joshua did so." (Joshua 5:13-15)

➤ **"For out of Jerusalem shall go forth a remnant,** and they that escape out of mount Zion: the zeal of the Lord of hosts shall do this." (2 Kings 19:31)

➤ "Therefore thus saith the Lord concerning the king of Assyria, He shall not come into this city, nor shoot an arrow there, nor come before it with shield, nor cast a bank against it. By the way that he came, by the same shall he return, and shall not come into this city, saith the Lord. For I will defend this city, to save it, for mine own sake, and for my servant David's sake. ¶And it came to pass that night, that the angel of the Lord went out, and smote in the camp of the Assyrians an hundred fourscore and five thousand: and when they arose early in the morning, behold, they were all dead corpses." (2 Kings 19:32-35)

➤ "And when the Lord saw that he turned aside to see, God called unto him out of the midst of the bush, and said, Moses, Moses. And he said, Here am I. And he said, Draw not nigh hither: put off thy shoes from off thy feet, for the place whereon thou standest is holy ground. Moreover he said, I am the God of thy father, the God of Abraham, the God of Isaac, and the God of Jacob. And Moses hid his face; for he was afraid to look upon God. ¶And the Lord said, I have surely seen the affliction of my people which are in Egypt, and have heard their cry by reason of their taskmasters; for I know their sorrows; And I am come down to deliver them out of the hand of the Egyptians, and to bring them up out of that land unto a good land and a large, unto a land flowing with milk and honey; unto the place of the Canaanites, and the Hittites, and the Amorites, and the Perizzites, and the Hivites, and the Jebusites." (Exodus 3:4-8)

➢ "And to the woman were **given two wings of a great eagle**, that she might fly into the wilderness, into her place, where she is nourished for a time, and times, and half a time, from the face of the serpent. (Revelation 12:14)

Commentary: Is it possible the Founders saw their land similar to that of a great eagle? Possibly!

Question: What did the Founders learn in their study of God's "perfect law of liberty?"

Answer: Many things that likely would have included the following … (For additional details on what the Founders learned in their study of God's perfect law of liberty the student is directed to the LDS Institute Manual, Exodus Chapter 20 – The Ten Commandments, free on the Gospel Library app)

• They learned that the major purpose of God is to make man free and to make possible the bringing about the immortality and eternal life for all mankind.

➢ "My doctrine is not mine, but his that sent me. If any man will do his will, he shall know of the doctrine, whether it be of God, or whether I speak of myself." (John 7:16-17)

Commentary: This scripture likely suggested to the Founders that if they were willing to turn to him, He would help them break free of King George III and England.

> **"If ye continue in my word, then are ye my disciples indeed; And ye shall know the truth, and the truth shall make you free."** (John 8:31-32)

Commentary: I believe the Founders likely believed they were indeed His disciples called to restore those freedoms He wanted all mankind to have through the creation of a new covenant nation – America.

> **"Stand fast therefore in the liberty wherewith Christ hath made us free, and be not entangled again with the yoke of bondage."** (Galatians 5:1)

Commentary: This scripture was a message to the Founders urging them to break the "yoke of bondage" of King George III and of the British Parliament.

- They learned that the Ten Commandments are the foundational and underlying laws of all civil (political) and religious law since they were first given via Moses and that they are applicable to all people and all nations. No nation or people are exempt. They are fundamental to mankind's relationship with God and in becoming perfect even as our Father in heaven is perfect.

> "Be ye therefore perfect, even as your Father which is in heaven is perfect." (Matthew 5:48)

- They learned that the Ten Commandments provides mankind with a better understanding of the three great priorities in life, these priorities being …
  - ✓ Our proper relationship to God, as explained in the first four commandments;
  - ✓ Our proper relationship with family,, as explained in the fifth commandment;
  - ✓ Our proper relationships with others, with five 'do not' or negative commandments.

- They learned that to better understand biblical law, they needed to understand certain basic characteristics of that law. These characteristics include:

✓ That the premises or principles of a given law are always declared and that these declarations are basic laws. The Founders learned that the Ten Commandments make such declarations and as such are the **basic or foundational law** that undergirds all other law; in this case the Mosaic Law that was soon to follow. "Thou shalt not steal" is an example of such a basic law. (Exodus 20:15 and reaffirmed in Deuteronomy 5:19)

✓ That those laws that flow from the basic or foundational laws are usually a form of "case law," that is, the illustration of the basic principles in terms of specific cases. They also learned that any specific case often illustrates the extent of the application of that law, that is, by citing a "case law" it reveals the jurisdiction or limits of that law.

✓ That law has as its purpose and direction **the restitution** of God's order.

Commentary: This is a fundamental principle that encourages Americans to get involved so that God's foundational laws deeply embedded in America's Foundational Documents can be preserved in their pristine beauty and application.

• Another characteristic they learned about God's Laws is that **they are primarily negative laws**; that eight of the Ten Commandments, as well as many of the Mosaic Laws are negative laws and deal with what ought not to be done rather than with what should be done. By understanding this negativity of God's laws the Founders better understood that God's laws to ancient Israel was not to shackle them but to guarantee the Israelites their greatest individual freedoms. A negative law prohibits the action, thus has a modest function, and limits the law and therefore the state; the enforcement agency is limited to just that particular law. Like the Ten Commandments, in America's Bill of Rights eight of ten are negative, thus literally providing all Americans the freedom to worship God according to their own conscience; to create a free press not controlled by the government; etc.

- They learned that **negative laws insure liberty**, and that except for the prohibited areas, **all of man's life is beyond the law.** This was a powerful lesson for the Founders to learn, and this should be a powerful lesson for all Americans in the 21st century. This lesson provides Americans with a better understanding of God's freedoms, that they are not restrictive but are truly liberating. The negativity of the law is the preservation of the positive life and freedom of man. Exodus 20:2 reads:
  - ➤ **"I am the Lord thy God, which have brought you out of the land of Egypt, out of the house of bondage"**

Commentary: This scripture declares that this law was to make them free and to keep them free – if they would simply be obedient to His laws and commandments.

- They learned that the law of Moses was:
  - ✓ a "preparatory gospel," a law that included the principles of repentance, baptism, remission of sins, and the laws of carnal commandments;'
  - ✓ a "very strict law;"
  - ✓ a law of performances and ordinances designed to keep the Israelites in remembrance of their God;
  - ✓ highly symbolic, filled with types and shadows all of which pointed toward Christ and His future Atonement;
  - ✓ "added to the gospel," not given as a substitute for the law;
  - ➤ "And the scripture, foreseeing that God would justify the heathen through faith, **preached before the gospel unto Abraham**, saying, In thee shall all nations be blessed." - (Galatians 3:8)
  - ➤ "Wherefore then serveth the law? It (Mosaic Law) was added because of transgressions, till the seed should come to whom the promise was made; and it was ordained by angels in the hand of a mediator." (Galatians 3:19)

✓ a "schoolmaster or tutor law" to bring wayward Israel to Christ.

➤ "But before faith came, we were kept under the law, shut up unto the faith which should afterwards be revealed. **Wherefore the law was our schoolmaster to bring us unto Christ, that we might be justified by faith.**" (Galatians 3:23-24)

• They learned that the principles taught by the Law of Moses are eternal in nature with the foremost eternal principle being that when one partakes of the Lamb's atoning sacrifice man is able to overcome and receive a forgiveness of one's sins.

• The Founders learned that God's 'perfect law of liberty' had been given to Moses on Mt. Sinai.

Question: How did the Bible influence America's Founding Fathers in creating a covenant nation?
Answer: There were fifty-six men who signed the Declaration of Independence and fifty-five men who participated in writing the Constitution (only thirty-nine signed it) – a total of one hundred and eleven men. There were a few who signed both documents, with likely about one hundred men, from twelve very divergent states (Rhode Island did not participate in the drafting of the Constitution) who were engaged in creating one or both of America's Foundational Documents. **Nearly all of these one hundred men were well versed in the Bible.**

Question: How would you describe the Bible to a person who has never seen or read a Bible?
Answer: I would hold a Bible in my hands and say to that person:

• This is the Bible, God's text book for life and salvation to help man overcome their natural self and strengthen their spiritual self so that each individual can choose the life that best suits them.

• This book is divided into four distinct sections:

- o Section one, Genesis 1 through Genesis 6, tells about the creation of the earth, the creation of man, the fall of man, and the eventual destruction of all mankind for his wickedness at the time of the flood, save eight souls aboard Noah's Ark.
- o Section two, the largest section, begins with Genesis 7 and goes through the end of the Old Testament, the book of Malachi. This section tells about the covenant God made with Abram, whose name was changed to Abraham, and was then told that he would be the father of many nations and given the priesthood of God.
- o Section three covers Matthew through Jude and tells of the mortal ministry of Jesus Christ and of his efforts to call his people to repentance; of how his people tried him and then crucified him; it tells of his burial in a tomb; of his literal resurrection from that tomb, a resurrection that broke the bonds of mortal death. It tells how Christ established his Church, the Church of Jesus Christ, via his apostles. And it tells how his own people, the Jews, had rejected him and then how his gospel, the Gospel of Jesus Christ, was given to the gentiles of the world via a Jewish convert named Saul who was then given the new name of Paul, the great Christian evangelist.
- o Section four is the Book of Revelation, a book written to provide insight into the future of the world, even to the time of Christ's second coming and of Christ's ruling on earth as its King for a thousand years.
- This book is essentially, from Genesis 7 through Jude, about a dysfunctional family, a family not unlike most earthly families but because of their human frailties was not able to fully overcome the temptations of the flesh. But because of the covenant God had made with Abraham, he kept loving them and giving them a reprieve from time to time. Then, after their disobedience became so flagrant, he literally destroyed the people he had freed from the Egyptians, scattered ten of the twelve tribes of Israel to locations

known only to him, before destroying the last two tribes, known as Judah, but always with a promise of gathering this dysfunctional family again in the last days.

- The first step in this gathering of Israel began in earnest in 1948 when the United Nations, strongly supported by then President Harry Truman, set apart a part of Palestine to be home to a portion of the world's homeless Jews, a nation known today as Israel, with a revival of that hatred that was initiated by Sarah when she had Hagar and Ishmael cast out into the wilderness.

- It was this book that became the spiritual guide for those gentiles known as Christians, and it was this book that crossed the Atlantic Ocean with the Pilgrims in 1620 and became the spiritual and governing foundation of the nation that is known as the United States of America. It is this book that inspired the Foundational Documents of these United States of America with God's "perfect law of liberty" embedded deeply in them, those laws of freedom and liberty that Jehovah himself wrote with his finger and gave to Moses to carry off Mt. Sinai and then used to govern nearly three million Israelites who had been enslaved by the Egyptian Pharaohs for over four hundred years.

- It is the book that has changed the lives of countless millions, including mine, as well as a book that can change the future of any nation that chooses to embrace its principles of freedom and liberty. This is also the book that literally changed this author's life – for the better, and led him to become a disciple of Jesus Christ and attempt to live his life as He would have had him live it. At age 86, he can say with great gusto, it has been a great and wonderful journey for nearly sixty years.

Question: Is there a 'best way' to study the Bible?
Answer: Yes, there is a 'best way' to study the Bible.

Donald S. Conkey

Question: What is that best way to study the Bible?
Answer: First, have a strong desire to read the Bible and learn why the Bible is known as God's 'text book' for (1) living a Christ-like life in mortality; (2) preparing for that eternal life after mortality; and (3) learning what God's "perfect law of liberty" is and how America's Founding Fathers found that law and were then inspired to embed this law deep into America's two foundational documents, America's Declaration of Independence and its Constitution, as amended.

Question: What are some of the ways one can study the Bible?
Answer: Most people, when they first begin to study the Bible, find it hard to follow and to fully understand and then quit and set it on the coffee table as a decorative piece.

My study habits of the Bible have changed since I first began my study of it in 1956. Then I read the words in the Bible. Today, thanks to modern technology, I read my Bible on my I-Pad on the **Gospel Library app,** a marvelous new tool that allows me to truly study and ponder the Bible. Especially helpful for me in my study of the Bible via the Gospel Library app is my immediate access to the Topical Guide, the Bible Dictionary and the LDS Institute student manuals for both the Old and New Testaments. This **Gospel Library app** has been a tremendous help in writing this book.

One of the beauties of the Gospel Library app is that it can go with me wherever I go. At my age I spend a lot of time in doctors' offices and often have waits. When this happens I open up my I-pad, bring up the scriptures or the Institute Manual and read and study. It is so easy and the app is available free to anyone who has access to an I-pad or I-phone. Today, the only thing between each individual reading and pondering the Bible is themselves – they must want to do it.

Question: Why would God covenant with America's Founding Fathers to create America as a 'covenant nation?'

Answer: Because, as we read in the words of Christ to his "other sheep" (John 10:16), America is a choice land, a land reserved for a people who would covenant with Him, as did America's Founding Fathers, to live by the principles of freedom and liberty the Lord embedded deeply into America's Declaration of Independence and Constitution. These two documents are powerful symbols of that covenant the Founders made with their Creator and Supreme Judge of the World, by men raised up for that very purpose of restoring the fullness and purity of His gospel of freedom and liberty, including living free in a nation whose laws are founded on God's "perfect laws of liberty." Once established, America's Constitution became a symbol of freedom to all other nations of the world and it has become a pattern for most other nations of the world today. As America's new government stabilized and became firmly founded on the laws of its Constitution, the gathering of Israel slowly began with Judah being the first tribe to begin gathering, beginning in 1948 with the creation of a modern Israel by the United Nations. It is a small nation, about the size of New Jersey, carved out of that land first given to the Israelites anciently by their Jehovah, a nation that has had untold attempts made by its enemies to destroy it, but with miracle after miracle preserving this small nation against unbelievable odds. This gathering of the tribe of Judah could not have happened without America first being created as a covenant nation and governed by those same laws that were first given to ancient Israel by Jehovah, via Moses. That covenant God made with Abraham is still alive and well but Americans must now step forward and take their place as the watchmen of man's freedoms and liberties - or those precious freedoms established and preserved by obedience to "the Laws of Nature and of Nature's God" could be lost once again, with mankind re-enslaved as they were prior to the creation of these United States of America as a land of freedom and liberty in 1789.

Question: What did the Founding Fathers have to say about the role of God in creating America?
Answer: Plenty! We will provide only a few of the hundreds of quotes available that provide solid support to the premise that God was involved in the creation of America as a Covenant Nation.

Quotes from George Washington:

- "Such being the impressions under which I have, in obedience to the public summons, repaired to the present station; it would be peculiarly improper to omit in this first official Act, **my fervent supplications to that Almighty Being who rules over the Universe, who presides in the Councils of Nations, and whose providential aids can supply every human defect,** that his benediction may consecrate to the liberties and happiness of the People of the United States, a Government instituted by themselves for these essential purposes: and may enable every instrument employed in its administration to execute with success, the functions allotted to his charge. In tendering this homage to the **Great Author** of every public and private good I assure myself that it expresses your sentiments not less than my own; nor those of my fellow-citizens at large, less than either. **No People can be bound to acknowledge and adore the invisible hand, which conducts the Affairs of men more than the People of the United States.** Every step, by which they have advanced to the character of an independent nation, seems to have been distinguished by some token of providential agency. And in the important revolution just accomplished in the system of their United Government, the tranquil deliberations and voluntary consent of so many distinct communities, from which the event has resulted, cannot be compared with the means by which most Governments have been established, without some return of pious gratitude along with an humble anticipation of the future blessings which the past seem to presage. These reflections, arising out of the present crisis, have forced themselves too strongly on my mind to be suppressed. You will join with me I trust in thinking, that there are none under the influence of which, the proceedings of a new and free Government can more auspiciously commence." (Paragraph two, Inaugural Address to Congress, 1789)

- "I dwell on this prospect with every satisfaction which an ardent love for my Country can inspire: **since there is no truth more thoroughly established, than that there exists in the economy and course of nature, an indissoluble union between virtue and happiness**, between duty and advantage, between the genuine maxims of an honest and magnanimous policy, and the solid rewards of public prosperity and felicity: **Since we ought to be no less persuaded that the propitious smiles of Heaven, can never be expected on a nation that disregards the eternal rules of order and right, which Heaven itself has ordained:** And since the preservation of the sacred fire of liberty, and the destiny of the Republican model of Government, are justly considered as deeply, perhaps as finally staked, on the experiment entrusted to the hands of the American people." (Paragraph four, Inaugural Address to Congress, 1789)

- "**Of all the dispositions and habits which lead to political prosperity, religion and morality are indispensable supports.** In vain would that man claim the tribute of patriotism, who should labor to subvert these great pillars of human happiness, these firmest props of the duties of men and citizens.... **Let it simply be asked, where is the security for property, for reputation, for life, if the sense of religious obligation desert the oaths which are the instruments of investigation in courts of justice?** And let us with caution indulge the supposition that morality can be maintained without religion. Whatever may be conceded to the influence of refined education…reason and experience both forbid us to expect that national morality can prevail in exclusion of religious principle."

- "And of the fatal tendency...to put, in place of the delegated will of the Nation, the will of the party; often a small but artful and enterprising minority…they are likely, in the course of time and things, to become potent engines, by which cunning, ambitious, and unprincipled men will be enabled to subvert the Power of the People and to usurp for themselves the reins of Government; destroying afterwards the very engines which have lifted them to unjust dominion…" (From Washington's Farewell Address to Congress in 1796)

Commentary: These are prophetic words by Washington that by 2014 have come to pass.

From Thomas Jefferson:
- "I shall need, therefore, all the indulgence I have heretofore experienced…I shall need, too, **the favor of that Being in whose hands we are, who led our forefathers, as Israel of old**, from their native land and planted them to a country flowing with all the necessities and comforts of life, **who has covered our infancy with his Providence and our ripper years with His wisdom and power,** and to whose goodness I ask you to join with me in supplications **that He will so enlighten the minds of your servants, guide their councils and prosper their measures that whatever they do shall result in your good,** and shall secure to you the peace, friendship and approbations of all nations." (From Jefferson's Second Inaugural Address to Congress in 2005)

From James Madison:
- "We have staked the whole future of American civilization, not upon the power of government, far from it. We have staked the

future of our political institutions upon the capacity of mankind for self-government; upon the capacity of each and all of us to govern ourselves, to control ourselves, **to sustain ourselves according to the Ten Commandments of God.**" (Encyclopedia of Quotations – page 411)

- "We have all been encouraged to feel in the guardianship and guidance of **that Almighty Being, whose power regulates the destiny of nations.**" (March 9, 1809, Inaugural Address)

From Abraham Lincoln:

- **"The philosophy of the school room in one generation will be the philosophy of government in the next [generation]."** (Lincoln was another of America's early prophets on the future of America.)

From Patrick Henry:

- "...Sir, we are not weak, if we make a proper use of the means **which the God of nature hath placed in our power.** Three millions of people, **armed in the Holy cause of Liberty,** and in such a country as that which we possess, are invincible by any force which our enemy can send against us. **Besides, sir, we shall not fight our battle alone. There is a just God who presides over the destines of nations;** Is life so dear, or peace so sweet, **as to be purchased at the price of chains and slavery? Forbid it, Almighty God!** I know not what course others may take, but as for me, **give me liberty or give me death."** (Spoken to the Second Virginia Convention on March 23, 1775, prior to the beginning of the Revolutionary War- page 287-288, America's God and Country Encyclopedia of Quotations by Federer.)

Chapter Three

America becomes a Covenant Nation

Opening commentary: Most Americans, especially those in my generation and in the preceding generation, have known in their hearts most of their lives that the America they are citizens of has been a blessed nation – but never asked why it was such a blessed nation. America has been greatly blessed because it is a politically covenant nation.

America became a covenant nation:

1. When fifty-six Founding Fathers signed the Declaration of Independence in July and August of 1776.
2. When thirty-nine Founding Fathers signed the Constitution on September 17, 1787.
3. When the thirteen states ratified the Constitution.
4. When George Washington took the Oath of Office as first President of the United States on April 30, 1789, with his left hand believed to be on the pages of chapter 28 of the Book of Deuteronomy and with his right hand raised to the square, and added four words **"so help me God."**

This covenant is renewed…

5. Every four years when the President of the United States takes the Oath of Office of the President of the United States **to preserve, protect and defend the Constitution of the United States** and then adds the same four words Washington added on June 30, 1789, **"so help me God."**
6. Each time any elected official in the United States takes the Oath of **Office to preserve, protect and defend the**

Constitution of the United States, often adding **"so help me God."**

The Oath of Office each president is required to take reads: "I do solemnly swear (or affirm) that I will faithfully execute the Office of the President of the United States and **will to the best of my Ability, <u>preserve, protect and defend the Constitution of the United States.</u>**" Washington was the first to add to this Oath "So help me God," but each president since Washington has followed Washington's example and added "so help me God."

Question: What is a covenant? What is a covenant nation?
Answer: To answer these two questions we need to know what a covenant is. My King James Bible dictionary provided this definition:

- A covenant "Sometimes denotes an agreement between persons (1 Sam. 23: 18) or nations (1 Sam. 11: 1); more often between God and man; but in this latter case it is important to notice that the two parties to the agreement do not stand in the relation of independent and equal contractors. God in his good pleasure fixes the terms, which man accepts. The same word is sometimes rendered "testament." The gospel is so arranged that principles and ordinances are received by covenant placing the recipient under strong obligation and responsibility to honor the commitment."

Then I looked up covenant in my Encarta Dictionary and read these two definitions:

- A covenant is "a solemn agreement that is binding on all parties."
- Under 'Mutual promises of God and Israelites' it says, "the promises that were made between God and the Israelites, who agreed to worship no other gods."

Question: Can America be considered a covenant nation using these two definitions?

Answer: Yes. Both the Bible and the Encarta dictionaries suggest America is a covenant nation.

Question: What word or phrases in these definitions suggest America is a Covenant Nation?

Answer: Two phrases in the Bible dictionary suggest that America is a covenant nation. The first phrase: "Sometimes denotes an agreement between persons or nations; more often between God and man; but in this latter case it is important to notice that the two parties to the agreement do not stand in the relation of independent and equal contractors." The second phrase: the "principles and ordinances are received by covenant placing the recipient under strong obligation and responsibility to honor the commitment."

Both of the Encarta definitions sustain the Bible definition.

Question: How did the signing of the Declaration of Independence by America's Founding Fathers cause America to become a covenant nation?

Answer: As one reads the Declaration of Independence they need to understand that in addition to being a declaration to separate the newly declared "United States of America" from their mother land, Great Britain, it is also an agreement, a covenant if you will, between God and those Founding Fathers who rushed forward to sign that world-changing document after its initial presentation on July 4, 1776. And the words of this document make it very evident that the parties to this declaration, the Founding Fathers (for America) and God are not equal partners: God fixed the terms of this covenant with America by implying that obedience to "the Laws of Nature and of Nature's God," proxy words for God's "perfect law of liberty," must be complied with. America's Founding Fathers accepted God's terms for this covenant with their signatures on that document, the Declaration of Independence.

Question: What words in the Declaration of Independence suggest a covenant with God?

Answer: There are several words and/or phrases that strongly imply this document is a covenant between God and America. Those primary words and phrases include:

1. In paragraph one the phrase "to assume among the Powers of the Earth, the separate and equal Station to which the Laws of Nature and of Natures God entitle them," ... immediately declares America's future independence and freedoms will depend on these two laws, **"the Laws of Nature and of Nature's God"** and that this entitlement comes from being equal before God with all other nations on earth.

Commentary: While this phrase, **'the Laws of Nature and of Nature's God**" had been used by other great thinkers of the world, few if any, other than perhaps Thomas Jefferson ever likely associated this phrase with God's "perfect law of liberty," words Jefferson would have long pondered, knowing, as a lifelong student of the Bible, this phrase would have meant that God's 'perfect law of liberty' was to be found in the Old Testament. Jefferson knew he could not use a Bible phrase so he in all likelihood substituted "the Laws of Nature and of Nature's God" for the apostle James' phrase "the perfect law of liberty." By associating these two phrases together Jefferson was telling his fellow Americans that by adopting the Declaration of Independence they, the Founders, were in effect adopting God's "perfect law of liberty" as the standard for their new nation, and then, as a covenant nation, America had become subject to those same blessings and curses that blessed ancient Israel in their good years and the curses when they rejected God's laws.

2. Jefferson's use of the words **"that all Men are created equal, and are 'endowed' by their 'Creator' with certain unalienable Rights"** in paragraph two again strongly suggests that he, Jefferson, had received divine assistance with the writing of this world-changing document. The Bible provides solid evidence that

God has been actively involved in the affairs of man from the beginning of the world. The words and activities of the Old Testament prophets provide powerful examples of this help. Biblical examples of this help include the following two scriptures from Daniel:

> "Thus Melzar took away the portion of their meat, and the wine that they should drink; and gave them pulse. As for these four children [Daniel, Hananiah, Mishael, Azariah], God gave them knowledge and skill in all learning and wisdom: and Daniel had understanding in all visions and dreams." (Daniel 1:16-17)

> And the king communed with them; and among them all was found none like Daniel, Hananiah, Mishael, and Azariah: therefore stood they before the king. And in all matters of wisdom and understanding, that the king enquired of them, **he found them ten times better than all the magicians and astrologers that were in all his realm."** (Daniel 1:19-20)

Commentary: As one studies the history of Daniel's time period one can see that in order for God to return the Jews to Jerusalem and **preserve his covenant with Abraham,** Isaac and Jacob, He raised up these four young Jews, princes of Judah, and gave them wisdom in all things in order to help prepare King Cyrus seventy years later to allow Ezra to return to Jerusalem and rebuild the temple, a powerful symbol to God's people, the people He would gather in these the latter-days and his covenant with Abraham.

> And the Lord spake unto Moses, saying, " I have called by name Bezaleel the son of Uri, the son of Hur, of the tribe of Judah: And I have filled him with the spirit of God, **in wisdom, and in understanding, and in knowledge, and in all manner of workmanship,** To devise cunning works, to work in gold, and in silver, and in brass, And in cutting of stones, to set them, and in carving of timber, to work in

64

all manner of workmanship. And I, behold, I have given with him Aholiab, the son of Ahisamach, of the tribe of Dan: and in the hearts of all that are wise hearted I have put wisdom, that they may make all that I have commanded thee." (Exodus 31:2-6)

Commentary: This verse reminds us of several parables where Christ makes it clear that not everyone receives the same talents when they enter mortality at birth. And God, in this case had prepared Bezaleel to build Solomon's Temple, in a manner similar to how he raised up Thomas Jefferson to write the Declaration of Independence; George Washington to win the Revolutionary War; James Madison to create a Constitution for the new United States of America; Abraham Lincoln to win a Civil War while freeing those held in bondage because of the color of their skin; and Martin Luther King to more fully implement the Emancipation Proclamation. Clear evidence that God is watching over America even today, He is watching as America gambles with its freedoms.

> "And Moses said unto the Lord, O my Lord, I am not eloquent, neither heretofore, nor since thou hast spoken unto thy servant: but I am slow of speech, and of a slow tongue. And the Lord said unto him, Who hath made man's mouth? or who maketh the dumb, or deaf, or the seeing, or the blind? have not I the Lord? Now therefore go, and I will be with thy mouth, and teach thee what thou shalt say." (Exodus 4:10-12)

Commentary: I suspect the Lord could have said much the same thing to Thomas Jefferson in that small rented room in Philadelphia in 1776, just as He had said these words to Moses, who was also reluctant to go and free the Israelites from the Egyptian Pharaoh.

> "And when Abram was ninety years old and nine, the Lord appeared to Abram, and said unto him, I am the Almighty God; walk before me, and **be thou perfect. And I will**

make my covenant between me and thee, and will multiply thee exceedingly." (Genesis 17:1-2)

Commentary: Or perhaps the Lord could have said to Jefferson in that room in Philadelphia what the Lord said to Abraham when Abraham, at age ninety-nine, and was told to go into a strange land and then covenanted with Abraham with these words.

> "To whom the word of the Lord came in the days of Josiah the son of Amon king of Judah, in the thirteenth year of his reign. It came also in the days of Jehoiakim the son of Josiah king of Judah, unto the end of the eleventh year of Zedekiah the son of Josiah king of Judah, unto the carrying away of Jerusalem captive in the fifth month." (Jeremiah 1:2-3)

> **"And the remnant that is escaped of the house of Judah** shall again take root downward, and bear fruit upward: **For out of Jerusalem shall go forth a remnant**, and they that escape out of mount Zion: the zeal of the Lord of hosts shall do this." (Isaiah 37:31-32)

Commentary: Did Jefferson perhaps see in Isaiah 37:31-32 that America just might be this "remnant" that had escaped out of Jerusalem and was about to put its roots down and produce gospel fruits. It's possible but we today will never know.

3. In paragraph five Jefferson declares that the Founding Fathers appealed "to the **Supreme Judge of the World** for the rectitude of our [their] intentions..." One need not guess who Jefferson's "Supreme Judge of the World" was. It was America's Founding Father's God, the God of Abraham, Isaac and Jacob.

Commentary: One only has to read Jefferson's words or his biography to fully understand just how much he admired the words of Christ in the New Testament, so his use of these words is fully in line with a man who loved Christ, and felt God's presence in that room when for seventeen nights he sat alone, with only the Holy Ghost prompting him, and wrote those immortal words of the Declaration of

Independence, the words that changed the world forever, and set the foundation for the creation of a written document that would promote freedom on earth once again.

4. In paragraph five, Jefferson again seeks "with a firm Reliance on the Protection of **divine Providence**" before they mutually pledged [covenanted] to each other their Lives, their Fortunes, and their Sacred Honor.

Commentary: Can anyone doubt whom Jefferson was seeking support from when he penned these words, "with a firm Reliance on the Protection of divine Providence"?

There are several other phrases that also strongly suggest divine support in Jefferson's choice of words. These phrases include:

5. "That to secure these Rights, Governments are instituted among Men, deriving their just Powers from the Consent of the Governed..."

Commentary: This phrase should be required memorization of every American – it is "We the People" who give the government their power – and "We the People" can alter that government with our vote and with personal involvement in our local, state and federal government. This we would call 'citizenship responsibility.' Have you checked your "Citizenship Quotient" lately?

6. "That whenever any Form of Government becomes destructive of these Ends, **it is the Right of the People** to alter or to abolish it, and to institute new Government, laying its Foundation on such Principles, and organizing its Powers in such Form, as to them shall seem likely to affect their Safety and Happiness."

Commentary: This phrase is a powerful reminder that we, under our Constitution, can still effect such needed change via our personal involvement and vote.

7. "Prudence, indeed, will dictate that Governments long established should not be changed for light and transient Causes: and according to all Experience hath shewn, that Mankind are more

disposed to suffer, while Evils are sufferable, than to right themselves by abolishing the Forms in which they are accustomed."

Commentary: There are two parts to this phrase. The first part cautions America not to be rash in wanting to change its government for "light and transient Causes." The second part reminds Americans that they need not be "disposed to suffer, while Evils are sufferable, than to right themselves by abolishing the Forms in which they are accustomed." He is strongly suggesting that when Evils in America become insufferable that we Americans have it in our power to change these 'sufferable Evils" by becoming involved in our government and voting out of office those that have caused such 'Evils.' These words make it clear that the Founding Fathers knew about good and evil – and warned about the evils to come to America as it began to mature and become a part of the evil world that surrounded them.

8. "But when a long Train of Abuses and Usurpations, pursuing invariably the same Object, evinces a Design to reduce them under absolute Despotism, **it is their Right, it is their Duty, to throw off such Government,** and to provide new Guards for their future Security."

Commentary: Jefferson listed twenty-seven "Abuses and Usurpations" King George III had put upon the colonies. It would not be difficult today to list at least twenty seven "Abuses and Usurpations" America's government has inflicted upon America in the past fifty years. Freedom loving Americans need to read and then reread this part of the Declaration of Independence, and more fully understand that the "Abuses and Usurpations" America is being afflicted with today **could lead to "absolute Despotism,"** and that it is not only the "Right" of freedom loving Americans to "throw off such Government" but that **it is "their Duty** to throw off such Government, and to provide new Guards for their future Security."

America's culture also strongly declares "America was/is a Covenant Nation"

Question: How does America's culture declare "America a covenant nation?"
Answer: America's covenant with God is all around us – it is with us on a daily basis; it is with us as we visit our national cemeteries; it is in our wallets and pocketbooks; it is on display when we visit our national capital; it is with us each time we sing the national anthem; it is with us in our churches as we sing of God's love for mankind; it is with us when we salute the flag of these Unites States of America; it is around us when we visit our national monuments.

Question: Is there any covenant symbolism found in the Seal of the United States of America?
Answer: Yes. Much! The Seal, both sides, is a very strong symbol of the covenant America's Founding Fathers made with God when they signed the Declaration of Independence. On the front of the Seal are the Latin words 'E pluribus Unum' meaning "Out of many one." The many are the thirteen states of the new United States of America. These thirteen states are reflected by the thirteen letters in E pluribus Unum; by the thirteen stripes in the flag; by the thirteen arrows in the eagle's claw; and by the thirteen leaves and branches in the Olive Branch. Even the thirteen stars grouped into a six-pointed star strongly suggest the Founders connection to ancient Israel and to the principles of freedom the Founders garnered from the Bible.

On the reverse side of the Seal we again see this covenant connection between the thirteen states and God in the pyramid – thirteen steps representing the thirteen states but leaving room for more states to be added, all being overseen by the "all seeing eye of God." Even the Latin words ooze of this special relationship between God and the Founding Fathers. The words "Annuit Coeptis" translates to "He (God) hath favored our undertaking." And the words "Ordo

69

Seclorum" translate to "New Order of the Ages," which America and its covenant with God became.

Other symbolism of America's covenant with God includes America's Liberty Bell, the Statue of Liberty, and Washington's Monument among many others and it is difficult not to understand that "America was and still is a covenant nation."

Question: Had God covenanted with others prior to covenanting with America?
Answer: Yes, on numerous occasions. The following scriptures show when such covenants were made with man. The first Biblical covenant recorded is the covenant God made with Noah. It reads:

> ➤ "And, behold, I, even I, do bring a flood of waters upon the earth, to destroy all flesh, wherein is the breath of life, from under heaven; and every thing that is in the earth shall die. **"But with thee will I establish my covenant**; and thou shalt come into the ark, thou, and thy sons, and thy wife, and thy sons' wives with thee." (Genesis 6:17-18)

After Noah's descendants began to falter God made a covenant with Abram, at age ninety-nine, and changed his name to Abraham. It reads:

> ➤ "And when Abram was ninety years old and nine, the Lord appeared to Abram, and said unto him, I am the Almighty God; walk before me, and be thou perfect. **And I will make my covenant between me and thee**, and will multiply thee exceedingly." (Genesis 17:1-2)

Isaiah spoke of the covenants to be made in these the last days with these words:

> ➤ "Incline your ear, and come unto me: hear, and your soul shall live; and I will make an **everlasting covenant** with you, even the sure mercies of David." (Isaiah 55:3)

From Jeremiah we read about covenants with these words, in two different chapters:

➢ "Behold, the days come, saith the Lord, **that I will make a new covenant with the house of Israel, and with the house of Judah**: Not according to the covenant that I made with their fathers in the day that I took them by the hand to bring them out of the land of Egypt; which my covenant they brake, although I was an husband unto them, saith the Lord: But this shall be the covenant that I will make with the house of Israel; After those days, saith the Lord, I will put my law in their inward parts, and write it in their hearts; and will be their God, and they shall be my people." (Jeremiah 31:31-33)

Commentary: Note how these words of the Lord indicate he will make a **'new covenant'** with the **house of Israel** – and with the **house of Judah**. This is a significant declaration. For many the term Israel, as in the nation of Israel in the Middle East, means this is the restoration of Israel in the Middle East. But it means for me that this was just the beginning of the gathering of Judah. The biblical term Israel includes all twelve tribes of Jacob, who were then known as Israel.

➢ "Behold, I will gather them out of all countries, whither I have driven them in mine anger, and in my fury, and in great wrath; and I will bring them again unto this place, and I will cause them to dwell safely: And they shall be my people, and I will be their God: And I will give them one heart, and one way, that they may fear me forever, for the good of them, and of their children after them: **And I will make an everlasting covenant with them,** that I will not turn away from them, to do them good; but I will put my fear in their hearts, that they shall not depart from me. Yea, I will rejoice over them to do them good, and I will plant them in this land assuredly with my whole heart and with my whole soul." (Jeremiah 32:37-41)

Donald S. Conkey

From Ezekiel we read about God's prophesied covenant about the reuniting of Israel and Judah:

> "And say unto them, Thus saith the Lord God; Behold, **I will take the children of Israel from among the heathen**, whither they be gone, and will gather them on every side, **and bring them <u>into their own land</u>**: And I will make them one nation in the land upon the mountains of Israel; and one king shall be king to them all: and they shall be no more two nations, **neither shall they be divided into two kingdoms any more at all:** Neither shall they defile themselves any more with their idols, nor with their detestable things, nor with any of their transgressions: but I will save them out of all their dwelling places, wherein they have sinned, and will cleanse them: so shall they be my people, and I will be their God. And David my servant shall be king over them; and they all shall have one shepherd: they shall also walk in my judgments, and observe my statutes, and do them. And they shall dwell in the land that I have given unto Jacob my servant, wherein your fathers have dwelt; and they shall dwell therein, even they, and their children, and their children's children for ever: and my servant David shall be their prince forever. **Moreover I will make a covenant of peace** with them**; it shall be an everlasting covenant** with them: and I will place them, and multiply them, and **will set my sanctuary** in the midst of them for evermore. My tabernacle also shall be with them: yea, **I will be their God, and they shall be my people.** And the heathen shall know that I the Lord do sanctify Israel, when my sanctuary shall be in the midst of them for evermore." (Ezekiel 37:21-28)

Commentary: It is likely that when Jefferson read this prophecy from Ezekiel he could have seen himself in a role of helping fulfill this prophecy in this new land that another prophet declared to be "a land

72

which is choice above all the lands of the earth." (Ether 1:42 – Book of Mormon)

Next we turn to Hebrews where Paul speaks about the **New Covenant** Christ established during his ministry with these words:

> ➢ "But now hath he obtained a more excellent ministry, by how much also **he is the mediator of a better covenant, **which was established upon better promises. **For if that first covenant had been faultless, then should no place have been sought for the second**. For finding fault with them, he saith, Behold, the days come, saith the Lord, **when I will make a new covenant with the house of Israel and with the house of Judah:** Not according to the covenant that I made with their fathers in the day when I took them by the hand to lead them out of the land of Egypt; **because they continued not in my covenant,** and I regarded them not, saith the Lord. For this is the covenant that I will make with the house of Israel after those days, saith the Lord; **I will put my laws into their mind, and write them in their hearts: and I will be to them a God, and they shall be to me a people:** And they shall not teach every man his neighbor, and every man his brother, saying, Know the Lord: for all shall know me, from the least to the greatest. For I will be merciful to their unrighteousness, and their sins and their iniquities will I remember no more. In that he saith, **A new covenant**, he hath made the first old. Now that which decayeth and waxeth old is ready to vanish away." (Hebrews 8:6-13)

Commentary: These are powerful words. This is the scripture where Christ, as quoted by Paul, declares that He, Christ, is the Jehovah of the Old Testament, with this phrase: "Not according to **the covenant that I made with their fathers in the day when I took them by the hand to lead them out of the land of Egypt;.**" It is also likely that the

Founding Fathers saw themselves in these scriptures uttered by Paul which would have given them a strong desire to listen to those promptings that come from above when one is in tune with the Spirit of God.

Question: Is there evidence that Christian churches believe God covenanted with America?
Answer: Yes. Covenant songs common to Christian Churches include:
- "How Great Thou Art"
- "Battle Hymn of the Republic"
- "A Mighty Fortress is our God"
- "Rock of Ages"
- "Faith of Our Fathers"
- "How Gentle God's Commands"
- "Cast Thy Burdens on the Lord"
- "Master, The Tempest is Raging"
- "Onward Christian Soldiers"
- "Silent Night"

Commentary: These songs all have one central theme – God, Jefferson's 'Nature's God,' 'Creator,' and 'Supreme Judge of the World,' the God of Abraham, Isaac and Jacob and of Christ. Most of these songs date back to the beginning of America as a new nation, one, "Battle Hymn of the Republic", was written during the early part of the Civil War, and all of them have uplifted and strengthened Americans during their personal and national challenges, in every generation since 1789, the year the United States of America became a separate and equal nation in the world, a nation led by God and destined to become the leader of the free world, and rescue the world from the tyrants of the world who enslaved their citizens.

Question: Are there other Christian scriptures that suggest America is a covenant nation?

Answer: Yes. The Church of Jesus Christ of Latter-day Saints, in addition to the Bible, have three other books they accept as the Word of God. The following two scriptures come from their Doctrines and Covenants and declare plainly that God was involved in the creation of the Constitution for very specific reasons. These two scriptures read:

> ➤ **"That mine everlasting covenant** might [once again] be established;" (D&C 1:22)

Commentary: These words were recorded on November 1, 1831, in Hiram, Ohio.

> ➤ "Therefore, he giveth this promise unto you, **with an immutable covenant** that they shall be fulfilled; and all things wherewith you have been afflicted shall work together for your good, and to my name's glory, saith the Lord. And now, verily I say unto you concerning the laws of the land, it is my will that my people should observe to do all things whatsoever I command them. **And that law of the land which is constitutional, supporting that principle of freedom in maintaining rights and privileges, belongs to all mankind, and is justifiable before me.** Therefore, I, the Lord, justify you, and your brethren of my church, in befriending that law which is the constitutional law of the land; And as pertaining to law of man, whatsoever is more or less than this, cometh of evil. **I, the Lord God, make you free, therefore ye are free indeed; and the law also maketh you free. Nevertheless, when the wicked rule the people mourn.** Wherefore, honest men and wise men should be sought for diligently, and good men and wise men ye should observe to uphold; otherwise whatsoever is less than these cometh of evil. And I give unto you a commandment that ye shall forsake all evil and cleave unto all good, that ye shall live by every

word which proceedeth forth out of the mouth of God."
(Doctrine &Covenants 98:3-11)

Commentary: These words were recorded on August 6, 1833 in Kirtland, Ohio, following the savage persecutions of their fellow members in Missouri;

> "And again I say unto you, those who have been scattered by their enemies, it is my will that they should continue to importune for redress, and redemption, by the hands of those who are placed as rulers and are in authority over you **— According to the laws and constitution of the people, which I have suffered to be established, and should be maintained for the rights and protection of all flesh, according to just and holy principles;** That every man may act in doctrine and principle pertaining to futurity, according to the moral agency which I have given unto him, that every man may be accountable for his own sins in the day of judgment. **Therefore, it is not right that any man should be in bondage one to another.** And for this purpose have I established the Constitution of this land, by the hands of wise men whom I raised up unto this very purpose, and redeemed the land by the shedding of blood."
> (D&C 101:76-80)

Commentary: These words were recorded on December 13, 1833, as the persecutions of their fellow church members in Missouri escalated. Note, even in the face of their persecutions, this church continued to support the laws of the land, even though they were being ignored by the elected leaders in Missouri, and how, even in the face of such hostility the declaration that "it is not right that any man should be in bondage one to another." This was thirty years before Lincoln would issue his Emancipation Proclamation.

From another of their books, the Book of Mormon, one can read of Lehi's prophecy about America. Lehi was a contemporary of Jeremiah and Ezekiel at the time Judah was being destroyed and led into captivity. This prophecy tells of another attempt by Jehovah to preserve the covenant He had made with Abraham. Said Lehi:

> "Wherefore, I, Lehi, prophesy according to the workings of the Spirit which is in me, that there shall none come into this land save they shall be brought by the hand of the Lord. **Wherefore, this land [America] is consecrated unto him whom he shall bring.** And if it so be that they shall serve him according to the commandments which he hath given, it shall be a land of liberty unto them; wherefore, they shall never be brought down into captivity; if so, it shall be because of iniquity; for if iniquity shall abound cursed shall be the land for their sakes, but unto the righteous it shall be blessed forever." (2 Nephi 1:6-7)

From Isaiah we read words that strongly support these words of Nephi. Isaiah 37:31-32 reads:

> "**And the remnant that is escaped of the house of Judah shall again take root downward**, and bear fruit upward: **For out of Jerusalem shall go forth a remnant,** and they that escape out of mount Zion: the zeal of the Lord of hosts shall do this." (Isaiah 37:31-32)

Commentary: As Americans watch the events unfolding around them in 2014, many wonder what is happening to them and to their beloved nation. Could it be that 'The God Factor" is at work, a work that is spelled out in the Bible and in these other scriptures?

America's Role as a Covenant Nation

Question: How many roles did God assign to America to fulfill?
Answer: At least three.

Question: What were the three known roles given to America to fulfill?
Answer: They were:

1. To restore God's basic principles of freedom to the world;
2. To be an example of a free people led by God;
3. To assist in the gathering of God's scattered people!

Question: Has America completed these three assignments yet?
Answer: No. America completed its first role when the Constitution was completed on September 17, 1787, and its Bill of Rights was added on December 17, 1791.

Its second assignment was to become an example to the world as a nation led by God. America is in the process of completing this assignment as an example to the world by sharing its Constitution with the world. At the time the Founding Fathers signed the newly crafted Constitution in 1787 the world was led by despotic rulers, enslaving their subjects both economically and spiritually. The ruler's word was law and could be changed on the spot by the ruler. America's written Constitution of law changed the world. Today, even though there are continual wars and rumors of wars making headlines, the world knows what real freedom is. America's Constitution has been emulated, albeit in different forms, by over 180 nations of the world.

The third assignment is a role still in play and will only be completed when God decides to speed up the gathering of the twelve tribes of Israel that were scattered and dispersed following Israel's destruction anciently.

And the flow of immigrants to America, once started has never stopped. We see this immigration, the dream to be free, continue on America's southern border in 2014. This assignment, while well under way, has slowed considerably since 1912 because as America matured it felt less dependency on God and began turning to their federal government, finally allowing the courts to cut its umbilical cord with God in the mid-1900s.

Question: Is America subject to the wrath of God as a Covenant Nation?

Answer: Yes. For more insights on this subject see chapter thirteen of this book.

Chapter Four

America's Declaration of Independence - A Covenant Document

Opening commentary: Ironically America's Declaration of Independence wears two hats. The hat seen by the secular eyes of the world is that of a document that only declared America to be a separate and equal nation among the nations of the world, a document that only opened the door for the world's enslaved to be freed from their economic and spiritual imprisonments.

But its second hat, that hat seen by those with the eyes that see beyond its words, the Declaration of Independence is more, much, much more. To those with eyes that see beyond its words it is a document drafted by a man raised up and inspired by God, Thomas Jefferson, to reintroduce to the world, with eight words, "the Laws of Nature and of Nature's God," the foundational principles of all law, those principles of freedom and liberty Jefferson had found in God's "perfect law of liberty." To those with the eyes to see beyond the words this document declares that "the Laws of Nature and of Nature's God" are America's two foundational laws, both near and long term, and that America will be blessed as a nation if it obeys the laws of Nature's God and cursed as a nation if these laws are ignored and/or trampled on.

Thus the Declaration of Independence declares itself to be a secular document that contains **the principles the Constitution was designed to preserve, protect and defend,** and **a spiritual document that foretells that the near and long term future of America's freedoms** are subject to America implementing and adhering to "the

Laws of Nature and of Nature's God," proxy words for God's "perfect law of liberty," the foundational principles and laws for all civilized nations.

July 4, 1776,
The day the United States of America declared its Independence

Question: What is America's Declaration of Independence?
Answer: America's Declaration of Independence is both a secular and spiritual document that was drafted in June of 1776 by Thomas Jefferson. It, as a secular document, declares the thirteen British Colonies in North America were now a separate and equal nation, cutting their umbilical cords with Great Britain to become one new and united independent nation. It is a written document, in final form, of fewer that three hundred words signed by fifty-six men who knew when they signed it they had just signed their own death warrant had they lost the Revolutionary War. These were brave men with families who could lose everything – and some did, some lost their families and some lost their lives.

It is a document so unique and world changing that in all probability, while Jefferson wrote down the words, the words were likely inspired by a higher divine source. I do not believe any human being, then or now, could have composed such a powerful document that would not only separate thirteen colonies from their motherland, Great Britain, **but would also become the foundational document for yet another very unique and divinely created document, the Constitution of the United States of America.** And because of its divine and spiritual origin it has become the target, as has America's Constitution, of those that feel it necessary to destroy both documents because they have literally changed the world and freed millions who were being held, then and now, in economic and spiritual bondage. These two documents are now under extreme attack and freedom loving Americans must quickly rally around them to preserve the America they love with its cherished freedoms and liberties.

To fully understand the efforts of those determined to destroy America and its freedoms Americans need to know the source of that opposition. A biblical reference to this source is given in Revelations 12 and reads:

> ➢ "And there was war in heaven: Michael and his angels fought against the dragon; and the dragon fought and his angels, And prevailed not; neither was their place found any more in heaven. And the great dragon was cast out, **that old serpent, called the Devil, and Satan, which deceiveth the whole world:** he was cast out into the earth, and his angels were cast out with him." (Revelation 12:7-9)

Thus we learn from the Revelations of John that there was a war in heaven, a war led by Jehovah on the good side and the Devil or Satan on the bad or evil side. Satan lost that war and was cast down "into the earth, and his angels were cast out with him" to earth to continue that war.

Isaiah also describes Lucifer (Satan) and his evil goals with these words in 14:12-17:

> ➢ "How art thou fallen from heaven, O Lucifer, son of the morning! how art thou cut down to the ground, which didst weaken the nations! **For thou hast said in thine heart, I will ascend into heaven, I will exalt my throne above the stars of God**: I will sit also upon the mount of the congregation, in the sides of the north: I will ascend above the heights of the clouds; I will be like the most High. Yet thou shalt be brought down to hell, to the sides of the pit. They that see thee shall narrowly look upon thee, and consider thee, saying, Is this the man that made the earth to tremble, that did shake kingdoms; That made the world as a wilderness, and destroyed the cities thereof; that opened not the house of his prisoners

Moses goes into more detail about the Devil and Satan and his goals with these words:

> "And I, the Lord God, spake unto Moses, saying: That Satan, whom thou hast commanded in the name of mine Only Begotten, is the same which was from the beginning, and he came before me, saying—Behold, here am I, send me, I will be thy son, and I will redeem all mankind, that one soul shall not be lost, and surely I will do it; wherefore give me thine honor. But, behold, my Beloved Son, which was my Beloved and Chosen from the beginning, said unto me—Father, thy will be done, and the glory be thine forever. Wherefore, because that Satan rebelled against me, and sought to destroy the agency of man, which I, the Lord God, had given him, and also, that I should give unto him mine own power; by the power of mine Only Begotten, I caused that he should be cast down; And he became Satan, yea, even the devil, **the father of all lies, to deceive and to blind men, and to lead them captive** at his will, even as many as would not hearken unto my voice." (Moses 4:1-4 – from *The Pearl of Great Price*)

To more fully comprehend that there are people today who actually want to destroy America, Google and read Saul Alinsky's 1960s' book, *Rules for Radicals*. Alinshy's book outlines a few basic rules on how to destroy America as a free nation **and his book is literally dedicated to Lucifer, the father of all evil** – he who led the rebellious in heaven, lost, and was cast out.

Question: Did Thomas Jefferson ever comment on the role the "Creator" and "Supreme Judge of the World" played in the creation of America?
Answer: Yes, many times. The following words are etched on the walls of The Jefferson Memorial located on the Washington D.C. mall.

- "God who gave us life gave us liberty. Can the liberties of a nation be secure when we have removed a conviction that these liberties are the gift of God? **Indeed I tremble for my country when I reflect that God is just, that his justice cannot sleep forever**. Commerce between master and slave is **despotism**. Nothing is more certainly written in the book of fate than these people are to be free. Establish the law for educating the common people. This it is the business of the state to effect and on a general plan."

- "We hold these truths to be self-evident: that all men are created equal, that they are endowed by their Creator with certain inalienable rights, among these are life, liberty, and the pursuit of happiness, that to secure these rights governments are instituted among men. We...solemnly publish and declare, that these colonies are and of right ought to be free and independent states...**And for the support of this declaration, with a firm reliance on the protection of divine providence, we mutually pledge our lives, our fortunes, and our sacred honor.**"

- "**I have sworn upon the altar of God eternal hostility against every form of tyranny over the mind of man.**"

This next quotation is from the letter Jefferson wrote to the Danbury Baptists. This is the letter the opponents of freedom, including the courts, used to develop their "separation of church and state" laws that have literally, in my opinion, cut the umbilical cord between America and its Creator and Supreme Judge. It's time for concerned Americans to step up and help reconnect America to its Creator and Supreme Judge of the world - the God of America's Founders.

- "Believing with you that religion is a matter which lies solely between man and his God, that he owes account to none other for faith or for worship, that the legislative powers of government reach actions only, and not opinions, I contemplate with solemn reverence that act of the whole American people which declared that their legislature should "make no law respecting an establishment of religion, or prohibiting the free exercise thereof," thus building a wall of separation between Church and State."

Question: What scriptures would have likely inspired and influenced Jefferson as he sat in his room in Philadelphia in June of 1776, having just been given the almost impossible task of writing a document of separation from their motherland – England?

Answer: There are many scriptures that likely inspired and influenced Jefferson. The following are but a few of those that could have inspired Thomas Jefferson and given him the strength and wisdom to draft America's new document of freedom, the Declaration of Independence.

> "And ye shall hallow the fiftieth year, **and proclaim liberty throughout all the land unto all the inhabitants thereof:** it shall be a jubilee unto you; and ye shall return every man unto his possession, and ye shall return every man unto his family." (Leviticus 25:10)

Commentary: It was this scripture that inspired the followers of William Penn, who founded the state of Pennsylvania, to create the Liberty Bell, the Liberty Bell that became another powerful symbol of freedom and liberty to not only the Patriots who created America but for all freedom-loving Americans since. This verse is inscribed on the Liberty Bell.

Another verse:

> "That be far from thee to do after this manner, to slay the righteous with the wicked: and that the righteous should be as the wicked, that be far from thee: **Shall not the Judge of all the earth do right?**" (Genesis 18:25)

Commentary: It is likely this verse inspired Jefferson to use the words he used in the last paragraph of the Declaration that declared the

Donald S. Conkey

Founders dependence on "The Supreme Judge of the World." The location of this verse also likely influenced Jefferson. Abraham was "standing before the Lord" and pleading for the residents of Sodom where his nephew Lot was living. Jefferson likely connected this verse with the other scriptures that indicated Moses had also pleaded with the Lord to keep him from destroying the Israelites who he had just rescued from 430 years of Egyptian slavery.

Next Jefferson would have likely pondered these two verses:

> "Wherefore ye shall do my statutes, and keep my judgments, and do them; **and ye shall dwell in the land in safety. And the land shall yield her fruit, and ye shall eat your fill, and dwell therein in safety.**" – (Leviticus 25:18-19)

> "And it shall come to pass in that day, that the Lord shall set his hand again **the second time to recover the remnant of his people**, which shall be left, from Assyria, and from Egypt, and from Pathros, and from Cush, and from Elam, and from Shinar, and from Hamath, and from the **islands of the sea** [could this include America?]. And he shall set up an ensign for the nations, and shall assemble the outcasts of Israel, and gather together the dispersed of Judah from the four corners of the earth." (Isaiah 11:11-12)

Commentary: Isaiah was privileged to see the future, the coming of the Lord in the meridian of time where he, Christ, initiated the gathering of both Israel, the lost ten tribes that were scattered, and Judah, who were dispersed after being taken captive about 600 BC. Americans are privileged to see the beginning of this gathering of Judah to their lands with the establishment of the State of Israel by the United Nations in 1948, but against great opposition from the Islamic nations – then and still today. This gathering of Israel has begun and is in progress even in our day.

Jefferson likely had also read, perhaps he even memorized, this verse from Isaiah:

> **"The Spirit of the Lord God is upon me;** because the
> Lord hath anointed me to preach good tidings unto the
> meek; he hath sent me to bind up the brokenhearted, to
> proclaim liberty to the captives, and the opening of the
> prison to them that are bound; To proclaim the acceptable
> year of the Lord, and the day of vengeance of our God; to
> comfort all that mourn;" – (Isaiah 61:1-2)

Commentary: Could the Founding Fathers have felt that Isaiah was
speaking directly to them as they brought forth the first nation in
centuries to have made a covenant with God, a nation that would
literally "proclaim liberty to the captives," the economic and spiritual
captives of the world – then, today, and in the future. **This is one of
America's covenant nation roles!**

Another verse Jefferson was likely very familiar with would be:

> "Then said Jesus to those Jews which believed on him, If
> ye continue in my word, then are ye my disciples indeed;
> **And ye shall know the truth, and the truth shall make
> you free.**" (John 8:31-32)

Commentary: This scripture was likely well known by all of the
Founding Fathers – it speaks volumes to the entire world and to all
those being held captive throughout the world even today, as were the
colonists in 1776.

Jefferson would have likely associated these next two verses with
the words of John 8:31-32:

> "Now the Lord is that Spirit: and where the Spirit of the
> Lord is, there is liberty." (2 Corinthians 3:17)

> "Stand fast therefore in the liberty wherewith Christ hath
> made us free, and be not entangled again with the yoke of
> bondage." (Galatians 5:1)

Commentary: These two scriptures, both recorded by the apostle
Paul, again spoke volumes about the potential of having a free nation
to live in and to raise a family in and to prosper by the sweat of one's
own work, as did Benjamin Franklin and others among the Founding

Fathers.

This next verse likely inspired Jefferson's phrase "the Laws of Nature and of Nature's God," the two laws Jefferson strongly implies are the cornerstone laws of America's freedoms and liberties.

> "But whoso looketh into the **perfect law of liberty,** and continueth therein, he being not a forgetful hearer, but a doer of the work, **this man shall be blessed in his deed**." (James 1:25)

Commentary: Both Thomas Jefferson and James Madison would have been very familiar with this scripture. It could have been the most powerful scripture that inspired Madison to press forward, against great odds, to create a written Constitution patterned after God's "perfect law of liberty."

Question: How was Thomas Jefferson chosen to write the Declaration of Independence?

Answer: On page 26 of *The Making of America* a book written by Dr. W. Cleon Skousen we read: "On June 7, 1776, Richard Henry Lee of Virginia introduced the fatal resolution in Congress calling for complete separation from Great Britain. Several states asked for a brief postponement of any final decision in order to get instructions from home. Meanwhile a special committee was appointed to write a formal declaration of independence. The committee consisted of Benjamin Franklin, John Adams, Roger Sherman, Robert Livingston, and Thomas Jefferson. Jefferson, after banter back and forth between he and John Adams, was given the assignment to draft the declaration."

After accepting this assignment, Jefferson, a self-declared lifelong student of the Bible, especially of the words of Christ, likely turned to his Bible for strength knowing the weight of this fast moving movement was now on his shoulders, and there found inspiration in the words of James 1:5-6, words that read:

> **"If any of you lack wisdom, let him ask of God,** that giveth to all men liberally, and upbraideth not; and it shall

be given him. But let him ask in faith, nothing wavering. For he that wavereth is like a wave of the sea driven with the wind and tossed." (James 1:4-5)

Commentary: It is my firm belief, though there is no known record of it, that after pondering these powerful words of James, Jefferson would have knelt in prayer, possibly fasting for spiritual strength, and asked God for the **wisdom** he would need to bring about His will. It would have been then that the **"dews of heaven"** would have begun to fall upon Jefferson and guide his quill as he drafted that initial draft of his world-changing document of freedom.

Question: How long did Thomas Jefferson take to write the Declaration of Independence?

Answer: Seventeen nights, with fifteen of the seventeen nights used to write the first two paragraphs. It took Jefferson seventeen **nights** to draft this document because he attended to his normal congressional duties during the day and would then return to his room and write from 6 p.m. to midnight on the declaration's draft.

Question: How did Jefferson organize the Declaration of Independence?

Answer: Into five distinct paragraphs.

Paragraph 1 is the introductory paragraph to the Declaration of Independence. In this paragraph Jefferson felt it appropriate to state clearly the reason the colonists were declaring their independence from the nation that had nurtured the thirteen colonies for so many years. As in real family life a child is born, becomes a teenager and struggles to become independent, still wanting a close relationship with their parents but knowing it is time to step out into the real world and do what all children must do, learn to live on their own. In this case these colonists wanted to become, as Jefferson stated, a part of the world's community of nations. Except in this instance the parents,

England, did not want their child to leave home and step out on their own.

The words Jefferson chose to use makes it evident that he fully understood that the laws the new nation would have to live by, as a "separate and equal" nation in the world community of nations, would be the same for them as it was for all other nations - the foundational laws of all civilized nations – **"the Laws of Nature and of Nature's God."** Jefferson fully understood, as did all the other fifty-five men who signed the Declaration of Independence, that these two foundational laws were the laws that Moses carried down off Mt. Sinai, the laws literally written by the finger of God. Jefferson was in effect declaring that the future success of this new nation, the United States of America, would be adherence and obedience to those Laws and Commandments referred to by the apostle James, in 1:25, as **God's "perfect law of liberty."**

It was in the writing of Paragraph 2 that Jefferson spent most of his seventeen nights. This is the paragraph where those **"just and holy principles"** are laid out that Jefferson had found while studying his Bible, those same **"just and holy principles"** that inspired James Madison to later call for a constitutional convention where these principles would become the very foundation of the Constitution that Madison and fifty-four other men created to govern a new nation with, so:

> ➤ "That every man may act in doctrine and principle pertaining to futurity, according to the moral agency which I have given unto him, that every man may be accountable for his own sins in the Day of Judgment." (Doctrine & Covenants 101:78)

Dr. W. Cleon Skousen identified on page 28 of his book, *The Making of America*, eight of those "just and holy" principles. These eight principles are:

- The Principle of "Sound Government." Sound government should be based on self-evident truths. These truths should be so obvious, so rational, and so morally sound that their authenticity is beyond reasonable doubt.
- The Principle of "Equal Station." The equal station of mankind here on earth is a cosmic reality, an obvious and inherent aspect of "the Laws of Nature and of Nature's God."
- The Principle of "Equal Rights." This presupposes (as a self-evident truth) that the Creator made human beings equal in their rights, equal before the bar of justice, and equal in God's sight. (Of course, individual attributes and personal circumstances in life vary widely.)
- The Principle of "Unalienable Rights." Those rights which have been bestowed by the Creator on each individual are unalienable; that is, they cannot be taken away or violated without the offender **coming under the judgment and wrath of the Creator**. A person may have other rights, such as those which have been created as a "vested" right by statute, but vested rights are not unalienable; they can be and often are altered or eliminated by various legislative bodies to adjust to changing times and needs, as is happening here in America in our day.
- Among the most important of the unalienable rights are the right to Life, the right to Liberty, and the right to pursue whatever course of life a person may desire in search of happiness, so long as they do not invade the inherent rights of others.
- The Principle of "Protection of Life and Property." The most basic reason for a community or a nation to set up a system of government is to assure its members and/or citizens that the rights of the people shall be protected and preserved.
- The Principle of the "Consent of the People." It follows then that no office or agency of government has any right to exist

91

except with the consent of the people or their elected representatives.

- It also follows then that if a government, either by malfeasance or neglect, fails to protect those rights – or, even worse, if the government itself begins to violate those rights – **then it is the right and duty of the people to regain control of their affairs and set up a form of government which will serve the people better.**

Jefferson had included one other principle in his initial draft, a principle addressing the future of slavery in the new nation, but it was rejected by several of the southern states after several days of very divisive debates. Jefferson attempted several times during his long years in government to address the slavery issue but was rebuked each time. It remained for Abraham Lincoln to end the slavery issue with the Emancipation Proclamation.

Paragraph 3 was relatively simple to write. It is the list of those twenty-seven abuses Jefferson named in his 1775 pamphlet, **"A Summary View of Rights of British America,"** a pamphlet that caused him to become well known throughout the colonies, and in Great Britain. King George was not pleased with Jefferson's summary. Each reader should ponder those twenty-seven abuses and then see if they can list twenty-seven similar abuses that America's government is saddling its citizens with today in 2014.

Paragraph 4 is a short paragraph that immediately follows the twenty-seven abuses Jefferson had listed in his 1775 pamphlet sent to King George III. This paragraph begins with "In every stage of these Oppressions we have Petitioned for Redress in the most humble Terms:" ... This paragraph reemphasizes the length and patience the colonists went through before declaring their independence on July 4, 1776.

Paragraph 5 is the paragraph where the Founding Fathers firmly declare their new nation, the United States of America, would be a 'covenant nation.' It is in this paragraph where Jefferson declares that the name of their new nation will be "the United States of America." It is in this paragraph where Jefferson openly appeals to God for help, with these words, words that are difficult to misunderstand whom he is addressing, words that read: **"We, therefore, the Representatives of the UNITED STATES OF AMERICA, in General Congress, Assembled, <u>appealing to the Supreme Judge of the World</u> for the Rectitude of our Intentions."** It is in this paragraph where Jefferson reinforces his appeal to the Supreme Judge of the world by openly declaring **"And for the support of this Declaration, with a firm Reliance on the Protection of divine Providence, we mutually pledge to each other our Lives, our Fortunes, and our sacred Honor."** Powerful, powerful words! How can reasonable citizens of these United States or officers of its courts miss seeing how openly dependent the Founding Fathers of America were on their God, the God of Abraham, Isaac and Jacob? Is there any wonder why America has as its motto "In God We Trust"?

These verses likely inspired Jefferson while he was writing the Declaration of Independence:

> ➤ "… would shew the king the interpretation. Then Daniel went to his house, and made the thing known to Hananiah, Mishael, and Azariah, his companions: That they would desire mercies of the God of heaven concerning this secret; that Daniel and his fellows should not perish with the rest of the wise men of Babylon. **Then was the secret revealed unto Daniel in a night vision**. Then Daniel blessed the God of heaven. Daniel answered and said, **Blessed be the name of God forever and ever:** for wisdom and might are his:" (Daniel 2:16-20)

Commentary: Note how these four young men, who had been obedient to the laws of God, and had been endowed by God with wisdom, **"blessed by the God of Heaven."** This showed their gratitude to their God in Heaven who had just blessed them. How many Americans do this today when their prayers are answered by an all-knowing God in Heaven? But Jefferson and the Founding Fathers were as grateful as were these four lads who openly declared their gratitude to God with the words in these two verses:

> "Wherefore king Darius signed the writing and the decree. ¶ Now when Daniel knew that the writing was signed, he went into his house; and his windows being open in his chamber toward Jerusalem, **he kneeled upon his knees three times a day, and prayed, and gave thanks before his God, as he did aforetime."** (Daniel 6:9-10)

Commentary: Remember Daniel and his friends were then living in captivity, yet they feared not their captive king but turned to their God, the God of Abraham, Isaac and Jacob, for help and after help came knelt in prayer and gave thanks before God.

> **"As many as I love, I rebuke and chasten:** be zealous therefore, and repent. Behold, I stand at the door, and knock: if any man hear my voice, and open the door, I will come in to him, and will sup with him, and he with me." (Revelation 3:19-20)

Commentary: Unfortunately far too many Americans do not want to believe that their Lord will rebuke or chasten them, or America. How wrong they are. America is being rebuked by God even today and those rebukes could become even more challenging in the days that lie ahead if or when more of God's curses are laid down on America because of its continued rejection of God's laws.

Question: Where did Jefferson find the eight Principles of Sound Government embodied in the Declaration of Independence?
Answer: During Jefferson's study of the history of ancient Israel he made a significant discovery. He learned that at one time the Israelites had practiced the earliest and most efficient forms of representative

government. He also learned that as long as the Israelites followed their fixed pattern of constitutional principles, they flourished. But when they drifted from those principles, disaster followed. After this study Jefferson referred to this constitutional pattern as **"ancient principles."** (From Skousen's *The Making of America*, page 27)

Question: What are the key phrases in Jefferson's Declaration of Independence?

Answer: The several key phrases, each followed by a scriptural verse or verses that could have inspired those phrases, include:

Phrase # 1:

- "When in the Course of human events, it becomes necessary for one people to dissolve the political bands which have connected them with another, and to assume among the powers of the earth, the separate and equal station to which **the Laws of Nature and of Nature's God** entitle them. A decent respect to the opinions of mankind requires that they should declare **the causes** which impel them to the separation."

The biblical scriptures that likely inspired these words would include:

- ➤ "When the most High divided to the nations their inheritance, when he separated the sons of Adam, he set the bounds of the people according to the number of the children of Israel." (Deuteronomy 32:8)
- ➤ "And the children of Israel, which were come again out of captivity, and all such as had separated themselves unto them from the filthiness of the heathen of the land, to seek the Lord God of Israel, did eat." (Ezra 6:21)
- ➤ "But whoso looketh into the perfect law of liberty, and continueth therein, he being not a forgetful hearer, but a doer of the work, this man shall be blessed in his deed." (James 1:25)
- ➤ "Ye shall have one manner of law, as well for the stranger, as for one of your own country: for I am the Lord your

God." (Leviticus 24:22)

Phrase # 2:

- The phrase, **"the Laws of Nature and of Nature's God,"** is a telling reference to the Creator, and to **the Creator's** known **Laws of Nature** and to the laws of **"Nature's God."** Jefferson, some believe, including this author, used this phase to declare these two laws as America two cornerstones of freedom and liberty.

Commentary: This is where we need to re-emphasize the enlightening words the Founders borrowed from William Blackstone's Commentary on British Law, words that clarify and solidify Jefferson's words. Said Blackstone,

- ✓ "the laws of human nature had been revealed by God, whereas the laws of the universe (natural law) must be learned through scientific investigation. Upon these two foundations, **the law of nature and the law of revelation**, depend all human laws."

A powerful lesson, a lesson ignored by today's judicial system. Note how Blackstone describes **"revelation"** as **a law equal to the law of nature**. Revelation is one of God's laws associated with prayer.

Phrase # 3: Jefferson begins paragraph two with this phrase:

- "We hold these truths to be self-evident, that all men are created equal, **that they are endowed by their Creator with certain unalienable Rights**, among these are Life, Liberty, and the pursuit of Happiness."

Commentary: The phrase **"endowed by their Creator"** is a powerful phrase, clear and **self-evident,** one the reader should find easy to comprehend and to help them better understand how the Founding Fathers unequivocally knew and understood God's role in the creation of their covenant nation.

The phrase **"unalienable rights"** makes reference to "rights given to every human being at birth by their Creator." But this is also a strong inference that there are also **"unalienable duties"** associated with citizenship, duties that are too often ignored by growing numbers of Americans.

Supportive biblical scriptures for this phrase would include:

➢ "So God created man in his own image, in the image of God created he him; male and female created he them. And God blessed them, and God said unto them, Be fruitful, and multiply, and replenish the earth, and subdue it: and have dominion over the fish of the sea, and over the fowl of the air, and over every living thing that moveth upon the earth." (Genesis 1:27-28)

➢ "And ye shall hallow the fiftieth year, and proclaim liberty throughout all the land unto all the inhabitants thereof: it shall be a jubilee unto you; and ye shall return every man unto his possession, and ye shall return every man unto his family." (Leviticus 25:10)

➢ "The heavens declare the glory of God; and the firmament sheweth his handywork." (Psalm 19:1)

➢ "Blessed is every one that feareth the Lord; that walketh in his ways. For thou shalt eat the labour of thine hands: happy shalt thou be, and it shall be well with thee." (Psalm 128:1-2)

➢ "For there is no respect of persons with God." (Romans 2:11)

Phrase # 4 reads:

• "That to secure these rights, Governments are instituted among Men, deriving their just powers from the consent of the governed,"

Biblical scriptures supporting this principle would include:

➢ "And Moses' father-in-law [Jethro] said unto him, The thing that thou doest is not good. Thou wilt surely wear away, both thou, and this people that is with thee: for this thing is too heavy for thee; thou art not able to perform it thyself alone. Hearken now unto my voice, I will give thee counsel, and God shall be with thee: Be thou for the people to God-ward, that thou mayest bring the causes unto God: And thou shalt teach them ordinances and laws, and shalt shew them the way wherein they must walk, and the work that they must do. Moreover thou shalt provide out of all the people able men, such as fear God, men of truth, hating covetousness; and place such over them, to be rulers of thousands, and rulers of hundreds, rulers of fifties, and rulers of tens: And let them judge the people at all seasons: and it shall be, that every great matter they shall bring unto thee, but every small matter they shall judge: so shall it be easier for thyself, and they shall bear the burden with thee. If thou shalt do this thing, and God command thee so, then thou shalt be able to endure, and all this people shall also go to their place in peace. So Moses hearkened to the voice of his father-in-law, and did all that he had said." (Exodus 18:17-24)

Commentary: These are the scriptures that the Founders found in Exodus that became the pattern for setting up a government of "We the People," the first three words of the Preamble to the Constitution, and reinforced by Abraham Lincoln who in his Gettysburg address referred to America's government as a government "of the people, by the people and for the people." (In John Wycliffe's 1384 English Bible Wycliffe stated: "This Bible is for the Government of the People, by the People, and for the People.")

> "Every man shall give as he is able, according to the blessing of the Lord thy God which he hath given thee. Judges and officers shalt thou make thee in all thy gates, which the Lord thy God giveth thee, throughout thy tribes: and they shall judge the people with just judgment. Thou shalt not wrest judgment; thou shalt not respect persons, neither take a gift: for a gift doth blind the eyes of the wise, and pervert the words of the righteous. That which is altogether just shalt thou follow, that thou mayest live, and

inherit the land which the Lord thy God giveth thee."
(Deuteronomy 16:17-20)

Commentary: This is a scripture that likely encouraged Jefferson's equality clause.

➤ "For unto us a child is born, unto us a son is given: and the government shall be upon his shoulder: and his name shall be called Wonderful, Counsellor, The mighty God, The everlasting Father, The Prince of Peace. Of the increase of his government and peace there shall be no end, upon the throne of David, and upon his kingdom, to order it, and to establish it with judgment and with justice from henceforth even forever. The zeal of the Lord of hosts will perform this." (Isaiah 9:6-7)

Commentary: Jefferson, in his writings, was open in his praise for the words of the Savior.

Phrase # 5 reads:

• "That whenever any Form of Government becomes destructive of these ends, **it is the Right of the People to alter or to abolish it,** and to institute new Government, laying its foundation on such principles and organizing its powers in such form, as to them shall seem most likely to effect their Safety and Happiness."

The following biblical scriptures show how the Lord allows a people to reject God's leadership and then ask for a government of their own choosing, even when God knows their new government will eventually destroy them as a nation and a people:

➤ "Then all the elders of Israel gathered themselves together, and came to Samuel unto Ramah, And said unto him, Behold, thou art old, and thy sons walk not in thy ways: now make us a king to judge us like all the nations. ¶ But the thing displeased Samuel, when they said, Give us a king to judge us. And Samuel prayed unto the Lord. And the Lord said unto Samuel, **Hearken unto the voice of the**

people in all that they say unto thee: for they have not rejected thee, but they have rejected me, that I should not reign over them." (1 Samuel 8:4-7)

➤ "Nevertheless the people refused to obey the voice of Samuel; and they said, Nay; but we will have a king over us; That we also may be like all the nations; and that our king may judge us, and go out before us, **and fight our battles**. And Samuel heard all the words of the people, and he rehearsed them in the ears of the Lord. **And the Lord said to Samuel, Hearken unto their voice, and make them a king**. And Samuel said unto the men of Israel, Go ye every man unto his city." (1 Samuel 8:19-22)

Commentary: These verses, all from 1 Samuel 8, tell a powerful story for those that have any doubt about the Lord removing himself from amongst his people. Americans, by their vote in recent elections, have indicated to the Lord that they no longer look to Him as their God, but have turned to their government for free handouts on most everything, a government whose policies are in the process of destroying the America I grew up in, just as Israel self-destructed from within anciently.

➤ "And ye were now turned, and had done right in my sight, in proclaiming liberty every man to his neighbour; **and ye had made a covenant before me in the house which is called by my name:** But **ye turned** and polluted my name, and caused every man his servant, and every man his handmaid, whom ye had set at liberty at their pleasure, to return, and brought them into subjection, to be unto you for servants and for handmaids. Therefore thus saith the Lord; Ye have not hearkened unto me, in proclaiming liberty, every one to his brother, and every man to his neighbour: behold, I proclaim a liberty for you, saith the Lord, to the sword, to the pestilence, and to the famine; and I will make you to be removed into all the kingdoms of the earth."

(Jeremiah 34:15-17)

Commentary: This is a powerful warning to all Americans who refuse to believe that their God would let them suffer. Not only did he let the Judeans suffer but he literally dispersed them.

A reading assignment: Read Jeremiah's Book of Lamentations. This book is a gruesome review of what happened to a nation who ignored the Laws and Commandments of their God. It is also prophecy fulfilling the words the Lord gave to Samuel in 1 Samuel 8.

Phrase # 6 is Jefferson's warning that applies to America in this 21st century. His words:

- "Prudence, indeed, will dictate that Governments long established should not be changed for light and transient causes: and accordingly all experience hath shewn, that mankind are more disposed to suffer, while evils are sufferable, than to right themselves by abolishing the forms to which they are accustomed."

Scriptures that likely inspired these words include: (This phrase is a condemnation on man's inability to become involved in making changes when changes are needed, and/or are justified.)

- ➤ "And he saith unto them, Whose is this image and superscription? They say unto him, Caesar's. Then saith he unto them, Render therefore unto Caesar the things which are Caesar's; and unto God the things that are God's." (Matthew 22:20-21)

- ➤ "Put them in mind to be subject to principalities and powers, to obey magistrates, to be ready to every good work, To speak evil of no man, to be no brawlers, but gentle, shewing all meekness unto all men. For we ourselves also were sometimes foolish, disobedient, deceived, serving divers lusts and pleasures, living in malice and envy, hateful, and hating one another." (Titus 3:1-3)

Phrase # 7: As Jefferson closes paragraph two he provides this powerful counsel to all Americans in our 21st century with these words:

- "But when a long train of abuses and usurpations, pursuing invariably the same Object evinces a design to reduce them under absolute **Despotism, it is their right, it is their duty**, to throw off such Government, and to provide new Guards for their future security. Such has been the patient sufferance of these Colonies; and such is now the necessity which constrains them to alter their former Systems of Government."

Jefferson likely felt the Spirit of the Lord rest upon him as he read these words in Isaiah?

- "The Spirit of the Lord God is upon me; because the Lord hath anointed me to preach good tidings unto the meek; **he hath sent me to bind up the brokenhearted, to proclaim liberty to the captives, and the opening of the prison to them that are bound;** To proclaim the acceptable year of the Lord, **and the day of vengeance of our God;** to comfort all that mourn; To appoint unto them that mourn in Zion, to give unto them beauty for ashes, the oil of joy for mourning, the garment of praise for the spirit of heaviness; that they might be called trees of righteousness, the planting of the Lord, that he might be glorified." (Isaiah 61:1-3)

Commentary: Powerful words of encouragement to Jefferson as he struggled for the perfect words.

The last paragraph is where the Declaration of Independence affirms America a covenant nation with their signatures on that document. Note in this paragraph to whom Thomas Jefferson and the Founding Fathers turn to, to call down the blessings of God, and of the heavens, to sustain these fifty-six men in their efforts to restore freedom and liberty to the world, as had Moses when he carried God's "perfect law of liberty" off Mt. Sinai anciently. Jefferson evoked the powers of heaven twice in this paragraph.

This paragraph reads:

- "We, therefore the Representatives of the UNITED STATES OF AMERICA, in GENERAL CONGRESS, Assembled, appealing to the Supreme Judge of the World for the rectitude of our intentions, do in the Name, and by Authority of the good People of these Colonies, solemnly publish and declare, that the United Colonies are, and of Right ought to be Free and Independent States, that they are Absolved from all political connection between them and the State of Great Britain, is and ought to be totally dissolved; and that as Free and Independent States, they have full Power to levy War, conclude Peace, contract Alliances, establish Commerce, and to do all other Acts and Things which Independent States may of right do. And for the support of this Declaration, with a firm reliance on the protection of divine Providence, we mutually pledge our Lives, our Fortunes and our sacred Honor."

Commentary: Jefferson, as were all fifty-six Co-Founders, was now dependent upon the Lord, even as were the ancient Israelites in Egypt; and as was Hezekiah and other biblical characters in time of need.

Scriptures that inspired Jefferson to seek the blessings of heaven likely included these powerful biblical verses:

The first scripture:

- "And it came to pass in process of time that the king of Egypt died: and the children of Israel sighed by reason of the bondage, and they cried, and their cry came up unto God by reason of the bondage. And God heard their groaning, **and God remembered his covenant with Abraham, with Isaac, and with Jacob**. And God looked upon the children of Israel, and God had respect unto them." (Exodus 2:23-25)

Commentary: Remember the colonists were literally in bondage, as had been the ancient Israelites, to Great Britain and King George III, so these two verses resonated well with Jefferson.

The second scripture:

> "If my people, which are called by my name, shall humble themselves, and pray, and seek my face, and turn from their wicked ways; then will I hear from heaven, **and will forgive their sin, and will heal their land**." (2 Chronicles 7:14)

Commentary: This is a scripture that every American should memorize.

The third scripture:

> "And for this cause Hezekiah the king, and the prophet Isaiah the son of Amoz, prayed and cried to heaven. ¶ **And the Lord sent an angel**, which cut off all the mighty men of valour, and the leaders and captains in the camp of the king of Assyria. So he returned with shame of face to his own land. And when he was come into the house of his god, they that came forth of his own bowels slew him there with the sword. Thus the Lord saved Hezekiah and the inhabitants of Jerusalem from the hand of Sennacherib the king of Assyria, and from the hand of all other, and guided them on every side." (2 Chronicles 32:20-22)

Commentary: This verse must have touched all of the Founding Fathers, not just Jefferson, and should have given them hope that if God would do what he did for Hezekiah, He would do the same for them as they labored to free themselves from the grips of tyranny.

The fourth scripture:

> "**As many as I love, I rebuke and chasten**: be zealous therefore, and repent. Behold, I stand at the door, and knock: if any man hear my voice, and open the door, I will come in to him, and will sup with him, and he with me." (Revelation 3:19-20)

Commentary: It is time America knocked once again on His door and let Him back into our personal lives and back into the fabric of our nation as well. I, along with millions of American, think it is now time for all freedom loving Americans to knock on His door – in humility, while praying and fasting.

Question: What would have been the price the Founding Fathers would have paid had they _not_ won the Revolutionary War and their new nation had not survived?

Answer: Had the Revolutionary War failed there is little doubt those fifty-six men would have been tried for treason. Under British law of that time that would have meant...

- "Being hanged by the head until unconscious.
- "Then cut down and revived.
- "Then disemboweled and beheaded.
- "Then cut into quarters.
- "Each quarter to be boiled in oil.
- "The remnants of the body were scattered abroad so that the last resting place of the offender would remain forever unnamed, unhonored, and unknown." (*The Making of America*, page 31)

Commentary: Cruel punishment! Yes! That punishment was cruel beyond all measures of modern-day standards! But the Founding Fathers knew the risks involved if their effort to separate from England had failed. This subject was uppermost on their minds as they pondered their future on that historic day on July 4, 1776. It is something all Americans should ponder even today, especially as they watch the atrocities being committed against Christians today in the Middle East and elsewhere around the world.

Had this effort to create a new nation failed, the land area now known as the United States of America quite likely would have continued to be ruled by the three powers then in America: England, France, and Spain. And America's history, and the world's history today, would have likely been quite different!

But the Founding Fathers were determined, and they were ready to fight a war if necessary, feeling very strongly that their efforts had been inspired by their God, the God of Abraham, Isaac and Jacob. That war was fought and won when the British gave up after the Battle of Yorktown in October 1781 – after God's powerful intervention, one of the many miracles Washington witnessed as he led a ragtag army against the world's most powerful Army at that time..

Question: Were there other biblical scriptures that could have inspired Jefferson?
Answer: Yes. Many! The following are but a few of the many that likely inspired Jefferson. Jefferson was a scriptorian who had created his own mini-Bible using only the words of the Lord.

> ➢ "So God created man in his own image, in the image of God created he him; male and female created he them." (Genesis 1:27)
> ➢ "Ye shall have one manner of law, as well for the stranger, as for one of your own country: for I am the Lord your God." (Leviticus 24:22)
> ➢ "The law of the Lord is perfect, converting the soul: the testimony of the Lord is sure, making wise the simple." (Psalm 19:7)
> ➢ "Stand fast therefore in the liberty wherewith Christ hath made us free, and be not entangled again with the yoke of bondage." (Galatians 5:1)

Commentary: Thomas Jefferson was a man spiritually and intellectually prepared, like Daniel, then endowed with wisdom to draft a document that would change the world, and would become the Foundational Document upon which the Constitution of the United States of America, with its Bill of Rights, would be founded. Thomas Jefferson's Declaration of Independence was America's first symbol of its covenant with the God of Abraham, Isaac and Jacob, a document that still inspires freedom-loving Americans to roll up their sleeves and become involved in preserving those freedoms and liberties so precious to all Americans.

Question: What words in the Declaration of Independence suggest a covenant with God?

Answer: There are several words and/or phrases that strongly imply this document helped create America as a covenant nation. Those primary words and phrases are:

1. In paragraph one the phrase: **"to assume among the Powers of the Earth, the separate and equal Station to which the Laws of Nature and of Natures God entitle them,"** … immediately declares America's future independence and freedoms will depend on these two laws, "the Laws of Nature and of Nature's God" and that **this entitlement comes from being equal before God with all other nations on earth.**

Commentary: This phrase, 'the Laws of Nature and of Nature's God" was used by other great thinkers of the world, but as a dedicated student of the Bible Jefferson likely was familiar with the apostle James' powerful reference to God's **"perfect law of liberty"** in James 1:25.

2. Jefferson's use of: **"that all Men are created equal, and are 'endowed' by their 'Creator' with certain unalienable Rights"** in paragraph two strongly suggests that he, Jefferson, had received divine assistance with the writing of this world-changing document. The Bible provides solid evidence that God has been actively involved in the affairs of man from the beginning of the world. The words and activities of the Old Testament prophets provide powerful examples of this help. Examples of this help include:

> "Thus Melzar took away the portion of their meat, and the wine that they should drink; and gave them pulse. As for these four children [Daniel, Hananiah, Mishael, Azariah], God gave them knowledge and skill in all learning and wisdom: and Daniel had understanding in all visions and

Donald S. Conkey

dreams." (Daniel 1:16-17)
- And the king communed with them; and among them all was found none like Daniel, Hananiah, Mishael, and Azariah: therefore stood they before the king. And in all matters of wisdom and understanding, that the king enquired of them, **he found them ten times better than all the magicians and astrologers that were in all his realm."** (Daniel 1:19-20)

Commentary: As one studies the history of Daniel's time period one can clearly see that in order for God to return the Jews to Jerusalem and **preserve his covenant with Abraham,** Isaac and Jacob, He had raised up these four young captive Jews, princes of Judah, and gave them wisdom in all things in order to help prepare King Cyrus to allow Ezra to return to Jerusalem and rebuild the temple, the singular powerful symbol of God's people whom he would gather in these latter-days.

- And the Lord spake unto Moses, saying, " I have called by name Bezaleel the son of Uri, the son of Hur, of the tribe of Judah: And I have filled him with the spirit of God, in wisdom, and in understanding, and in knowledge, and in all manner of workmanship, To devise cunning works, to work in gold, and in silver, and in brass, And in cutting of stones, to set them, and in carving of timber, to work in all manner of workmanship. And I, behold, I have given with him Aholiab, the son of Ahisamach, of the tribe of Dan: and in the hearts of all that are wise hearted I have put wisdom, that they may make all that I have commanded thee;" (Exodus 31:2-6)

Commentary: This verse reminds believers of several of Christ's parables where He makes it clear, very clear, that not everyone receives the same talents when they enter mortality at birth. And God, as in this case, had prepared Bezaleel to build Solomon's Temple, similar to how God raised up Thomas Jefferson to write the

Declaration of Independence; George Washington to win a difficult war and become America's first president; James Madison to create a Constitution of law for the new United States of America; Abraham Lincoln to win a Civil War while freeing those held in bondage because of the color of their skin; and Martin Luther King to more fully implement the Emancipation Proclamation. Clear evidence that God is ever watching America, even today He is watching as America gambles with its freedoms.

> ➤ "And Moses said unto the Lord, O my Lord, I am not eloquent, neither heretofore, nor since thou hast spoken unto thy servant: but I am slow of speech, and of a slow tongue. And the Lord said unto him, Who hath made man's mouth? or who maketh the dumb, or deaf, or the seeing, or the blind? have not I the Lord? Now therefore go, and I will be with thy mouth, and teach thee what thou shalt say." (Exodus 4:10-12)

Commentary: I suspect the Lord could have said much the same thing to Thomas Jefferson, a man of few words, in that small rented room in Philadelphia, just as God said these words to Moses, who too was very reluctant to go and free the Israelites.

> ➤ "And when Abram was ninety years old and nine, the Lord appeared to Abram, and said unto him, I am the Almighty God; walk before me, and be thou perfect. **And I will make my covenant between me and thee,** and will multiply thee exceedingly." (Genesis 17:1-2)

Commentary: Or perhaps the Lord could have said to Jefferson in that room in Philadelphia what the Lord said to Abraham when Abraham, at age ninety-nine, and was told to go into a strange land and then covenanted with Abraham with these words.

> ➤ "To whom the word of the Lord came in the days of Josiah the son of Amon king of Judah, in the thirteenth year of his reign. It came also in the days of Jehoiakim the son of Josiah king of Judah, unto the end of the eleventh year of

Zedekiah the son of Josiah king of Judah, unto the carrying away of Jerusalem captive in the fifth month." (Jeremiah 1:2-3)

Commentary: Or perhaps the word of the Lord came to Jefferson as it came to Jeremiah as it is declared in Jeremiah 1:2-3 with these words.

3. In paragraph five Jefferson declares that those Founding Fathers appealed "to the **Supreme Judge of the World for the rectitude of our [their] intentions…**" One need not have to guess who Jefferson's "Supreme Judge of the World" was. It was America's Founding Fathers' God, the God of Abraham, Isaac and Jacob.

Commentary: One only has to read Jefferson's words, or his biography to fully understand just how much he admired the words of Christ in the New Testament, so his use of these words is fully in line with a man who loved Christ, and felt God's presence in that room for seventeen nights when he sat alone, with the Holy Ghost prompting him, and wrote those immortal words of the Declaration of Independence, the words that changed the world forever, and set the foundation for the creation of a written document that would establish God's "perfect law of liberty" once again on earth.

4. And again in paragraph five, Jefferson asks for help with these words: "**with a firm Reliance on the Protection of divine Providence**" before they mutually pledged [covenanted] to each other their Lives, their Fortunes, and their Sacred Honor.

Commentary: Can anyone doubt who Jefferson was seeking support from when he penned these words, "with a firm Reliance on the Protection of divine Providence."

There are several other powerful phrases that also strongly suggest divine support in Jefferson's choice of words. These phrases include:
Phrase # 1:

> **"That to secure these Rights, Governments are instituted among Men, deriving their just Powers from the Consent of the Governed…"**

Commentary: This phrase should be required memorization of every American – it is "We the People who give the Government their power – and "We the People" can alter that Government with our vote and with personal involvement in our local, state and federal government. This we would call 'citizenship responsibility.' What is your "Citizenship Quotient?"

Phrase # 2:

"That whenever any Form of Government becomes destructive of these Ends, **it is the Right of the People** to alter or to abolish it, and to institute new Government, laying its Foundation on such Principles, and organizing its Powers in such Form, as to them shall seem likely to effect their Safety and Happiness."

Commentary: The message in this phrase is that when Government becomes destructive to our freedoms and liberties **"it is the Right of the People to alter or to abolish it, and to institute new Governments, laying its Foundation on such Principles, and organizing its Powers in such form, as to them seem likely to effect their Safety and Happiness."** A powerful reminder that we, under our Constitution can still effect such needed change via our involvement and vote.

Phrase # 3:

"Prudence, indeed, will dictate that Governments long established should not be changed for light and transient Causes: and according to all Experience hath shewn, that Mankind are more disposed to suffer, while Evils are sufferable, than to right themselves by abolishing the Forms in which they are accustomed."

Commentary: There are two parts to this phrase. The first part cautions America not to be rash in wanting to change its government for **"light and transient Causes."** The second part reminds Americans that they need not be "disposed to suffer, while Evils are sufferable, then to right themselves by abolishing the Forms in which they are accustomed." Jefferson strongly suggests that when Evils in America become insufferable that we Americans have it in our power to change these 'sufferable Evils" by becoming involved in our government and voting out of office those that have caused such 'Evils.'

Phrase # 4:

> "But when a long Train of Abuses and Usurpations, pursuing invariably the same Object, evinces a Design to reduce them under absolute Despotism, **it is their Right, <u>it is their Duty, to throw off such Government,</u>** and to provide new Guards for their future Security."

Commentary: Jefferson listed twenty-seven "Abuses and Usurpations" King George III had put upon the colonies. It would not be difficult today to list at least twenty-seven "Abuses and Usurpations" America's government has inflicted upon its people in the past fifty years. Freedom-loving Americans need to read and then reread this part of the Declaration of Independence, and more fully understand that the "Abuses and Usurpations" America is being afflicted with today **could lead to "absolute Despotism,"** and that it is not only the "Right" of freedom-loving Americans to "throw off such Government" but that **it is "their Duty"** to throw off such Government, and to provide new Guards for their future Security through the ballot box.

A careful reading of the Bible tells us the United States of America is a covenant nation. The writings of America's Founding Fathers tell us America is a covenant nation. America's culture – its history; its national anthem; its Pledge of Allegiance, its National Monuments; the United States Seal; its patriotic songs; its sacred religious music, and America's Foundational Documents, the Declaration of Independence and its Constitution, as amended all strongly and authoritatively declare that the United States of America is a covenant nation.

And so I too declare America a **Covenant Nation** – a nation subject to those same blessings and curses, including the wrath of God, as ancient Israel was subject to as a Covenant Nation anciently.

Chapter Five

America's Revolutionary War Years

Opening commentary: There have been scores of books written on the Revolutionary War Years and these books are available to all persons interested in that war. But few if any of these books mention how God was involved, per the writings of America's Founding Fathers themselves, in that war. This book, however, declares that 'America is a covenant nation' and is written to explain that without **"The Hand of God"** Washington and his "ragtag army" could not have won the "Revolutionary War;" and how often 'a God-provided miracle' was needed to keep Washington and his army moving forward to victory.

A Chronology of the Revolutionary War years - 1775 to 1883

The real challenges General George Washington faced are evident as one follows this chronology. The challenges to preserve America's liberties by our generation today will be equally challenging and they won't be challenges that will be solved in a day. And the challenges to preserve America's freedoms and liberties today will be no less challenging than those Washington and his fellow Founders faced as they struggled to create a covenant nation where God could reintroduce to the world his 'perfect law of liberty' through America's Declaration of Independence whose pure and holy principles of freedom would be protected by the written laws established by a new form of government, a Republican form of government "of the people, by the people and for the people."

1775

- **February:** Massachusetts was declared in **'open rebellion'** by King George III.
- **April 19:** 250 British soldiers and ninety minutemen were killed near Lexington, Massachusetts. The Revolutionary War began on this day in 1775. There would be no turning back after this.
- **May 10:** Ethan Allen and Colonel Benedict Arnold, with eighty-three troops, captured Fort Ticonderoga in New York State.
- **May:** America's Second Continental Congress met in New York City as renegade representatives of a nation that did not yet exist. It would be a year later before America would declare its independence from Great Britain.
- **June 15:** George Washington was named commander-in-chief of a "Continental Army" that was created by a renegade Congress for a nation that did not yet exist. Remember this was a Congress of men from thirteen separate colonies taking things into their own hands. This must have been a frightful experience for those involved, as it will be for those who take on a task few even want to think about, but a task that must be done if America's freedoms and liberties are to be preserved by that same 'spirit of liberty' that fortified America's Founding Fathers.
- **June 17:** The first major Revolutionary War battle was fought at Bunker Hill.
- **July 3:** Washington took command of a 'ragtag army,' minutemen from New England.
- **November 13:** The American army captured Montreal, Canada, and invited the French Canadians into their new loosely-formed Union. Their invitation was rejected!
- **November 15:** The American forces were badly defeated near Quebec in Canada.

1776

- **January:** Thomas Paine wrote his famous pamphlet "Common Sense" to support the colonists' cause. Paine's pamphlet became a strong motivator in encouraging the colonists to separate from England. George Washington later used Paine's words to motivate and rally his troops during a very difficult time of the war.

- **March 17:** The British evacuated Boston, taking over 1,000 Tories (Loyalists) with them to Nova Scotia. The Tories remained 'loyal' to the king of England. During the Revolutionary War Tories often sided with England and fought against General Washington and his troops. Following the Revolutionary War the Tories were harassed by the winning Patriots and many were forced to leave their homes and farms and move to Canada.

- **June 12:** A congressional committee was appointed by the Continental Congress to draft a constitution. John Dickinson was named chairman of this committee. (This committee drafted the Articles of Confederation.)

- **Early June:** The Congress named a committee to draft a declaration of separation from England. The final draft became the Declaration of Independence. Thomas Jefferson was one of the five members of the committee and was asked to draft the document. He did!

- **June:** The British navy attempted to capture Charleston, South Carolina, and induce Loyalists to fight against the 'rebels.' They failed in that first attempt but tried again and succeeded.

- **July 4:** The Declaration of Independence was adopted unanimously by the fifty-six members of America's second Continental Congress. With the signing of that document America became dependent on their "Creator" and "Supreme Judge of the World" and caused it to become a covenant nation.

- **August:** The British Parliament authorized an army of 55,000 men, an army that included 30,000 hired German mercenaries to be sent to America. This event outraged the American Patriots and made them even more determined to separate. This may be comparable to the progressive movement's efforts during the past 100 years to make America subservient to the United Nations.

- **August 22:** General Howe landed on Long Island with 32,000 superbly armed and equipped troops. Washington evacuated his troops from Long Island under cover of darkness – in a dense fog. (Was Washington saved by another divine intervention? Many called it a miracle!)

- **September:** General Howe took New York City, a town of 22,000, second only to Philadelphia in the colonies. When General Howe entered New York City, its large Tory citizenry, estimated to be two-thirds of the citizens, turned out to greet and welcome General Howe and his British army.

- **September 21:** New York City went up in flames. The Tories blamed their 'rebel' neighbors and became an angry mob and 'strung up' many rebels, without trial, and even threw a few of their 'rebel' neighbors screaming into the leaping flames.

- **September 22:** Nathan Hale, famous for his line, "I only regret that I have but one life to give for my country," was hung, without trial, by General Howe.

- **October 28:** General Howe, after defeating Washington, a defeat that could have ended the infant war, changed course and allowed Washington to escape across New Jersey. (Another divine intervention)

- **December 23:** Washington rallied his bedraggled troops by reading them a stirring message written by Thomas Paine. Paine's message created a renewed sense of commitment into the troops regarding their "mission" at Valley Forge.

- **December 26:** Washington's troops captured 1,000 Hessian troops at Trenton, New Jersey. This was Washington's first major victory. General Howe, in New York, taking the winter off, was furious and ordered General Cornwallis, then at Princeton, New Jersey, to Trenton, New Jersey, to destroy Washington. Washington escaped! (Another miracle!)

1777

- **January 3:** Washington captured Princeton, New Jersey, General Cornwallis' headquarters. This victory saved the war for the Americans. (Another divine intervention!)
- **Winter-Spring:** The British and their hired Hessian troops burned, looted and raped the surrounding countryside during the winter of 1777. Their excuse was that this was an eighteenth century soldier's privilege. The local Tories had been given writs of immunity from the British but the Hessians could not read English, and to the Hessians looting was all the same, friend or foe, it didn't make any difference. This caused the Tories to begin rethinking their support of the British cause.
- **Winter-Spring:** Washington was forced to stay in Morristown, New Jersey, due to the sickness of his troops: smallpox and starvation diets. His troops dwindled to only 3,000, but his victories at Trenton and Princeton, New Jersey, brought in new recruits, helping Washington rebuild his army to 9,000 men. The French, to support the American cause, sent 22,000 muskets to help the Americans. Washington greatly appreciated France's help.
- **Summer, Early Fall:** Fort Ticonderoga was recaptured by Britain's General Burgoyne. However Burgoyne's Indian troops captured, and then scalped an American girl named Jane McCrea. This incident inflamed the American Patriots causing them to flock to their militia posts, volunteering to fight. This was a huge boost for Washington's forces.
- **Summer:** General John Stark, a hero at Bunker Hill, agreed to

lead his New Hampshire troops against General Burgoyne. Vermont's Green Mountain Boys then joined Stark.

- **August 15:** General Stark encountered three hundred seventy-four German mercenaries out foraging for cattle, horses, and food near Bennington, Vermont. Only nine Germans escaped death or capture. Later, another German foraging unit suffered 230 dead, wounded or captured. These were badly needed victories to boost Washington's troops' sagging morale.

- **September 11:** Washington's troops were badly defeated by the British troops at Brandywine, 50 miles south of Philadelphia.

- **September 19:** The British lost six hundred troops at Freeman's Farm in New York. At Freeman's Farm Daniel Morgan's frontiersmen climbed trees and with their Kentucky long rifles "picked off" British officers and artillerymen. Benedict Arnold's military leadership skills stood out and were noticed by both the soldiers and officers.

- **September 26:** Britain's General Howe and his troop occupied Philadelphia.

- **October 4:** Washington's forces were again defeated by the British at Germantown, 50 miles south of Philadelphia.

- **October 7:** The Patriots defeated the British for a second time at Freeman's Farm.

- **October 17:** England's General Burgoyne retreated from the Freeman's Farm battle to Saratoga. At Saratoga Burgoyne's troops were surrounded by General Washington's troops and Burgoyne was forced to surrender five thousand British and German troops. **This was a major victory** for Washington's cause as it was the battle that allowed Benjamin Franklin, America's ambassador to France to convince France that the Americans could win their 'unwinnable' war with Great Britain. France then declared war on Great Britain, its long time enemy. The French then began to provide Washington

118

needed money and military equipment, funds and materials badly needed to fight this war. (Another divine intervention?)

- **November 14:** The Articles of Confederation were finally approved, but they had been watered down and provided little support to General Washington. The completed Articles required all thirteen states to approve every decision made, an impossible task for any organization, especially a government running a war.

- **December 19:** Washington's army retired to its winter quarters at Valley Forge. A vivid report of this experience at Valley Forge was described by author Leckie, in his book, *The Wars of America*. He wrote: "Soldiers at Valley Forge went hungry because nearby farmers preferred to sell to the British in Philadelphia for hard cash, because New York's grain surplus was diverted to New England civilians and the British in New York City, and because Connecticut farmers refused to sell beef cattle at ceiling prices imposed by the state. Soldiers went half naked because merchants in Boston would not move government clothing off their shelves at anything less than profits ranging from 1,000 to 1,800 percent. Everywhere in America there was a spirit of profiteering and a habit of graft that made Washington grind his teeth in helpless fury. In response to his appeals, Congress passed the buck by authorizing him to commandeer supplies. This he was reluctant to do among a people supposed to be trying to throw off the yoke of a tyrant. When he was forced to do it, the results confirmed his fears."

1778

- **Winter:** Disloyalty was evident in Washington's officer corps. Several ranking officers felt they were better qualified than Washington to lead the army. These events caused great strain on Washington and on his loyal officers. (Individual pride and jealously destroy many good causes, as is witnessed in Washington D.C. today in 2014.)

- **Early in 1778,** and for nearly two long years, the British War Office had mobilized Indian tribes on the western frontier. These Indians, led by Britain's Sir John Butler, were terrorizing (using tactics modern day terrorists use to terrorize the world today) the settlements along the outlying frontier. Congress was ineffective and could do little to stop those murderous raids. The entire frontier was up in arms, demanding protection. Virginia's Governor Patrick Henry sent a 25-year-old frontiersman named George Roger Clark, along with 125 men, to wipe out the British outposts and return calm to the frontier.

- **May:** British army's General Howe and his brother Admiral Howe both resigned their commands. Howe's replacement, Sir Henry Clinton, soon abandoned Philadelphia in an effort to shore up the British defenses around New York City, fearing a large French fleet he believed was heading to New York. When Clinton left Philadelphia the Tories living in Philadelphia were terrified. General Howe suggested they make peace with the Patriots whom they had mistreated during the pomp and pageantry of the previous winter.

- **February 6:** The United States and France signed an alliance pact. France became an even bigger factor in the war, sending more equipment, money and troops to America. (Another divine intervention?)

- **June 28:** The Battle at Monmouth, New Jersey, between the British and Washington's troops ended in a draw.

- **November:** The British sent Colonel Archibald Campbell south, with 3,500 troops, to capture Savannah in Georgia.

- **December 29:** The British attacked and captured Savannah Georgia.

1779

- **June 16:** Spain declared war on Great Britain. This declaration added new pressures on Great Britain. The British then **redeployed its navy** to protect its holdings in Gibraltar and Minorca. It also weakened Britain's naval strength in the West Indies. France became bolder and captured a number of British vessels. Naval action by the French in the West Indies required General Clinton to dispatch eight thousand regulars from New York to the West Indies. This provided Washington's army badly needed relief. (Another divine intervention)

- **Summer:** With Indian raids continuing in western New York and western Pennsylvania General John Sullivan was sent to the frontier by Congress with five thousand men to make a direct attack on the Indian settlements. Sullivan destroyed at least forty of the Iroquois villages of the Five Nations of the Long House, dispersing most of their people. The Iroquois never recovered from this "affliction of desolation."

- **October 3:** The French failed to retake Savannah, losing eight hundred and fifty troops in the attempt. Savannah was now being defended by local Tories and this victory in Savannah Georgia brought other Tories out of their "closets" throughout the south.

- **Fall:** Times were so difficult that Alexander Hamilton, then an aid to General Washington, wrote: **"We begin to hate the country for its neglect of us. The country begins to hate us for our oppression of them."** Difficult times for all involved! Establishing and, preserving liberty is never easy. There will always be opposition. Opposition is a natural law!

1780

- **Spring:** Great Britain played its trump card in the south! Encouraged by the large Tory turn out in support of the British in the south, General Clinton again targeted Charleston, South

Carolina. Charleston fell and five thousand five hundred Patriot prisoners were captured. Following this campaign the southern Tories developed a repulsive reputation for their continuing **"atrocities to colonial prisoners."** Then, noting the new British emphasis on the south, the Congress appointed General Gates, against Washington's strong opposition, to lead their southern army, and appointed Baron Johann de Kalb, a Bavarian and volunteer from France as second in command. Baron de Kalb was a brilliant and experienced military man and attracted many Patriots to volunteer throughout the south. But then a numerically superior American force was soundly defeated at Camden South Carolina by Britain's General Cornwallis. During this battle General Gates **literally abandoned his troops.** Baron de Kalb stayed and with six hundred troops fought the British to a moral victory. But de Kalb died in that battle and this British victory was followed two days later with another victory. Britain's good news continued. Up north **Benedict Arnold defected and became a Loyalist,** and came close to betraying General Washington's army into British hands at West Point, New York – but didn't. (Another divine intervention!)

- **October 7:** Finally, at Kings Mountain North Carolina, a major victory was won by the Americans forces. This victory turned the tide of the Revolutionary War. General Cornwallis, in his effort to capture North Carolina, put Major Patrick Ferguson in charge of his flanking troops. Major Ferguson, one of the most hated persons in the south, had a passion for engaging in merciless pillaging of all who fell in his way. Ferguson was killed at Kings Mountain. This battle at Kings Mountain marked the beginning of the end for the British in the South.

1781

- **January 1:** Mutiny broke out in General Washington's northern army – the issue, no pay in a year. Washington had to resort to strong measures: he had two of the ring leaders shot. A near disaster was averted.

- **January 17:** Morale was lifted when General Daniel Morgan's troops killed or captured nine-tenths of the British army led by the Tories "terrible" Tarleton.

- **March 15:** Over thirty percent of General Cornwallis' troops were killed in one of the bloodiest battles of the war at Guilford Courthouse near the western foothills of North Carolina.

- **Spring-Summer:** The war continued to seesaw back and forth. General Cornwallis finally abandoned North Carolina and left for Virginia where he met "turn-coat" Benedict Arnold who had mobilized seventeen hundred Tory volunteers. British General William Phillips had also sent General Cornwallis reinforcements from New York. This gave General Cornwallis 7,200 men, all concentrated around Yorktown, Virginia. Cornwallis had turned Yorktown, a small tobacco shipping port on the York River, into a powerful naval and military base.

Yorktown - The Final Battle

Great Britain's Sir Henry Clinton had fortified New York while waiting for the French fleet to land troops and attack his army in New York. And General Cornwallis had assembled his troops near Yorktown waiting to be reinforced by the British navy sailing down from New York. The French fleet, however, sailing up from the West Indies changed the British plans. The French fleet, instead of sailing to New York as Clinton had prepared for, sailed into the Chesapeake Bay area where there were deeper ports. In route the two navies met and a great naval battle ensued. The French navy outnumbered the British navy with 24 ships and 1,700 guns, to Britain's 19 ships and 1,400 guns. The French navy routed the British navy. (Was this another divine intervention? Yes.)

Meanwhile General Cornwallis' 7,200 troops were trapped against the York River at Yorktown. The French fleet prevented General Cornwallis from receiving his badly needed supplies from New York by "bottling up" Chesapeake Bay while Washington's army of 16,000 men, including 5,000 French troops, moved down from the north and surrounded Cornwallis' army on the York River. The British dug in, and prepared to fight. And fight they did!

Yorktown, one of God's real miracles

- **October 9:** The French navy fired on the British troops, followed by Washington's batteries. General Washington ignited the first shot fired by his troops. It was a deadly battle and included hand-to-hand combat by Alexander Hamilton's brigade that attacked a British redoubt - An earthen fortification within a fortification.

- **October 16:** After seven days and nights of fighting a terrified General Cornwallis made a desperate attempt to cross the York River to reach Gloucester. His plan was to fight his way northward until he could escape along the coast. But it was not to be. He loaded his men into boats commandeered along the York River. But when Cornwallis reached the center of the river **a virtual hurricane suddenly arose and blew all his boats back to Yorktown.** After this General Cornwallis was heard to say: **"that it even looked like God was on Washington's side."** Many think He was! (Another divine intervention!)

- **October 17:** A teenaged Redcoat drummer appeared on a British parapet (a protective wall) amidst the cannonading and beat the drum calling for a parley (meeting). The guns fell silent, and the parley began. The terms: unconditional surrender!

- **Noon, October 19:** Two lines formed on the Yorktown battlefield, one headed by Washington, the other by their French allies. General Cornwallis refused to come out to present his sword to Washington, but had his subordinate, General O'Hare, present the sword of defeat. General Washington then had O'Hare present the sword to his subordinate, General Benjamin Lincoln. The sword ceremony was the signal for the British to march forward and surrender their weapons as they acknowledged themselves to be captured prisoners of War. The British marched to a tune titled "The World Turned Upside Down."

The news of General Cornwallis' surrender at Yorktown had a devastating impact on England. The king wanted to continue, but the English people's hearts were no longer in this war.

The Revolutionary War was virtually over
1782

With the actual fighting over there was a move among the army to ask for retribution from Congress for the lack of pay, poor food, no uniforms, etc. The army felt there was only one man who could give them their due: General George Washington. They wanted to **make Washington their King** and have him serve as King George I of the United States.

The restlessness among the army troops continued through the rest of 1782 and on into the early months of 1783.

- **November 30:** A preliminary Peace Treaty was signed between the United States and the British.

1783

- **February 3:** The definitive treaty was signed. On this same day, treaties were signed between Britain, France, Spain, and the Netherlands, who had also entered the war. None of these European nations gained substantially from this war. The United States gained much. England lost almost everything!

- **March 10:** A circular was brought to Washington's attention calling for a military revolt and setting up of a military dictatorship, with or without General Washington. Washington called a meeting of his officers and pleaded with them for reason and patience. He reviewed their grievances and expressed a determination to work with Congress for a just solution, but he denounced any and all who would attempt to **"open the floodgates of civil discord and deluge our rising empire in blood."** (Anarchy is never far from liberty's door.)

- **March 10:** As Washington read a letter from Congress he reached into his pocket and brought out a pair of glasses few had ever seen him wear. He explained: **"Gentlemen, you will permit me to put on my spectacles, for I have not only grown gray but almost blind in the service of my country."** This simple statement achieved what all of Washington's rhetoric and arguments had not been unable to achieve. The officers were in tears. (It's important for all Americans to remember that following America's successful war the French had their own revolution – but it ended differently – such as America's could have ended if it wasn't for George Washington and Washington's faith in God. America's experiment led to freedom and liberty. The French revolution led to Napoleon and many years of harsh tyranny.)

Historians have since emphasized that the whole American experiment hung on this one speech at Newburgh, New York. Jefferson, a year later, wrote:

- **"The moderation and virtue of a single character** (George Washington) **probably prevented this revolution from being closed, as most others have been by a subversion of that liberty it was intended to establish."**

This was a powerful statement and it was also another probable divine intervention.

- **April 15:** Congress ratified the preliminary peace treaty.

126

- **September 3:** The United States and Great Britain signed the final peace treaty in Paris.
- **November 25:** The British left New York for England.
- **December 4:** Washington went to Fraunces' Tavern in New York to bid his officers farewell and there embraced each one of his officers.
- **December 23:** Washington reported to Congress in Annapolis and resigned his commission and left for home, arriving home at Mt. Vernon on Christmas Eve 1783.

The Founding Fathers speak out on
America's new found freedoms

The first three presidents of the new United States expressed strong opinions on how and why America won its Revolutionary War. They spoke often of those virtues required of a people if they were to prosper and maintain their newly won freedom. Here are a few of their comments:

- George Washington: From his inaugural address: **"There exists in the economy and course of nature an indissoluble union between virtue and happiness....we ought to be no less persuaded that the propitious smiles of Heaven can never be expected on a nation <u>that disregards the eternal rules of order and right which Heaven itself has ordained.</u>"** ... From Washington's farewell address: **"Of all the dispositions and habits which lead to political prosperity, religion and morality are indispensable supports."** Later he would say: **"reason and experience both forbid us to expect that national morality can prevail in exclusion of religious principles. It is substantially true, <u>that virtue and morality are a necessary [foundation] of popular government.</u>"**

- John Adams: **"We have no government...capable of contending with human passions unbridled by morality and religion."**

Donald S. Conkey

Later he wrote: **"Liberty can no more exist without virtue than the body can live without the soul."**

- Thomas Jefferson: **"passions and appetites are parts of human nature, but so are 'reason and moral sense.'**

Edmond Burkes thought's on liberty

The Founding Fathers learned these lessons on virtue and morality from their knowledge of history, and from one of their mentors, the great English philosopher Edmond Burke. Burke said this about liberty: **"Men are qualified for civil liberty in exact proportion to their disposition to put moral chains on their appetites. Society can not exist unless a controlling power upon the will and appetite be placed somewhere, and the less of it there is within, the more there must be without. It is ordained in the eternal constitution of things, that men of intemperate minds cannot be free. Their passions forge their fetters."** (P. 83 *America's God and Country*, Federer)

Question
Was America created by chance or by divine intervention?

In the nearly 240 years since the Revolutionary War, that began at Lexington, Massachusetts on April 19, 1775, historians have written thousands of books on the War that ended, against great odds, with an American victory, and the birth of a new nation.

Historians have provided the world with two schools of thought on why the American Revolution was fought, and on how the insurgents, (the colonists/patriots) won this difficult war with Great Britain. One group of contemporary historians, especially the progressive's "politically correct" historians, write their history from a point of view that 'America's time had come,' that a small group of 'radical' colonists, tired of tyrannical kings and taxation without representation

128

felt it was time for the colonies to break from their mother land, Great Britain, and form a new nation, with self-representation and taxation only with representation. They exclude all references to God's influence, divine assistance, divine intervention, or to America being a covenant nation.

The other group, including a small but growing number of contemporary historians, write their history from the perspective that the creation of America was not by accident but by a "divinely guided plan" that brought victory to Washington and his ragtag army after nearly eight long years of fighting what should have been an 'unwinnable war.'

This second group, including Alexis de Tocqueville, the French historian, uses the writings of the Founding Fathers to support their writings citing specific writings of Washington, Adams, and Jefferson, to give emphasis to Jefferson's points on 'divine intervention.'

In 1789 President George Washington was asked to proclaim a national day of public thanksgiving to encourage Americans to acknowledge: **"with grateful hearts, <u>the many signal favors of Almighty God,</u> especially by affording them the opportunity peaceably to establish a constitution of government for their safety and happiness."** This was to acknowledge God's Hand in America's victory!

One cannot fully comprehend the history of America's founding without understanding Washington was a man of deep faith, often pleading with God for divine assistance, especially when no other help was available from the colonies or from the Continental Congress. His pleas to God were heard, many times, and God's help came, often, according to his writings.

Washington's notes indicate he unashamedly turned to and received help from a source higher than himself. He also recorded in his journal, on many occasions, when and how his prayers were heard, and of the "miracles" extended to him and to his armies by "divine intervention" in times of serious crisis. It was this **"divine**

129

intervention" from "Nature's God," according to Washington, that helped his armies prevail, against great odds. It is difficult to read these records and not think of the words written by the prophets about America, and its destiny as "a beacon of freedom" for enslaved people all around the world. The Founders, in pondering the prophesies of Isaiah, felt his words resonated with them and saw themselves fulfilling Isaiah's prophesies.

Well-documented sources of where the Founding Fathers found their unique ideas of freedom show that fully one-third of their ideas on government discussed at the Constitutional Convention came from the writings of Moses, especially from his Book of Deuteronomy.

These emerging historians that support the "divine intervention" principle draw from Moses' and Isaiah's writings to support their writings on how the Founding Fathers were able to accomplish so much in such a short time, while changing world history forever.

The Founders believed in the principle of **"divine intervention"** and that it was real. Their writings verify this. They had read about "divine intervention" in their Bibles and they had seen "divine intervention" in their own lives during the Revolutionary War, especially George Washington, the one leader who was constantly on his knees pleading for God's "divine intervention."

The Founders were well versed in the Bible, and were fully aware that God had, on many occasions, intervened on behalf of those pleading for deliverance from bondage through their prayers. They were aware of how God had sent Moses to free and liberate the Israelites from their Egyptian bondage. They also knew God spoke to Moses saying:

> ➤ "I have surely seen the afflictions of my people which are in Egypt, and have heard their cry by reason of their taskmasters; for I know their sorrows." The Founders had also read how God had "divinely intervened" in the cause of Hezekiah, following his and Isaiah's prayers for deliverance from the Assyrians, by sending "an angel

which cut off all the mighty men of valour, and the leaders and captains in the camp of the king of Assyria. ..." (2 Chronicles 32:20-22)

Jefferson was especially aware of the pleadings of both the Israelites and of Hezekiah as he had just listed his 27 grievances against King George III, "prayers if you will," that literally ended up in the Declaration of Independence as twenty-seven charges against the king and the parliament of England.

The Founders were likely aware of the following scriptures: one set from Deuteronomy the other from Isaiah, prophecies that prophesy that the Israelites will be scattered but that a remnant of them will be planted elsewhere in the field and there put down roots and bring forth fruit. These scriptures read:

➤ **"For the Lord thy God is a consuming fire, even a jealous God**. ¶ When thou shalt beget children, and children's children, and ye shall have remained long in the land, **and shall corrupt yourselves**, and make a graven image, or the likeness of any thing, and shall do evil in the sight of the Lord thy God, to provoke him to anger: I call heaven and earth to witness against you this day, **that ye shall soon utterly perish from off the land** whereunto ye go over Jordan to possess it; ye shall not prolong your days upon it, but shall utterly be destroyed. And the Lord shall scatter you among the nations, and ye shall be left few in number among the heathen, whither the Lord shall lead you. And there ye shall serve gods, the work of men's hands, wood and stone, which neither see, nor hear, nor eat, nor smell." (Deuteronomy 4:24-28)

➤ "And the remnant that is escaped of the house of Judah shall again take root downward, and bear fruit upward: **For out of Jerusalem shall go forth a remnant,** and they that escape out of mount Zion: the zeal of the Lord of hosts shall do this." (Isaiah 37:31-32)

The following words were written by the son of Lehi, a Jewish contemporary of Zedekiah, who was then king of Jerusalem during the time Jerusalem was taken into captivity. His words provide these other historians with documentation showing God knew the future role of America and helped America's Founding Fathers establish America. These other historians believe it was Lehi who led the remnant that escaped Jerusalem. His words read:

> ➤ "And it came to pass that I beheld that the Gentiles who had gone forth out of captivity did humble themselves before the Lord; and the power of the Lord was with them. And I beheld that their mother Gentiles were gathered together upon the waters and upon the land also, to battle against them. And I Nephi beheld that the power of God was with them, and also that the wrath of God was upon all those that were gathered together against them to battle. ...And I beheld that the Gentiles that had gone out of captivity were delivered by the power of God, out of the hands of all other nations." (1 Nephi 13 – Book of Mormon)

As one reads the chronology of the Revolutionary War and ponders the odds of Washington winning that war with his ragtag army, no navy, and no effective central government, not even a willingness on the part of the Continental Congress to provide Washington's army desperately needed men, clothing, food, equipment, and pay; this passage takes on a powerful new meaning: that God can, has, and does **"intervene"** in the affairs of righteous men and women who have humbled themselves before Him, and have asked in prayer for deliverance – as had the Founding Fathers, especially George Washington.

While there is no known record of God sending an angel or angels to intervene, Washington was aware that the Lord had sent the "**captain of His host**" to assist Joshua after he crossed the River Jordon to 'cleanse Canaan.'

> ➢ "And it came to pass, when Joshua was by Jericho, that he lifted up his eyes and looked, and, behold, there stood a man over against him with his sword drawn in his hand: and Joshua went unto him, and said unto him, Art thou for us, or for our adversaries? And he said, Nay; but as **captain of the host of the Lord** am I now come. And Joshua fell on his face to the earth, and did worship, and said unto him, What saith my lord unto his servant?" (Joshua 5:13-14)

Commentary: This scripture from Joshua strongly suggests the Lord was aware of Washington and his men and was watching over them. Remember it was General Cornwallis who said, as he surrendered his troops to Washington at Yorktown, "that even God is on his [Washington's] side."

Freedom loving Americans today would do well to ponder those divine experiences recorded by the Founding Fathers telling of their total dependence on God, especially on the divine help George Washington received in answer to his pleading prayers, as they face off against an enemy as powerful as the enemies Washington faced, maybe more so, with similar pitfalls standing in their paths; who will do anything to destroy this nation and its liberties – and are doing it.

Question: Were the colonists united in their fight for religious and economic freedoms?

Answer: No, they were not! But under such conditions one would think that a people fighting a war to create a new nation would be united. Not so! The American colonists were badly divided. The doctrine of opposition in all things, as old as life itself, was in full effect in colonial America during the Revolutionary War. The principle of Murphy's Law: "if anything can go wrong, it will," was also in full effect.

133

This principle is better understood when one understands that the population of the colonies in 1776 was estimated to be approximately 3,700,000 with sixty-one percent English, ten percent Irish, and eight percent Scottish. Most white colonists were Anglo-Saxon. The racial percentage was eight-one percent white and nineteen percent black, of whom ninety-six percent were slaves.

George Washington had the foresight to see what was coming and called for a Constitutional Convention, but he was rebuffed. He then wrote to John Jay these words: **"What a triumph for the advocates of despotism to find that we are incapable of governing ourselves, and that systems founded on the basis of equal liberty are merely ideal and fallacious."** In our efforts to restore sanity to America Americans need to be continually reminded that what they have embarked upon, the preservation of their liberty, will be filled with many disheartening challenges, likely more losses than wins – but, like Washington's tactics of hit and run while always moving forward.

But little did Washington know that the greatest test of the "**great American experiment**" lay directly ahead, and that his personal involvement would be inescapable? A similar scenario may lie ahead for all who embark on a similar journey today, as they set out on their journey to 'preserve' America's freedoms and liberties,

But it was still a time of crisis for America, as it is today as America struggles to remember its past and realize that its freedoms can be lost through neglect and rejecting the "the Laws of Nature and of Nature's God." **Another miracle would be needed, as will be needed in our day!** But where would that miracle come from? It came, and it came from the same source that had helped Washington win his seemingly 'unwinnable' war – the same source that will be needed to bring America back to where it needs to be – **America's God, the Founder's "Creator and Supreme Judge of the World."**

Now we will see just how that miracle came about!

Chapter Six

America's Post-Revolutionary War Years
1783 – 1789

Opening commentary: This chapter explains that even though the war had been won by General George Washington, with his ragtag army winning a war against unbelievable odds, the several years following the war were equal to, or worse than, the war itself. During the war they knew their enemy – the British. **After the war their enemy came from within.** Their Congress was ineffective, the nation had no executive under the Articles of Confederation, the soldiers who had been so heroic during the war were being treated badly, had not been paid, and had little to eat, and wore rags for clothes. Food was scarce, there were riots among the people, and farmers closed down the courts that were foreclosing on their farms. **Rebellion was in the air.** The new nation was close to mutiny and anarchy.

Question: What was the document being used to govern the new nation during this time period?
Answer: The Articles of Confederation. Remember, when the thirteen colonies declared their independence from Great Britain in July 1776, they were still thirteen independent colonies, with no constitution or document to guide them in their quest for freedom, or in governing a new nation. Each colony had its own government, its own British appointed governor, and its own legislature. Each state was jealous of its own sovereignty and was afraid of a strong central government,

having lived under British rule for years. (For additional details of this time period read chapters 4 and 5 of Dr. W. Cleon Skousen's *The Making of America.*)

Question: What were the Articles of Confederation, how were they created, and how did they work?

Answer: By the time the thirteen colonies in America adopted their Declaration of Independence in 1776 they had been meeting as a confederation of states for nearly two years They had met together to discuss mutual concerns, without authority from England, and without any formal constitution.

During the Second Congress in early 1776, just before they drafted and signed the Declaration of Independence, that Congress decided to organize under a formal charter. On June 12, 1776, one day after the appointment of the committee to write the Declaration of Independence, a committee of thirteen members of Congress, delegates appointed by their colonial legislatures, was appointed to draft a governing document. It never was intended to be a **"people's constitution,"** simply a compact among the states. But this was a necessary step for the colonies to take in order to end up eleven years later with a new and unique workable Constitution.

John Dickinson was appointed chairman of that thirteen-man committee. A draft was written. The initial draft by Dickinson included an outline for a national government, but many of the delegates and states took exception to many of the concepts of a national government, and whittled away at it, watering it down until it was little more than a compact between the various states. The haggling continued until November 15, 1777, when congress agreed to accept a severely watered-down version of Dickinson's draft. It emphasized **"perpetual union"** but merely coordinated the states instead of consolidating the thirteen sovereignties into a genuine union. The approved document was then sent to the states for ratification.

For more detailed information regarding the Articles of Confederation read Dr. Skousen's *The Making of America.*

Question: Was there anything missing in the Articles of Confederation?
Answer: Yes, they were weak and **did not** provide:

- For any executive to speak with one voice for all of the states in time of emergency. This lack of executive power created many problems for George Washington as Commander of the army.
- For a federal judiciary with general jurisdiction to handle federal cases other than those involving boundary disputes, piracies, and crimes on the high seas.
- For any means of enforcing the decrees of Congress except by sending out an army to declare war on the offending state.
- For the authority to regulate interstate commerce. After the Revolutionary War this problem became the fuse that could have blown the new Unites States to pieces.
- Any authority to regulate foreign commerce except through treaties with foreign nations.
- The authority to tax. This left the Congress and its armed forces completely dependent upon the states to voluntarily meet their assessment, which they did not do.

In spite of their deficiencies, and as weak as they were, the Articles were brilliant as far as they went. They actually contained some of the most elemental principles that were later incorporated into the Constitution. The British quickly perceived the weaknesses of the American political structure and recognized the well-nigh hopeless task of mobilizing the resources of a people trying to operate as thirteen independent sovereign states. King George and the British Parliament expected to bring back the wayward Americans, regardless of cost. The British held out hope for this reconciliation until they were defeated in the War of 1812.

Author's Note: The following paragraphs include a few moments in the history of the United States that need to be better understood if Americans are to fully understand the challenges America's Founding Fathers faced when they were birthing America as a free and covenant nation.

Question: How was Washington able to hold the nation together?
Answer: By his strong dominating personality, with sheer determination – and with God's help.

Seven months after Yorktown and long before the peace treaty was signed, Washington received a most disturbing letter from one of his officers, Colonel Lewis Nicola. The letter outlined the abuse and neglect the army had received from the Congress as well as from the states during the war years. He outlined a long list of complaints suffered by the men who had risked their lives many times to throw off the British yoke, and were yet lucky enough to still be alive. They were in rags. They had not been paid. Their food was so scanty it was not fit to be served as slop to pigs.

Colonel Nicola pleaded with Washington to become King George I of the United States, and assured Washington the army would put him in office. This was to be a military coup. Washington was horrified that such a sentiment festered among his troops. He responded with a letter, signed by his aides, that this temptation to abandon the revolution and return to Ruler's Law would nullify everything for which the Revolution had been fought.

Ten months after the Nicola letter a circular began appearing among the men and it came to the attention of Washington on March 10, 1783. It called for a military revolt and the setting up of a military dictatorship. Washington called for a meeting of his officers on March 15 and reviewed their grievances and expressed a determination to work with the Congress for a just solution, but he emphatically denounced any and all who would attempt "to open the floodgates of civil discord and deluge our rising empire in blood."

The officers were still sullen and silent. His plea had failed. Finally he pulled out a letter from his pocket and tried to read it, but couldn't. Biographer James T. Flexner describes what followed.

"The officers stirred impatiently in their seats, and then suddenly every heart missed a beat. Something was the matter with His Excellency. He seemed unable to read the paper. He paused in bewilderment. He fumbled in his waistcoat pocket. And then he pulled out something that only his intimates had seen him wear. A pair of glasses! He explained, **"Gentlemen, you will permit me to put on my spectacles, for I have not only grown gray but almost blind in the service on my country."**

"This simple statement achieved what all Washington's rhetoric and all his arguments had been unable to achieve. The officers were instantly in tears, and, from behind the shining drops, their eyes looked with love at the commander who had led them all so far and long."

"Washington quietly finished reading the congressional letter, walked out of the hall, mounted his horse, and disappeared from the view of those who were staring out the window."

"As those who had fought beside Washington in the heat of many battles pondered his words, they voted unanimously (with one abstention) to support their leader in his peaceful, constructive approach to solving their problems."

Historians have since emphasized that the whole American experiment (a government of free people) hung on this one speech at Newburgh, New York. A year later Thomas Jefferson wrote a paragraph of special praise about Washington, saying,

- **"The moderation and virtue of a single character have probably prevented this revolution from being closed, as most others have been, by a subversion of that liberty it was**

139

intended to establish." (For additional insight into this singular incident read Skousen's *The Making of America*, pages 105-106.)

There was a strong need for a Constitutional Convention

As the war subsided with the signing of the peace treaty in 1783 **the perils of freedom increased.** The country needed just what George Washington and James Madison later called it – a miracle. The country was already drifting down that swift current of **internal revolution** which France would follow just a few years later during their French Revolution, after which they turned to the dictator Napoleon. The Founders knew they had to somehow halt the explosive forces which were tearing apart the states and threatening to shatter the fragile union.

Both England and Spain expected the United States to collapse. Both of these nations were waiting offshore for signs of internal disintegration and were ready to move in and retake America. Even many Americans expected the United States to collapse. There was widespread talk of an imminent civil war. It seemed the "weak and helpless government" was unable to defend its sovereignty against Britain, Spain, or the Native Americans. There was talk of forming three new confederations, one for each section – New England, the Middle States, and the South.

The signs of Internal Revolt were everywhere

- On January 1, 1781, over 2,400 soldiers mutinied. They killed an officer and launched a protest march to Philadelphia to vent their anger on Congress. Washington intercepted them at Trenton and worked out an accord, but he lacked the resources to provide any genuine solutions to their truly legitimate complaints.

- About the same time, some of the New Jersey troops mutinied and two of their leaders had to be shot before order was restored.

- During June 1783 a body of about one hundred soldiers from Pennsylvania stormed the seat of Congress in Philadelphia and terrified the members so much they fled to Princeton and then to Annapolis for safety. The Congress never restored the seat of government to Philadelphia again.

- After the peace treaty, the foremost business interests in the nation seriously considered uniting with the army to set up a military dictatorship in order to save the country from total ruin. Historian Flexner writes: "Out of this seemingly desperate situation there hatched a desperate expedient, which was spread from one mind to another by letter and conversation and semi- public toast...." It nearly cost America its freedom.

Up and down the Atlantic seaboard Americans were suffering the depths of a paralyzing depression. Taxes were of a grave concern. In desperation, the people finally resorted to the same measures of defense they had used against the Coercive Acts of George III. Mobs of farmers assembled to prevent the courts from sitting, so there would be no more judgments for debts. They held conventions to pool their grievances and draft petitions. They appointed committees of correspondence between counties.

Unable to solve their immediate problems, state officials had the governor issue a proclamation against "unlawful assemblies" and had the militia sent out to disperse them. The desperate farmers pushed reluctant Daniel Shays into chairmanship of a committee which was determined to prevent the supreme court of Massachusetts from sitting at Springfield, lest it indict the rebelling farmers. On January 24, 1787, a force of 1,100 men led by Shays entered Springfield to seize the courthouse and the federal arsenal. They suddenly found themselves enveloped in a withering blast of artillery fire, which killed and wounded a number of the poorly armed rebels. They were attacked again at Petersham and dispersed again. Fourteen were sentenced to death, but when things cooled down they were pardoned or given short sentences. Shays escaped to Vermont.

Public opinion throughout the United States recognized the serious implications of Shays rebellion. It became apparent that raw freedom **without economic stability** was certainly not the **"pursuit of happiness"** Americans had been talking about during the Revolutionary War. It was obvious there had been serious mistakes made in dealing with the fiscal policies of the infant republic. The worst of these was cranking up the engine of inflation.

Question: Why did Washington lament the State of the New Nation?
Answer: Because he feared Anarchy was taking over the nation, a return to "Ruler's Law."
On November 5, 1786 Washington commented to James Madison,

- "No day was ever more clouded than the present.... We are fast verging to anarchy and confusion.... How melancholy is the reflection.... What stronger evidence can be given of the want of energy in our government than these disorders? ... A liberal and energetic constitution, well guarded and closely watched to prevent encroachments, might restore us."

On December 26, 1786, Washington wrote General Henry Knox these words.

- "I feel, my dear General Knox, infinitely more than I can express to you, for the disorders, which have arisen in these states. Good God! Who ... could have foreseen, or ... predicted them?"

On February 3, 1787 Washington wrote,

- "If ... any person had told me that at this day I should see such a formidable rebellion ... as now appears, I should have thought him a bedlamite, a fit subject for a madhouse."

Times were difficult but these were times for testing, and these challenging times would eventually lead to a constitutional convention. The nation had reached its lowest level of humiliation. Alexander Hamilton listed a number of problems the nation faced such as:

- The Articles of Confederation gave the Central Government No Power to Act.
- The Articles lacked Fundamental Power for a Sound Government.
- There was no power to raise revenue.
- There was an immediate need for a Stronger Union, and the United States was too weak to be **"feared or respected."**
- The Articles did not allow for majority rule, nor did they have the power to carry out any congressional decrees while disinterested states ignored the decrees of Congress.
- The Articles allowed the states to veto congress.
- Some states were starting to trade with other states like they were foreigners.

The states were coming closer and closer to the needed Constitutional Convention as the Confederation began to collapse economically, with the states failing to support the congress, and with a total political dissolution being approached.

The need for a constitutional convention became more evident with each passing day. And it was about to happen.

Chapter Seven

America's Constitutional Convention

Opening commentary: Chapter seven describes why a constitutional convention was needed and how God's covenant with America was involved in preparing George Washington and James Madison, the "Father of the Constitution," to find needed solutions for the common needs of the newly created United States of America.

This chapter will provide 21st century Americans, concerned about America's future as a free nation, a much better understanding of the monumental challenges they face today as they battle **to preserve, not create, America's freedoms.** These 21st century challenges, though different in many ways, are similar to the challenges the Founding Fathers faced in 1787. Freedom will always be under attack from Satan and his minions. And freedom-loving Americans will always be needed as watchmen/women to guard against the loss of those freedoms that God gave America when he orchestrated the creation of America as a covenant nation, a nation that embedded God's "perfect laws of liberty" deeply into America's world-changing documents, its Declaration of Independence and Constitution.

Question: Who authorized the Constitutional Convention, and why?
Answer: The Congress called for the convention. They called for the convention because there were events happening that could have led the new nation into anarchy and/or a civil war. Conditions were getting out of hand. Many of the Founding Fathers thought anarchy would happen.   Conditions had deteriorated so much that Alexander Hamilton called for and succeeded in getting his state of New York to

pass a resolution calling for a constitutional convention in 1782. When Hamilton was elected to Congress in 1783 he immediately began campaigning for the convention. Washington, on March 28, 1785, realizing that to preserve the new union something had to change, lobbied his state of Virginia. Relations were so bad between Maryland and Virginia over fishing rights that Washington himself had already intervened by asking delegates from both states to meet at his Mount Vernon home to mediate their differences.

As conditions continued to deteriorate, the Congress, on February 21, 1787, officially extended an invitation to the several states (13) to send special delegates to Philadelphia on May 14, 1787. There were seventy-three delegates invited; only fifty-five attended. The states had not provided travel money and many of the delegates had to borrow money to attend the convention. Congress's instructions to the delegates was to **"modify, or patch up"** the Articles of Confederation to make **"the federal constitution adequate to the exigencies of government, and the preservation of the union."** The Congress knew the country was in trouble, deep trouble, but little did they suspect that before the delegates would complete their assignment they, the delegates, would come up with an entirely new system of government under a completely new and unique constitution. A people's government!

Question: Who were the fifty-five men who established an entirely new form of government?
Answer: In terms of experience and professional training, the fifty-five delegates represented a cross-section of the most capable men in the country. They included:

- Two were college presidents (William S. Johnson and Abraham Baldwin).
- Three were or had been college professors (George Wythe, James Wilson, and William C. Houston).
- Four had studied law in England.

- Thirty-one were members of the legal profession, and several of them were judges.
- Nine had been born in foreign countries and knew the oppressions of Europe from first-hand experiences.
- Twenty-eight had served in Congress, and most of the rest had served in state legislatures.
- Nineteen or more had served in the army, seventeen as officers. Four had been on Washington's staff.

Dr. Samuel Eliot Morison of Harvard wrote: "Practically every American who had useful ideas on political science was there except John Adams and Thomas Jefferson, (both were on foreign missions) and John Jay, busy with the foreign relations of the Confederation. Jefferson contributed indirectly by shipping to James Madison and George Wythe from Paris sets of Polybius and other ancient publicists who discoursed on the theory of "mixed government" on which the Constitution was based. The political literature of Greece and Rome was a positive and quickening influence on the Convention delegates."

For a short biography for each of the fifty-five delegates read Skousen's *The Making of America*, pages xv through xxix. Aside from their quality of experience another attribute of the fifty-five delegates was their age. Their average age was forty-one.

- Five (including Charles Pinckney) were under thirty.
- One (Alexander Hamilton) was thirty-two.
- Three (James Madison, Gouverneur Morris, and Edmund Randolph) were within a year of being thirty-five. Only four members had passed sixty, and Benjamin Franklin, at eighty-one, was the oldest member by a gap of fifteen years.

Question: Of the fifty-five delegates, which are the most remembered?

Answer: The following fifteen. For a more in-depth biography of these men read Dr. Skousen's *The Making of America*, pages 138 – 153.

- George Washington, Virginia: 1732 – 1799, was forty-two when named General of the Army. He died at age sixty-seven.
- Benjamin Franklin, Pennsylvania: 1706 – 1790, was eighty-one when the Constitutional Convention began.
- James Madison, Virginia: 1751 – 1836, was thirty-four when the Constitutional Convention convened.
- Edmund Randolph, Virginia: 1753 – 1813, was Governor of Virginia.
- Alexander Hamilton, New York: 1757 – 1804, was born in the West Indies.
- Gouverneur Morris, New York: 1752 – 1816, wrote the final draft of the Constitution.
- Robert Morris, Pennsylvania: 1734 – 1806, was born in England. Was the Confederation's financial genius during the war.
- George Mason, Virginia: 1725 – 1792, was one of the three who refused to sign the initial Constitution that led to the establishment of America's Bill of Rights.
- George Wythe, Virginia: 1726 – 1806, was the mentor of Thomas Jefferson.
- James Wilson, Pennsylvania: 1742 – 1798, born in Scotland and had a strong legal mind.
- John Dickinson, Delaware: 1733 – 1808, was the penman of the revolution.
- Roger Sherman, Connecticut: 1721 – 1793, businessman, lawyer.
- John Rutledge, South Carolina: 1739 – 1800, Governor of South Carolina.

- Charles Pinckney, South Carolina: 1757 – 1824, Governor of South Carolina.
- Charles Cotesworth Pinckney, South Carolina: 1746 – 1825, Attorney General of South Carolina.

Question: When did the convention actually convene?

Answer: Congress called for the convention to convene on May 14, 1787. But on May 14 only two states, with their delegates, had shown up – Pennsylvania, the host state, and Virginia, the home state of both George Washington and James Madison, prime movers for the convention. This delay in delegates arriving turned out to be a real blessing. (Perhaps a miracle) Remember, Congress's charge to the delegates was simple, modify the existing Articles. Nothing more, nothing less, simply modify and adjust the Articles of Confederation and make them more effective in governing the thirteen states. However Madison and Washington both felt that "patching up" the Articles would not do what was needed to be done to save the struggling nation, a nation very close to internal anarchy, and possibly civil war.

It was at this time that Madison proposed to Washington that the convention, contrary to their charge, throw out the Articles and begin anew, to find a better way. Washington agreed. Madison also won the support of his Virginia delegation, eventually winning the support of the entire convention. A new day was about to begin.

Madison took advantage of this eleven-day grace period to review some new ideas with Washington and other members of the Virginia delegation. This was the period when Madison formulated the Convention's Agenda with what became known as Virginia's "Fifteen Resolves."

When the full Convention convened Madison was ready to begin discussions with his fifteen resolves which included forty-one specific issues. These forty-one issues were presented as an agenda by the Virginia delegation and vigorously debated. Twenty-eight of the issues were accepted by the delegates. Eleven were rejected. Two were toss-ups. The delegates then voted to throw out the Articles of Confederation and begin from scratch and create a new form of government, "line upon line, and precept upon precept." (Isaiah 28:10 & 13)

This is where the educational background of the delegates was vital. It was necessary for these men to see beyond their day, and grasp the meaning behind Madison's proposals. Also remember Thomas Jefferson had been Madison's mentor for several years by then, so we are seeing the wisdom and training of Jefferson brought into full view with Madison's proposals. For a full review of these forty-one issues the reader is referred to pages 155-156 in Skousen's *The Making of America*. Recommended reading! This book is also recommended as a Freedom Library book!

Question: When did the Convention officially open?
Answer: On May 25, 1787, in Philadelphia, Pennsylvania.

Question: Where were John Adams and Thomas Jefferson when this convention convened?
Answer: Both men were still fully involved as ministers representing America in Europe. John Adams was in England, Thomas Jefferson in France. Even though Jefferson was in France his influence was still being felt in the convention. As Madison's mentor Jefferson had sent him over 100 books from France on various philosophies of government.

Question: What were the Convention's first two orders of business?
Answer: The first order was to elect a convention president. Washington was immediately and unanimously elected the Convention president. The second order of business was to adopt a set of rules to

govern the Convention business. They adopted six very effective rules. These six rules were:

- The proceedings were to be conducted in secret. This was to prevent false rumors or misinformation from spreading across the country while the Founders were still threshing out the formula which would solve the problems plaguing the nation. Guards were posted at the doors, and no one was admitted without signed credentials.
- Each state was to be allowed one vote, and the majority of the delegation from a state had to be present and in agreement in order to have its vote counted.
- Many times during the proceedings a poll was taken of the individual delegates to see how they stood, but the rule was adopted that none of these votes was to be recorded lest delegates be embarrassed if they later changed their minds as the discussion progressed.
- Each delegate could speak only twice on each issue until after everyone else had been given the opportunity to speak. And no one could speak more than twice without special permission of the convention members.
- Everyone was expected to pay strict attention to what was being said. There was to be no reading of papers, books, or documents while someone was speaking.
- All remarks were to be addressed to the president of the convention and not to the members of the convention. This was to avoid heated polemics between individuals engaging in direct confrontation.

Note that the Convention **was a 'closed session.'** No visitors or press were allowed. It was now up to these fifty-five delegates. America would rise or fall with these men, and their wisdom, and their willingness to negotiate, compromise, and come to a consensus of opinion on matters that would determine the fate of America, its citizens, and the world for years to come, even to our day in 2014.

This is often the case when hard decisions have to be made by mere people. These were the men God had prepared and raised up for this event. America was about to become a covenant nation in reality.

Question: What was the Convention's "Committee of the Whole"?
Answer: This **"Committee of the Whole"** was created by the delegates to give them latitude in debating important issues. It was a procedure whereby the delegates could listen to the ideas of others, and then pick and choose between ideas without having to make a commitment for or against any given idea. It served the delegates well. When the **"Committee of the Whole"** was needed, the delegates **"resolved"** themselves, stepping outside of their delegate duties. Washington would step off the podium and hand the gavel over to another delegate and any issue before the convention that needed to be openly discussed was discussed on an informal 'committee format' instead of in a 'formal format.' The delegates used this "talk it out" format until a substantial agreement could be agreed upon, and a consensus of opinion agreed upon, before **"resolving back into their convention role,"** and officially voting on the matter previously decided in the "informal committee." This procedure was extremely important with this body of fifty-five intelligent men from many different walks of life and experiences.

Question: Was compromise ever used in the Convention?
Answer: Yes. Many times! Compromise is an integral component of consensus politics.

Question: What were the issues where compromise was used during the Convention?
Answer: There were three issues that required statesmanship and compromise in order for the convention to move forward, and succeed to the extent it did. These three issues were: slavery; regulation of commerce; and the apportionment of representation for each state. All

three of these issues were worked out on the basis of genuine compromise, since a consensus or general agreement could not be reached.

Other issues were hotly debated, with vote after vote taken, to no avail. The issue of how to elect the president required six days of debate and sixty ballots to resolve. These were troubling times for Washington who had hoped for great things from this convention.

Question: How many plans for a constitution were submitted?
Answer: Three. The plans submitted were the Virginia Plan, the New Jersey Plan, and the Hamilton Plan. On June 19, 1787, James Madison gave a moving speech in which he said the convention must come up with a **"Constitution for the ages"** and that the Virginia Plan was the only plan that would stand the test of time. Following this speech the New Jersey Plan was voted down and the Hamilton Plan was abandoned.

Question: What was the Virginia Plan?
Answer: It provided for:
- Two branches for the legislature.
- The legislative powers would be derived from the people.
- A single executive.
- A majority of the legislature can act.
- Removal of the executive by impeachment.
- The establishment of inferior federal courts.

Question: Today each State has two U.S. Senators. Where did two Senators come from?
Answer: It was a compromise suggested by Roger Sherman of Connecticut, and was called the "Connecticut Compromise." The compromise was necessary because the convention was looking for a formula to elect representatives to the Congress. The problem was that the small states (Delaware, Connecticut, Massachusetts, etc) were

determined to have one vote for each state as provided in the Articles of Confederation. The large states (New York, Virginia, Pennsylvania, etc.) were equally determined to have one man one vote representation. **Neither side would give in on this issue.**

On July 16, 1787, the convention finally agreed to accept the compromise suggestion by Roger Sherman that each state have equal representation in the Senate, thus two Senators per state, regardless of state size or population, but that the House of Representatives would be apportioned to each state according to population. This suggestion was made three separate times during the heated debates before it was finally accepted. **A major compromise**!

Question: After coming to a consensus on a new Constitution, what was left to do?

Answer: The final draft was given to two committees, a "Committee on Detail," and a "Committee on Style." By July 26 the principle issues had been sufficiently settled to put the Constitution in rough form. The draft was given to the new "Committee on Detail" with instructions to have it in final form by August 6. This committee completed its role and sent it back to the convention floor for review. It took from August 6 to September 8 to hammer out the final details, and during this four-week period eleven of the delegates left for home, leaving only forty-four delegates on the floor. It had been a long hot summer.

On September 8, the amended draft was again in need of refinement so it was sent to another committee, the "Committee on Style" for a final rewrite. Gouverneur Morris, a Pennsylvania delegate, chaired this committee. He was a highly skilled lawyer and it took only four days to put the Constitution into the form it came from the Convention. This is when the Constitution's Preamble was added by Gouverneur Morris.

When the new draft was read to the Convention, some delegates continued to raise new issues. There were eighteen new issues raised during the next three days. However, the vast majority of the delegates were satisfied with the draft as it had been written. The final step was to turn over the final draft to a skilled penman to be inscribed in its final form.

Question: When was the Constitution signed, and by how many delegates?

Answer: The Constitution, in its final form, was signed on September 17, 1787, by thirty-nine delegates. Remember, eleven delegates had left for home in August, thinking everything was over. Three delegates, Elbridge Gerry of Massachusetts, George Mason of Virginia, and Edmund Randolph of Virginia, refused to sign the Constitution as it was presented because it did not include a "Bill of Rights." Because of their strong opposition to the Constitution without a set of rights attached, Washington agreed this would be the first order of business in the first Congress. He kept his word and asked the states for suggestions. A long list was submitted. This list was reduced to seventeen by James Madison and further reduced to twelve by the Congress. These twelve amendments were sent to the states for ratification. Ten were ratified. On December 15, 1791 America's "Bill of Rights," became an official part of the Constitution. Ironically, one of the two amendments not approved in 1791 was adopted as the 27th amendment in 1992.

After the thirty-nine men signed the document Washington submitted the new Constitution to Congress for their approval, along with a cover letter explaining the Convention's reasoning. The Congress discussed it for a few days and then sent it to the thirteen states for ratification. Remember Rhode Island had never sent delegates to this convention.

When Benjamin Franklin signed the Constitution he wept. Later, as the delegates were signing, Benjamin Franklin referred to a picture of the sun on the back of Washington's chair. He said:

- "I have ... often, in the course of the sessions ... looked at that [sun] behind the president without being able to tell whether it was rising or setting. But now at length, I have the happiness to know that it is a rising, and not a setting sun."

It is very important to remember and understand that America's Constitution didn't just happen one day when several men sat down and decided to create a new Constitution for a new nation. The reader can see from this brief review that there is opposition in all things, especially against good things whenever man's freedoms are involved. It is also important to understand that when honest men and women, with character, set their minds on accomplishing something good, one can see the Hand of God in their midst.

Question: Was the Constitution of the United States divinely inspired?

Answer: The delegates themselves believed it was divinely inspired and told the world it was inspired with their writings. In reporting to Jefferson, James Madison wrote*:*

- "the spiritual elements of **a genuine "miracle"** were present in the final hours which made the adoption of the Constitution possible."

Dr. W. Cleon Skousen, in his book *The Majesty of God's Law*, referred to Madison's "spiritual elements" words as the **"Diamond Dust of Heaven."**

George Washington wrote these words to Benjamin Franklin:

- "No one can rejoice more than I do at every step the people of this great country take to preserve the Union.... **The great Governor of the Universe [God] has led us too long and too far on the road to happiness and glory to forsake us in the midst of it."**

Washington reported to Congress that on at least sixty-seven occasions,

155

- "that except for the intervention of God the consequences of those contests would have been different."

Every delegate to the convention knew that there was something being manifested in a most spectacular way. Skousen illuminates this incident more on page 445 of his book, *The Majesty of God's Law.* (A recommended Freedom Library Book)

Benjamin Franklin's words to his fellow delegates were...

- "Our prayers, Sir, were heard – and they were graciously answered. All of us who were engaged in the struggle must have observed frequent instances of superintending Providence in our favor." In pleading with the delegates to call upon God for guidance Franklin said, "In this situation of this assembly, groping, as it were, in the dark to find political truth, and scarce able to distinguish it when presented to us, how has it happened, Sir, that we have not hitherto once thought of humbly applying to the Father of Lights to illuminate our understanding?"

While unseen by Franklin, God was in their midst and His influence was being felt from the beginning to the end of that Convention. God's "perfect law of liberty" was now being restored – the first of God's three major goals for his new covenant nation had been set in motion.

Each of the delegates expressed similar thoughts regarding the inspiration they felt as they toiled long hours under difficult conditions. Those testimonies by America's Founding Fathers were powerful, but perhaps the strongest confirmation that God had had a hand in creating America's new Constitution through the wise men He had raised up, endowed and inspired is found in these words, words accepted as latter-day scripture by members of The Church of Jesus Christ of Latter-day Saints, and words that were recorded in 1833 in Kirkland, Ohio, in a book known as their Doctrine and Covenants:

> "And that law of the land which is constitutional, supporting that principle of freedom in maintaining rights and privileges, **belongs to all mankind,** and is justifiable before me.... And as pertaining to law of man, whatsoever is more or less than this, cometh of evil. **I, the Lord God, make you free, therefore ye are free indeed; and the law also maketh you free.** Nevertheless, when the wicked rule, the people mourn. Wherefore, honest men and wise men should be sought for diligently, and good men and wise men ye should observe to uphold; otherwise whatsoever is less than these cometh of evil." (D&C 98:5-10)

In a later chapter of this book we read of God's purpose for the Constitution with these words:

> "According to the laws and constitution of this people, which I have suffered to be established, and should be maintained for the rights and protection of all flesh, according to just and holy principles.... Therefore, it is not right that any man should be in bondage one to another. And for this purpose have I established the Constitution of this land, by the hands of wise men whom I raised up unto this very purpose, and redeemed the land by the shedding of blood." (D&C 101:77-80)

These are words that strongly clarify for me God's intentions regarding the Constitution of these United States of America.

Another miracle of this convention is that fifty-five delegates survived through four months of heavy intellectual debate and then came up with a structure of government which completely repudiated practically everything they had been taught as loyal Englishmen. Note what the Founders had rejected from their English tutors: (The following list is from Dr. W. Cleon Skousen's magnificent book, *The Majesty of God's Law*, pages 448 & 449 – and used with permission)

• In spite of Hamilton's eloquent plea they wanted nothing to do

157

with a monarchy, not even a limited monarchy. They saw what happened to the Israelites when they demanded a king (1 Samuel 8) so they could be "like all the other nations." The Israelites never recovered from that fatal political blunder.

- They rejected the idea of a prime minister being selected from amongst the members of Parliament.
- They rejected the idea of the cabinet being selected from amongst the members of Parliament.
- They rejected the idea of having the members of Parliament serve as the executive administrators in charge of various departments of government. (cabinet)
- They rejected the British idea of an "unwritten constitution."
- They rejected the idea that the acts of Parliament would automatically become the supreme law of the land even though they may violate some of the most fundamental provisions of their unwritten constitution.
- They rejected the idea of the upper chamber of the legislature being a House of Lords occupied by a body of lifetime aristocrats.
- They rejected the British idea of a "unitary" republic where all power was concentrated in the central government.
- They rejected the idea of the national government being allowed to nullify the laws of the local governments even when there was no constitutional issue involved.
- They rejected the idea of the national executive being allowed to dissolve the legislature before it had finished its session.
- They rejected the British coinage system and chose a system based on the dollar instead of the pound.
- They rejected the doctrine of primogeniture – an old feudal law – which required a parent to bestow his entire estate on the eldest son whether he was competent or not.
- They rejected the doctrine of entail estates – another old feudal law – which required large tracts of land (sometimes millions

of acres) to be maintained intact by the same family because of important feudal obligations to the king or some high ranking lord or baron. This was designed to preserve the English feudal society and prevent a father from dividing his estate among his children and grandchildren.

- They eventually got around to rejecting the authority of the legislature to select a certain religious denomination as the official church of the state or the realm, and then tax the people to support that church whether they were members or not.
- The Founders also **tried** to get rid of serfs and slaves, but the circumstances in two states (Georgia and South Carolina) forced them to postpone this decision. As everyone knows, that was the biggest mistake the Founders made. The inspiration was right but they allowed themselves to be talked out of it.

The Founders didn't achieve perfection with their document, but they came closer to "the perfect law of liberty" than had any nation in more than 5,000 years. In coming this close to God's "perfect law of liberty" America's Founding Fathers established a covenant nation with God, very similar to how Israel became a covenant nation – and subject to those same blessings, curses and wraths that Jehovah declared would come upon Israel when they obeyed his laws, statutes and commandments, and the curses that would come if they disobeyed those laws, statutes and commandments. And when Israel turned to idolatry He allowed the ten tribes, Israel, to be captured, then scattered, and later when Judah followed in the path of Israel, idolatry, He allowed Judah and Jerusalem to be captured and taken into captivity. This action by God is referred to as the wrath of God. To get a better understanding of the results of this destruction of Judah and Jerusalem, the reader is encouraged to read Jeremiah's Book of Lamentations in the Bible. But Isaiah's words about a remnant escaping from Jerusalem should not be forgotten.

Chapter Eight

America's Constitution – A Covenant Document

Opening commentary: This chapter describes just how unique the Constitution of the United States is and that the Founding Fathers believed deeply within themselves that there was something very special about the work they had just completed in "Constitutional Hall" in Philadelphia during the summer of 1787. Please read the Constitution again before beginning this chapter.

Question: What is the Constitution of the United States?
Answer: As defined in Article VI of the Constitution, the Constitution is the "Supreme Law" of the United States of America. It is a "written" document of law that all states in the Union, and their people, <u>**"covenant to live by."**</u> **The President of these United States, when he takes his Oath of Office, covenants to "preserve, protect and defend the Constitution of the United States."** All elected officials, both in federal and state governments take an Oath to uphold the Constitution of the United States of America as the Supreme Law of the land. **This Oath is a covenant with the God of America, thus America is a covenant nation,** especially for those who add "so help me God." And those who take this Oath with tongue-in-cheek or with their fingers crossed behind their backs will one day find themselves being held accountable before God's eternal Court of Justice for complicity in attempting to destroy God's covenant nation.

The Oath of Office was written into the Constitution to assure Americans today that the United States of America was indeed established as a covenant nation. Every individual who enters America's Armed Forces takes a similar Oath to defend the Constitution of the United States. And each time an American recites the Pledge of Allegiance to the Flag of the United States of America and utter the words, "under God," they too are acknowledging that this nation, the United States of America, is a covenant nation.

Upon completion of the Constitution it was then signed by thirty-nine of the fifty-five men who had been sent to the convention by the congress. The congress debated it for only a few days, adopted it, and then sent it to the thirteen states in the new Union for Ratification according to Article VII of the newly drafted Constitution.

The Constitution consists of three parts.

- Part one is the original Constitution, including the Preamble, which was signed on September 17. 1787, and then ratified by the thirteen states.

- Part two are the "Ten Amendments" that George Mason, Edmund Randolph, and Elbridge Gerry caused to be added to the Constitution on December 15, 1791, and known today as America's "Bill of Rights."

- Part three are the seventeen amendments that have been added to the Constitution since December 15, 1791, two of which offset one another, thus leaving only fifteen additional amendments that have been added in 225 years. A remarkable feat.

Question: What is unique about the Constitution of the United States of America?

Answer: Several things about the government formed by America's Constitution are extremely unique. It is:

- A government established on the ancient principles of government first established by ancient Israel, principles the Founders found in their Bibles.

- A "People's Government."

- A government where the power of government comes from the people. Not since ancient Israel was set up had a nation's power originated with the people.
- A government where the powers are divided among three branches of government – legislative, executive, and judicial – with strong checks and balances that defines and limits the power of each branch, checks that are 'written into its Constitution.'
- A government where the central government was initially limited, and where the states retained their power to govern at the state and county level.
- A government designed to make the states sovereign in their realm of responsibility, and the federal government sovereign in its realms.
- A government that declares in its Constitution that no monarchy (king) will ever reign in these United States of America.
- A government that requires its executive to be chosen by "the people," not chosen from among members of Parliament, as is the case in Canada, Great Britain, and other parliamentary forms of government.

Question: How was the <u>initial</u> Constitution laid out, or organized?
Answer: The Founding Fathers organized the Constitution into **Two Parts.**

- **Part One** is the Preamble, America's Mission Statement of six unique goals for America.
- **Part Two** is the body of the Constitution containing the seven Articles, plus the twenty-seven Amendments that are accepted as the Supreme Law of the Land, establishing **"the Rule of Law"** as the foundational support of America's freedoms.

Question: Who wrote the Preamble to the Constitution, and how did it come about?

Answer: Gouverneur Morris, Chair of the Committee on Detail, wrote the Preamble as his committee was completing their assignment to arrange the Constitution into its final form. Morris felt few people would bother to read the text of the Constitution so he wanted to set forth in the Preamble the six magnificent objectives the Founders intended this form of government to attain. As it turned out this was the first time these six criteria for sound government had ever been recorded.

Political scientists still marvel at what Morris accomplished with only fifty-two words – everything important which should have been included – six goals – were included, and nothing superfluous which should have been left out was included. (Another divine intervention)

The Preamble begins with seven covenant words, **"We the People of the United States."** These seven words define where the power of the United States government comes from – the American people. The last twelve words of the Preamble read **"do ordain and establish this Constitution for the United States of America."**

Between these beginning (We the People) and ending words are listed the six goals the Founders wanted America to strive for. These goals were to:

- Form a more perfect Union.
- Establish justice.
- Insure domestic Tranquility.
- Provide for the common defense of the nation.
- Provide for the general Welfare.
- Secure the blessings of liberty to ourselves and our posterity.

The biblical verses that suggest a biblical foundation for these six goals include:

1. "To form a more perfect union …"

➢ "And he said unto Moses, Come up unto the Lord, thou,

and Aaron, Nadab, and Abihu, and seventy of the elders of Israel; and worship ye afar off. And Moses alone shall come near the Lord: but they shall not come nigh; neither shall the people go up with him. ¶ And Moses came and told the people all the words of the Lord, and all the judgments: and all the people answered with one voice, and said, **All the words which the Lord hath said will we do.**" (Exodus 24:1-3)

Commentary: This last phrase is the **'covenant'** that the Israelites made with Jehovah that day.

> "Gather the people together, men, and women, and children, and thy stranger that is within thy gates, that they may hear, and that they may learn, and fear the Lord your God, and observe to do all the words of this law: And that their children, which have not known anything, may hear, and learn to fear the Lord your God, as long as ye live in the land whither ye go over Jordan to possess it." (Deuteronomy 31:12-13)

Commentary: This law was for the **'stranger'** as well as for the native, and strongly emphasized educating the children to "learn to fear your God." America's education leaders should read this verse and begin teaching the children as did America from 1789 to about 1910, the year America's pride began telling them they knew more about educating children than God did. And America's educational system has never regained its initial effectiveness of training their youth the needed correct principles of life so they, the youth, can learn to govern themselves effectively as adults.

> "Therefore shall a man leave his father and his mother, and shall cleave unto his wife: and they shall be one flesh." (Genesis 2:24)

Commentary: Can any biblical verse make it any clearer that marriage is between a man and a woman.

> "Behold, how good and how pleasant it is for brethren to

dwell together in unity!" (Psalm 133:1)

➤ "And said, For this cause shall a man leave father and mother, and shall cleave to his wife: and they twain shall be one flesh? Wherefore they are no more twain, but one flesh. What therefore God hath joined together, let not man put asunder." (Matthew 19:5-6)

Commentary: Another Bible verse that clarifies an issue that is dividing America today.

2. "To establish justice ..."

➤ "Defend the poor and fatherless: do justice to the afflicted and needy. Deliver the poor and needy: rid them out of the hand of the wicked." (Psalm 82:3-4)

➤ "To do justice and judgment is more acceptable to the Lord than sacrifice." (Proverbs 21:3)

➤ "Thus saith the Lord God; Let it suffice you, O princes of Israel: remove violence and spoil, and execute judgment and justice, take away your exactions from my people, saith the Lord God." (Ezekiel 45:9)

➤ "Then Peter opened his mouth, and said, Of a truth I perceive that God is no respecter of persons: But in every nation he that feareth him, and worketh righteousness, is accepted with him." (Acts 10:34-35)

3. "To ensure domestic tranquility ..."

➤ "And I will give peace in the land, and ye shall lie down, and none shall make you afraid: and I will rid evil beasts out of the land, neither shall the sword go through your land." (Leviticus 26:6)

4. "Promote the general welfare ..."

➤ "This book of the law shall not depart out of thy mouth; but thou shalt meditate therein day and night, that thou mayest observe to do according to all that is written therein: for then thou shalt make thy way prosperous, and then thou shalt have good success." (Joshua 1:8)

➤ "Then shalt thou prosper, if thou takest heed to fulfil the statutes and judgments which the Lord charged Moses with concerning Israel: be strong, and of good courage; dread not, nor be dismayed." (1 Chronicles 22:13)

➤ "She stretcheth out her hand to the poor; yea, she reacheth forth her hands to the needy." (Proverbs 31:20)

5. "Provide for the common defense ..."

➤ "When thou goest out to battle against thine enemies, and seest horses, and chariots, and a people more than thou, be not afraid of them: **for the Lord thy God is with thee**, which brought thee up out of the land of Egypt. And it shall be, when ye are come nigh unto the battle, that the priest shall approach and speak unto the people. And shall say unto them, Hear, O Israel, ye approach this day unto battle against your enemies: let not your hearts faint, fear not, and do not tremble, neither be ye terrified because of them; **For the Lord your God is he that goeth with you, to fight for you against your enemies, to save you.**" (Deuteronomy 20:1-4)

Commentary: This message is as valid today for defenders of truth and freedom as it was in the days of Moses. If people get involved in this battle to preserve America's freedoms, God will be with them, even as He was with the ancient Israelites and America's Founding Fathers.

➤ "And all this assembly shall know that the Lord saveth not with sword and spear: for the battle is the Lord's, and he will give you into our hands." (1 Samuel 17:47)

➤ Or what king, going to make war against another king, sitteth not down first, and consulteth whether he be able with ten thousand to meet him that cometh against him with twenty thousand? Or else, while the other is yet a great way off, he sendeth an ambassage, and desireth conditions of peace." (Luke 14:31-32)

6. "Secure the blessings of liberty to ourselves and our posterity…"

➤ "And God sent me before you to preserve you a posterity in the earth, and to save your lives by a great deliverance." (Genesis 45:7)

➤ "And in the days of these kings shall the God of heaven set up a kingdom, which shall never be destroyed: and the kingdom shall not be left to other people, but it shall break in pieces and consume all these kingdoms, and it shall stand for ever. Forasmuch as thou sawest that the stone was cut out of the mountain without hands, and that it brake in pieces the iron, the brass, the clay, the silver, and the gold; the great God hath made known to the king what shall come to pass hereafter: and the dream is certain, and the interpretation thereof sure." (Daniel 2:44-45)

➤ "And ye shall know the truth, and the truth shall make you free." (John 8:32)

➤ "Stand fast therefore in the liberty wherewith Christ hath made us free, and be not entangled again with the yoke of bondage." (Galatians 5:1)

Commentary: These last two verses likely struck home hard with the Founding Fathers.

Question: How is Part Two or body of the Constitution laid out?
Answer: It is divided into seven Articles. Each Article provides guide lines for one particular segment of government. These seven Articles, in chronological order, are:

Article I: Article I outlines how the first Branch of government, the Legislative Body, is organized. It is subdivided into nine sections. It is the longest Article in the Constitution.

Article II: Article II outlines how the second Branch of government, the Executive Branch, the President, is elected, defines his powers, etc. It is subdivided into four sections.

Article III: Article III outlines how the third Branch of government, the Judiciary Branch, is organized, and lists the powers and responsibilities Congress has been given.

Article IV: Article IV outlines how the states shall deal with one another as separate entities within the Union. It is subdivided into four sections.

Article V: Article V outlines how the Constitution can be amended.

Article VI: Article VI provides for paying all debts, and declares "the Constitution, and all laws made Pursuant thereof, shall be the Supreme Law of the Land."

Article VII: Article VII defines how the Constitution can be amended.

Question: What are the powers and responsibilities of Congress – the House - the Senate?

Answer: Article I deals with the First Branch of Government, the Congress – and defines how Congress is to be established and the powers delegated to the House of Representatives and to the Senate, who together make up "the Congress." It has seven sub-sections. A review is provided for each sub-section under Article I.

Section 1 states: All legislative Powers herein granted shall be vested in a Congress of the United States, which shall consist of a Senate and House of Representatives.

"Supportive scriptural verse[s]"

➤ "And Moses came and called for the elders of the people, and laid before their faces all these words which the Lord commanded him. And all the people answered together, and said, **All that the Lord hath spoken we will do**. And Moses returned the words of the people unto the Lord. And the Lord said unto Moses, Lo, I come unto thee in a thick cloud, that the people may hear when I speak with thee, and believe thee forever. And Moses told the words of the people unto the Lord." (Exodus 19:7-9)

Commentary: The Israelites, like the Founding Fathers, covenanted to do all the Lord said.

"...which shall consist of a senate..."

➤ "And the Lord said unto Moses, Gather unto me seventy men of the elders of Israel, whom thou knowest to be the elders of the people, and officers over them; and bring them unto the tabernacle of the congregation, that they may stand there with thee. And I will come down and talk with thee there: and I will take of the spirit which is upon thee, and will put it upon them; **and they shall bear the burden of the people with thee,** that thou bear it not thyself alone." (Numbers 11:16-17)

"...and a House of Representatives..."

➤ "How can I myself alone bear your cumbrance, and your burden, and your strife? Take you wise men, and understanding, and known among your tribes, and I will make them rulers over you. And ye answered me, and said, The thing which thou hast spoken is good for us to do. So I took the chief of your tribes, wise men, and known, and made them heads over you, captains over thousands, and captains over hundreds, and captains over fifties, and captains over tens, and officers among your tribes. And I charged your judges at that time, saying, Hear the causes between your brethren, and judge righteously between every man and his brother, and the stranger that is with him. Ye shall not respect persons in judgment; but ye shall hear the small as well as the great; ye shall not be afraid of the face of man; for the judgment is God's: and the cause that is too hard for you, bring it unto me, and I will hear it. And I commanded you at that time all the things which ye should do." (Deuteronomy 1:12-18) (Also see Exodus 18)

Commentary: Americans, who look, can see these biblical verses in operation in every state of the union today, and at every level of government.

Section 2 defines: Where the members of the House of Representatives shall come from; what the requirements for office shall be; their terms of office; and how vacancies shall be filled. This section states the number of representatives each of the original thirteen states was initially entitled to. (In 1787 a Representative was to represent thirty thousand people. In 2014 each Representative represents approximately 700,000 people.)

Section 3 defines: The Senate of the United States: two from each state; the requirements for office; the term of office, six years; how their terms were to be determined; how each Senator was to be selected by their state legislature (changed by the 17th amendment); how the Senate body was to be organized; how the Vice President of the United States is to preside over the Senate, but without a vote, unless to break a tie; and the Senate's power to impeach Officers of the United States, including the President of the United States of America.

"Supportive scripture verse[s]"

> "And the Lord said unto Moses, Gather unto me seventy men of the elders of Israel, whom thou knowest to be the elders of the people, and officers over them; and bring them unto the tabernacle of the congregation, that they may stand there with thee." (Numbers 11:16)

Section 4 defines: The times, places and manner of holding elections for Senators and Representatives, and when the Congress shall meet.

Section 5 defines: How each House shall develop its own rules of conduct; punish its members for disorderly Behaviour; and how a member can be expelled. It declares each House shall keep a journal of its proceedings and publish its journal from time to time; and that neither House can adjourn for more than three days without the consent of the other House.

Section 6 defines: The compensation the Senators and Representatives shall receive for their services; how it is be paid; how in all Cases, except Treason, Felony and Breach of the Peace, members of Congress shall be privileged from Arrest during their Attendance at the Session; and their limitation to be appointed to any civil Office while in elective office.

Section 7 states: That all Bills for raising Revenue **shall originate** in the House of Representatives; how the Senate may propose or concur with Amendments as on other Bills; how Bills, once passed by both Houses, must go to the President for his approval; and how a presidential veto can be overridden by both Houses.

One phrase in Section 7 of paragraph two is indicative of the influence the Bible had on America's founding Fathers. This phrase reads: "If any Bill shall not be returned by the President within ten days **(Sundays excepted)** …" This phrase brings into play one of the three more powerful tools the Lord has provided to preserve, protect and defend America's freedoms - keeping the Sabbath day holy, as declared in Exodus 20:8-11.

"Supportive scripture verse[s]"
  ➤ "Remember the Sabbath day, to keep it holy. Six days shalt thou labour, and do all thy work: But the seventh day is the Sabbath of the Lord thy God: in it thou shalt not do any work, thou, nor thy son, nor thy daughter, thy manservant, nor thy maidservant, nor thy cattle, nor thy stranger that is within thy gates: For in six days the Lord made heaven and earth, the sea, and all that in them is, and rested the seventh day: wherefore the Lord blessed the Sabbath day, and hallowed it." (Exodus 20:8-11)

Section 8 lists: The eighteen allowed duties the congress is empowered to do.
  1. "...lay and collect taxes...**but all...shall be uniform throughout the Unites States**..."

"Supportive scripture verse[s]"
  ➤ "And all the tithe of the land, whether of the seed of the land, or of the fruit of the tree, is the Lord's: it is holy unto the Lord. And if a man will at all redeem ought of his tithes, he shall add thereto the fifth part thereof. And concerning the tithe of the herd, or of the flock, even of whatsoever passeth under the rod, the tenth shall be holy unto the Lord. He shall not search whether it be good or bad, neither shall he change it: and if he change it at all, then both it and the change thereof shall be holy; it shall not be redeemed. These are the commandments, which the Lord commanded Moses for the children of Israel in Mount Sinai." (Leviticus 27:30-34)
  ➤ "Will a man rob God? Yet ye have robbed me. But ye say, wherein have we robbed thee? In tithes and offerings. Ye

are cursed with a curse: for ye have robbed me, even this whole nation. Bring ye all the tithes into the storehouse, that there may be meat in mine house, and prove me now herewith, saith the Lord of hosts, if I will not open you the windows of heaven, and pour you out a blessing, that there shall not be room enough to receive it." (Malachi 3:8-10)

Commentary: Over the years the United States has given generously of its wealth to the needy of the world, in cash, defense, and stores. This is in line with America's Covenant to live God's law of tithing.

2. Pay the debts and provide for the common Defense and general Welfare of the United States, while declaring all Duties, Imposts and Excises **shall be uniform throughout the United States;**

3. Borrow Money on the credit of the United States;

4. Establish a uniform rule of Naturalization, and uniform Laws on the subject of Bankruptcies throughout the United States;

5. Coin Money, regulate the Value thereof, and of foreign Coin, and fix the Standards of Weights and Measures;

➤ "Ye shall do no unrighteousness in judgment, in meteyard, in weight, or in measure. Just balances, just weights, a just ephah, and a just hin, shall ye have: I am the Lord your God, which brought you out of the land of Egypt." (Leviticus 19:35-36)

➤ "The law of the Lord is perfect, converting the soul: the testimony of the Lord is sure, making wise the simple." (Psalm 19:7)

6. Provide for the Punishment of counterfeiting the Securities and current Coin of the United States;

7. Establish Post Offices and post Roads;

8. Promote the Progress of Science and useful Arts, by securing for limited Times to Authors and Inventors the exclusive Right to their respective Writings and Discoveries;

9. Constitute Tribunals inferior to the Supreme Court;

➢ "And let them judge the people at all seasons: and it shall be, that every great matter they shall bring unto thee, but every small matter they shall judge: so shall it be easier for thyself, and they shall bear the burden with thee. If thou shalt do this thing, and God command thee so, then thou shalt be able to endure, and all this people shall also go to their place in peace. So Moses hearkened to the voice of his father-in-law, and did all that he had said. And Moses chose able men out of all Israel, and made them heads over the people, rulers of thousands, rulers of hundreds, rulers of fifties, and rulers of tens. And they judged the people at all seasons: the hard causes they brought unto Moses, but every small matter they judged themselves." (Exodus 18:22-26)

10. Define and punish Piracies and Felonies committed on the high Seas, and Offenses against the Law of Nations;

➢ "Behold, I have taught you statutes and judgments, even as the Lord my God commanded me that ye should do so in the land whither ye go to possess it. Keep therefore and do them; for this is your wisdom and your understanding in the sight of the nations, which shall hear all these statutes, and say, Surely this great nation is a wise and understanding people. For what nation is there so great, who hath God so nigh unto them, as the Lord our God is in all things that we call upon Him for? And what nation is there so great, that hath statutes and judgments so righteous as all this law, which I set before you this day?" (Deuteronomy 4:5-8)

11. Declare War, grant Letters of Marque and Reprisal, and Make Rules concerning Captures on Land and Water;

12. Raise and support Armies;

13. Provide and maintain a Navy;

14. Make Rules for the Government and Regulation of the land and naval Forces;

15. Provide for calling forth the Militia to execute the Laws of the Union, suppress Insurrections and repel Invasions;

➤ "And Samuel told all the words of the Lord unto the people that asked of him a king. And he said, This will be the manner of the king that shall reign over you: He will take your sons, and appoint them for himself, for his chariots, and to be his horsemen; and some shall run before his chariots. And he will appoint him captains over thousands, and captains over fifties; and will set them to ear his ground, and to reap his harvest, and to make his instruments of war, and instruments of his chariots." (1 Samuel 8:10-12)

16. Provide for organizing, arming, and disciplining, the Militia, and for governing such Part of them as may be employed in the Service of the United States, ...;

17. Exercise exclusive Legislation in all Cases whatsoever, over such District (not exceeding ten Miles square [the District of Columbia) ... and to exercise like Authority over all Places purchased by the Consent of the Legislature of the State in which the Same shall be, for the erection of Forts, Magazines, Arsenals, dock-Yards and other needful things;

18. Make all Laws which shall be necessary and proper for carrying into Execution the foregoing Powers, and all other Powers vested by this Constitution in the Government of the United States, or in any Department or Officer thereof.

Section 9: Is the **"thou shall not"** section that limits the powers of the Congress. It states:

• The slavery issue could not be resolved by compromise;
• The Privilege of the Writ of Habeas Corpus shall not be suspended, unless ...;
• No Bill of Attainder or ex post facto Law shall be passed;
• No Capitation, or other indirect, Tax shall be laid unless in

Proportion to the Census ...;

- No Tax or Duty shall be laid on Articles exported from any State;
- No Preference shall be given by any Regulation or Revenue to the Ports of one State over another ...;
- No Money shall be drawn from the Treasury ... without an Appropriation ...;
- No Title of Nobility shall be granted by the United States: And no Person holding office ... shall accept any present, Emolument, Office, or Title ... from any King or foreign State.

Section 10 limits: What each State can or cannot do regarding the laying of Imposts or Duties on Imports or Exports.

- ➤ "For thou didst separate them from among all the people of the earth, to be thine inheritance, as thou spakest by the hand of Moses thy servant, when thou broughtest our fathers out of Egypt, O Lord God." (1 Kings 8:53)

Question: What is Article II?
Answer: Article II deals with the Second Branch of Government, the Executive Branch, and...

how the executive Power shall be vested in a President of the United States of America; defines who can become the President, or Vice President, their term of office, compensation, the transfer of Power to the Vice President should the President be removed from office, or not be able to function in his office, and the Oath of Office he shall take before he enters the office of the presidency. This Oath of Office reads:

- **"I so solemnly swear (or affirm) that I will faithfully execute the Office of President of the United States, and will to the best of my Ability, preserve, protect and defend the Constitution of the United States."**
- ➤ "Take you wise men, and understanding, and known

among your tribes, and I will make them rulers over you." (Deuteronomy 1:13)

It then makes these declarations. It:

1. Establishes the Electoral College system for electing a President;
2. Declares the President shall be the Commander in Chief of the Army and Navy – the Militia of the several states, when called into actual Service ...;
3. He shall have the Power, by and with the Advise and Consent of the Senate, to make Treaties, provided two-thirds of the Senate concur ...;
4. He shall, again with the Advise and Consent of the Senate, appoint Ambassadors, other public Ministers and Consuls, Judges of the supreme Court, and all other Officers of the United States ...;
5. He shall have Power to fill all Vacancies that may happen during the Recess of the Senate, by granting Commissions which shall expire at the End of the next Session;
6. He shall provide to Congress Information on the State of the Union on a Timely basis;
7. He shall receive Ambassadors and other public Ministers;
8. He shall take Care that the Laws be faithfully executed, and shall Commission all the Officers of the United States;
9. The Impeachment process for all civil Officers of the United States.

These are all powerful duties and responsibilities and are necessary to govern a free people.

Question: What is Article III?

Answer: Article III deals with the Third Branch of Government, the Judiciary Branch. It states, or defines:

- That the judicial Powers of the United States shall be vested in one supreme Court, and in such inferior Courts as the Congress may from time to time ordain and establish;

- How the Judges, both of the supreme and inferior Courts, shall hold their Offices during "good Behaviour (for life)," and their compensation.
- ➢ "Judges and officers shalt thou make thee in all thy gates, which the Lord thy God giveth thee, throughout thy tribes: and they shall judge the people with just judgment. Thou shalt not wrest judgment; thou shalt not respect persons, **neither take a gift: for a gift doth blind the eyes of the wise, and pervert the words of the righteous.**" (Deuteronomy 16:18-19)
- The judicial Power shall extend to all Cases, in Law and Equity, arising under this Constitution, the Laws of the United States, and Treaties ...;
- Where the supreme Court shall have original and/or appellate Jurisdiction;
- That the Trial of all Crimes, except in Cases of Impeachment, shall be by Jury; and that such Trial shall be held in the State where said Crimes shall have been committed ...;
- Treason against the United States, and details relating to such Treason Crimes.

Question: What does Article IV provide for?
Answer: Article IV deals with the relationship of one State with another State, and how the laws of one State shall provide...

- The Full Faith and Credit in each State to the public Acts, Records, and judicial Proceedings of every other State; and prescribes the Manner in which such Acts, Records and Proceedings shall be proved;
- The Citizens of each State entitlement to all Privileges and Immunities of Citizens in the several States;
- How New States may be admitted into the Union by Congress;
- Congress with the Power to dispose of and make all needful

Rules and Regulations respecting the Territory or other Property belonging to the United States ...;

- That the United States shall guarantee to every State in the Union a Republican Form of Government, and shall protect them (the several states) against Invasion; and on Application of the Legislature, or the Executive (when the Legislature cannot be convened) against domestic Violence.

➤ "Take you wise men, and understanding, and **known among your tribes**, and I will make them rulers over you. And ye answered me, and said, The thing which thou hast spoken is good for us to do. So I took the chief of your tribes, wise men, and known, and made them heads over you, captains over thousands, and captains over hundreds, and captains over fifties, and captains over tens, and officers among your tribes." (Deuteronomy 1:13-15)

Question: What does Article V provide for?
Answer: Article V provides for Amending the Constitution and the details of approval, etc.

Question: What does Article VI provide for?
Answer: Article VI defines four powerful principles for any free people.

- **Principle # 1:** The new Government agreed to pay all debts the Confederation had entered into.
- ➤ "Avoiding this, that no man should blame us in this abundance which is administered by us: Providing for honest things, not only in the sight of the Lord, but also in the sight of men. (2 Corinthians 8:20-21)
- **Principle # 2:** Defines what the "Supreme Law of the Land" is, and who shall take an Oath to uphold it.
- **Principle # 3:** That all federal Senators and Representatives, and all State Legislatures, and all executive and judicial

Officers, both of the United States and of the several States, shall be bound by Oath or Affirmation, to support the Constitution.

➢ "If a man vow a vow unto the Lord, or swear an oath to bind his soul with a bond; he shall not break his word, he shall do according to all that proceedeth out of his mouth." (Numbers 30:2)

• **Principle # 4:** No religious Test shall ever be required as a Qualification to any Office or public Trust under the United States.

Question: What does Article VII provide for?
Answer: Article VII provides for two things:

• It defines the Ratification process of the Constitution.
• It declares the Constitution done, gives the date completed, names the thirty-nine men who signed it on September 17, 1787, and that it was attested to by William Jackson, the Convention's secretary.

➢ "The Spirit of the Lord God is upon me; because the Lord hath anointed me to preach good tidings unto the meek; he hath sent me to bind up the brokenhearted, to proclaim liberty to the captives, and the opening of the prison to them that are bound; To proclaim the acceptable year of the Lord, and the day of vengeance of our God; to comfort all that mourn;" (Isaiah 61:1-2)

Chapter Nine

Ratifying America's New Constitution

Opening commentary: This chapter explains how the Constitution was to be ratified and of the strong opposition it received in several states. This ratification process brought the people of each state into the covenanting process – no longer was the Constitution the Constitution of the few, it was the Constitution – the Law – of the nation – a covenant nation.

Question: What was the process for ratifying the new Constitution?

Answer: To make changes in the Articles of Confederation required unanimous consent of all thirteen states. An almost impossible rule! However the Founders, in their wisdom, in Article VII of their new constitution, provided for a **"more common sense"** ratification process. It states: "The Ratification of the Conventions of nine States, shall be sufficient for the Establishment of this Constitution between the States so ratifying the Same."

Several convention delegates were also members of Congress so when the Constitution reached Congress for its approval, these delegate/congressmen were there to answer vital questions – and help smooth over any ruffled feathers of their fellow congressmen. Remember the Constitutional Convention was a "closed door convention" so few people knew much about the new Constitution. After reviewing and approving the new Constitution, Congress sent it out to the thirteen states for ratification under the terms of Article VII.

Question: What was the reaction of the general public to the new document?
Answer: Mixed and cautious.
Commentary: Because the document was different from anything any of the people had ever lived under before, they were curious, and for some it was too much for them to comprehend, a government with checks and balances between equal but interdependent branches of government.

Question: Was there opposition to the new Constitution?
Answer: Yes, heavy opposition. In Virginia word spread quickly (even without cell phones and twitter) that George Mason had refused to sign the new Constitution, as had their governor Edmund Randolph and another delegate, Elbridge Gerry of Massachusetts. Most of the states soon became bitterly divided over the new document. Today our people are divided as Democrats and Republicans. Over this debate the states were divided between the Federalists, those favoring the new Constitution, and the Anti-Federalists, those opposed to the new Constitution.

The greatest opposition came from the people in North Carolina, New York, and southern and western Virginia, with pockets of opposition in South Carolina and western Pennsylvania.

Question: What caused the people to study and ponder this new document?
Answer: Its many new and unique features.

The new and unique features in the new Constitution created a climate of controversy that caused thousands of the people to study this new controversial document for themselves. This created a healthy debate among the people, and finally led to its ratification. This was a time when opposition, strong opposition, led to a better understanding of the new document, and then to the Constitution's ratification.

Question: What issues created the strongest opposition to the new Constitution?

Answer: The several issues that bothered the people the most were the following:

Issue # 1: The new constitution did not contain a **"Bill of Rights."** George Mason refused to sign it for this reason alone. The Founders felt that because the new constitution would be one of limited government, the protection of rights would not be needed. Mason soon convinced many Virginians, including Patrick Henry, the "Give me Liberty or give me Death" patriot, that a set of rights **"written-into"** the Constitution was necessary. They did not want to rely on a set of **"implied rights."** This issue was resolved when Washington, in its first session of the new congress, requested the states to submit suggestions. There were 189 suggestions submitted. Ten made it into the Constitution, as America's "Bill of Rights."

Issue # 2: Many felt the office of the President was too powerful. Mason preferred a weak President shackled with constitutional chains.

Issue # 3: George Mason felt the office of Vice President was superfluous – a completely unnecessary expense.

Issue # 4: There was no specific provision for a cabinet or council to guide the President.

Issue # 5: George Mason saw the federal courts as a very real threat to the independence and integrity of the state courts. This concern has been verified by the passage of time. Jefferson was also among the first to see a real flaw in the judicial appointment system of the new Constitution.

Question: How did the Founders 'sell' the new Constitution against such strong opposition?

Answer: They organized a grassroots educational program.

The Governor of New York, John Clinton, a strong believer in states' rights, strongly opposed the new Constitution and wrote a series of newspaper articles under the name of Cato. To defend the Constitution and its new features Alexander Hamilton began answering Clinton's questions in a series of articles titled "The Federalist." His series of articles were instrumental in educating the people on the positive merits of the new Constitution. As the people became more involved they demanded more answers for their questions. Hamilton then asked James Madison and John Jay to help him in writing the Federalist Papers. They accepted and the three of them then wrote a large number of the pamphlets that would soon be distributed throughout the states. The eighty-five Federalist Papers that were published were one of the main factors in educating the people on the need for, and the merits of, the new Constitution.

But it was also the personality of the delegates who pitched in and sold the people on the need for a Constitution to replace the defective Articles of Confederation. Hamilton was a powerful influence in getting New York to ratify it – but only by a 30 yes, 27 no vote.

Thomas Jefferson, from France, wrote:

- "The example of changing a constitution by assembling wise men of the state, instead of assembling armies, will be worth as much to the world as former examples we have given them (such as the Declaration of Independence). The Constitution is ... unquestionably the wisest ever yet presented to men."

John Adams wrote from London:

- "the greatest single effort of national deliberation that the world has ever seen."

Question: How long did it take to ratify the Constitution?
Answer: From September 17, 1787, until June 21, 1788, nine months, when the ninth state, New Hampshire, ratified it.

The ratification chronology was:

- Delaware, on December 6, 1787, ratified it with a

unanimous vote.

- Pennsylvania, on December 12, 1787, ratified it with a vote of 46 yes, 23 no.
- New Jersey, on December 18, 1787, ratified it with a unanimous vote.
- Georgia, on January 2, 1788, ratified it with a unanimous vote.
- Connecticut, on January 9, 1788, ratified it with a vote of 140 yes, 40 no.
- Massachusetts, on February 6, 1788, ratified it with a vote of 187 yes, 168 no.
- Maryland, on April 26, 1788, ratified it with a vote of 63 yes, 11 no.
- South Carolina, on May 23, 1788, ratified it with a vote of 149 yes, 73 no.
- New Hampshire, on June 21, 1788, was the ninth state to ratify, with a close vote, 56 yes, 46 no.

Per the terms of Article VII of the new Constitution the new nation was born when nine states ratified it, New Hampshire being the ninth state. However, several big states, and rogue Rhode Island, were still debating this issue. The leaders knew the new nation could not function without New York, Virginia, and North Carolina. So they continued to wait for these important states to finish their ratification process. They did, in this order.

- Virginia, on June 26, 1788, ratified it with a vote of 87 yes, 79 no – an 8 vote margin.
- New York, on July 26, 1788, ratified it with a vote of 30 yes, 27 no. This was a bitter battle. A three vote margin.
- North Carolina had strong opposition, and had to hold two conventions to get a positive vote, but on November 21, 1789, nearly 16 months later, North Carolina ratified it with a vote of 194 yes, 77 no.
- Rhode Island, often called the "Rogue State," did not ratify until May 29, 1790, and then only with a narrow vote of 34

yes, 32 no. A two vote margin! Again note the importance of one vote.

Question: What happened following the Ratification of the New Constitution by the States?
Answer: The new government began to take shape, in this chronological order...

- January 7, 1789. Presidential electors were chosen by each state – some by the legislatures, some by the people themselves. (Note that North Carolina and Rhode Island had yet to ratify the Constitution.)
- April 1, 1789. The House of Representatives convened with 59 elected Representatives present.
- April 6, 1789. The Senate was organized.
- April 6, 1789. A joint session of the two bodies was held to see who would become the President. The results were no surprise. George Washington was elected unanimously with 69 electoral votes, and John Adams was named Vice President with 34 electoral votes.
- April 15, 1789. The Gazette or Annals of Congress began its publication. Today this paper is called the Congressional Record.
- April 30, 1789. George Washington was inaugurated in the Senate Chamber of Federal Hall in New York City. **Because of the damages to his Mt. Vernon estate, and an eight year absence, Washington had to borrow money to attend his own inaugural. This was the day that the United States of America was actually born, having been conceived on July 4, 1776.**
- September 11, 1789. President Washington appointed Alexander Hamilton Secretary of Treasury.
- September 24, 1789. The federal court system was set up with the Supreme Court at the head, one federal district in each

state, and three federal circuit courts of appeals.

- September 26, 1789. John Jay was appointed the first Chief Justice of the United States Supreme Court.
- September 26, 1789. Former Virginia Governor Edmund Randolph was appointed Attorney General of the United States. And Thomas Jefferson, who had returned from France, was appointed Secretary of State.
- September 29, 1789. President Washington created the United States Army, with 1000 soldiers.

The new government was set in order by Washington and the Congress and with the others who were brought in to fill cabinet spots, etc. America was on its way to becoming a mighty nation, a Standard of Freedom to the entire world, just as God intended for His covenant nation.

Question: When was the Bill of Rights adopted?
Answer: On December 15, 1791, the ninth state ratified the first ten amendments to the constitution. God's "perfect law of liberty" was now embedded in the Constitution. Task one was completed.

Donald S. Conkey

Chapter Ten

Amending America's Constitution

Opening commentary: This chapter shows how the Constitution of the United States can be amended, by the will of the People, and that it has been amended seventeen times since December 15, 1791, when America's first ten amendments, America's Bill of Rights, became a part of the Constitution. Even though the amendment process can be done quickly, amending the Constitution generally is a long and difficult task, requiring a lot of patience and a lot of time. Before beginning this chapter read Article V and Article VII of the Constitution again. Article V provides the details on how to amend the Constitution, Article VII provides the guidelines on how an amendment is ratified.

Question: What caused the first Ten Amendments to be added after the Constitution was ratified?
Answer: The refusal of three delegates to sign the Constitution when it was signed on September 17, 1787. Those three men were George Mason, Governor Edmund Randolph, both of Virginia, and Elbridge Gerry of Massachusetts. These men believed the basic rights of man must be written into the Constitution while the other delegates believed the Constitution was broad enough to cover their concerns. These three insisted. Then Washington agreed the first order of business, when the new Congress convened, would be to request suggestions from the thirteen states to protect the rights of man. There were 189 suggested amendments submitted. These 189 were reduced to seventeen by Madison. The seventeen were reduced to twelve and

were sent to the thirteen states for ratification. Ten were ratified. The first ten amendments provide(s):

Amendment 1:

Declares **America's five basic freedoms**: religion, speech, a free press, the right to petition the government, and the right to peaceably assemble!

➤ "Conscience, I say, not thine own, but of the other: for why is my liberty judged of another man's conscience?" (1 Corinthians 10:29)

➤ "And if it seem evil unto you to serve the Lord, choose you this day whom ye will serve; whether the gods which your fathers served that were on the other side of the flood, or the gods of the Amorites, in whose land ye dwell: but as for me and my house, we will serve the Lord." (Joshua 24:15)

➤ "And ye shall hallow the fiftieth year, **and proclaim liberty throughout all the land unto all the inhabitants** thereof: it shall be a jubilee unto you; and ye shall return every man unto his possession, and ye shall return every man unto his family." (Leviticus 25:10)

Amendment 2:

The right to keep and bear arms:

➤ "Wherefore take unto you the whole armour of God, that ye may be able to withstand in the evil day, and having done all, to stand. Stand therefore, having your loins girt about with truth, and having on the breastplate of righteousness; And your feet shod with the preparation of the gospel of peace; Above all, taking the shield of faith, wherewith ye shall be able to quench all the fiery darts of the wicked. And take the helmet of salvation, and the sword of the Spirit, which is the word of God:" (Ephesians 6:13-17)

Amendment 3:

That no soldier, in time of peace, shall be quartered in any house, without owner's consent.

Amendment 4:

For the right of people to be secure in their persons, houses, papers, and effects, against unreasonable searches and seizures, with no warrants issued without probable cause...

> "Finally, my brethren, be strong in the Lord, and in the power of his might. Put on the whole armour of God, that ye may be able to stand against the wiles of the devil." (Ephesians 6:10-11)

Amendment 5:

That no person shall be held to answer for a capital, or otherwise infamous crime, unless on a presentment or indictment of a Grand Jury ... nor shall private property be taken for public use without just compensation. A Grand Jury is made up of citizens in the local county, citizens who are neighbors, of all ages, who sit once a month to listen to the county prosecutor present the evidence they have against an accused individual. The Grand Jury plays an important role in America's judicial system.

> "Nicodemus saith unto them, Doth our law judge any man, before it hear him, and know what he doeth?" (John 7:50-51)

Amendment 6:

That in all criminal prosecutions, the accused shall enjoy the right to a speedy and public trial, by an impartial jury of the State ... wherein the crime was committed...

Amendment 7:

That suits at common law, where the value in controversy shall exceed twenty dollars, the right of trial shall be preserved...

Amendment 8:

That excessive bail shall not be required, nor excessive fines imposed, nor cruel and unusual punishment inflicted.

Amendment 9:

That the enumeration in the Constitution of certain rights shall not be construed to deny or disparage others retained by the people!

Amendment 10:

That the powers not delegated to the United States by the Constitution, nor prohibited by it to the States, are reserved to the States respectively, or to the people.

Question: When was the first and the last Amendment adopted since 1791?

Answer: Amendment XI was the first amendment ratified after 1791. It was adopted on February 7, 1795, four years after the Bill of Rights was ratified. Amendment XXVII was ratified May 7, 1992. It was one of the twelve amendments submitted on September 25, 1789, but failed to get ratified and then waited 201 years to be finally ratified.

The next seventeen Amendments were ratified as follows:

Amendment 11:

Ratified February 7, 1795: It clarified a judicial issue.

Amendment 12:

Ratified June 15, 1804: It redefined how the President and Vice President were elected. This Amendment was later modified by the 20th Amendment.

Amendment 13:

Ratified December 6, 1865: Slavery and Involuntary Servitude were outlawed.

> ➤ "And if a **stranger** sojourn with thee in your land, ye shall not vex him. But the stranger that dwelleth with you shall be unto you as one born among you, and thou shalt love him as thyself; for ye were strangers in the land of Egypt: I am the Lord your God." (Leviticus 19:33-34)

> ➤ "And if a stranger shall sojourn among you, and will keep the Passover unto the Lord; according to the ordinance of

191

the Passover, and according to the manner thereof, so shall he do: ye shall have **one ordinance, both for the stranger, and for him that was born in the land."** (Numbers 9:14)

➢ "Stand fast therefore in the liberty wherewith Christ hath made us free, and be not entangled again with the yoke of bondage." (Galatians 5:1)

➢ "Therefore, it is not right that any man should be in bondage one to another." (D&C 101:79)

Amendment 14:

Ratified July 9, 1868: Clarifies who are citizens of the United States; removing language on who was eligible to vote; declared those who engage in insurrection or rebellions against the United States are not eligible to hold public elective office; and clarified what constituted public debt.

Amendment 15:

Ratified February 3, 1870: Clarified that the right to vote could not be denied because of race, color, or previous condition of servitude.

Commentary: The passage of this amendment was a major step forward in implementing the fullness of God's "perfect law of liberty."

Amendment 16:

Ratified February 3, 1913: This amendment instituted America's present graduated income tax laws.

Commentary: Prior to the passage of this amendment, which really opened the door to the corruption of elected officials and uncontrolled spending, all tax revenue, except during a short period in the 1860s, was based on a consumption tax, paid equally by all citizens at the time of purchase of a product.

Amendment 17:

Ratified April 8, 1913: Senators, who had previously been elected by their state legislatures, would in the future be elected by the people of their state. This destroyed the state's effective powers.

Commentary: Passage of this amendment fractured the checks and balances the Founders had so carefully established in the Constitution. This amendment destroyed the ability of the states to check excessive authority by the federal government.

Amendment 18:

Ratified January 16, 1919: Outlawed the manufacture and sale of alcoholic beverages.

Amendment 19:

Ratified August 18, 1920: Women were given the right to vote following the Suffrage Movement.

Amendment 20:

Ratified January 23, 1933: Defines who shall become President in the case a President-elect dies; and initiates a seven-year time limit for Ratification of an Amendment.

Commentary: This was an important amendment. It limited to seven years the time allowed to pass an amendment. It has been very effective in stopping bad amendments from becoming law in recent years.

Amendment 21:

Ratified December 5, 1933: It repealed the Eighteenth Amendment.

Amendment 22:

Ratified February 27, 1951: Limits the terms of office a President can serve to two.

Commentary: This amendment was passed because F.D. Roosevelt ran for and was elected four times.

Amendment 23:

Ratified March 29, 1961: Gave the District of Columbia the right to elect electors!

Amendment 24:

Ratified January 23, 1964: Made poll taxes illegal!

Amendment 25:

Ratified February 10, 1967: Clarified who shall become President in case of the death of a sitting president, or their removal from office for cause.

Amendment 26:

Ratified July 1, 1971: Gave the right to vote to eighteen year olds!

Amendment 27:

Ratified May 7, 1992: Set when a Congressional pay raise may go into effect.

Question: What two amendments changed the "original intent" of the Founding Fathers?

Answer: Amendments XVI and XVII reversed very basic principles established by the Founding Fathers. Prior to the passage of the 16th amendment in 1913 federal revenue was raised, except for a short time after the Civil War, by consumption taxes, equal upon everyone at the time of a purchase, and known today as the "Fair Tax."

The passage of the 17th Amendment destroyed a vital check, which the Founding Fathers had established to control the power of the Federal Government. Prior to the passage of this amendment Senators were elected by their respective state legislatures, with their major role to support and defend "States Rights." Since 1913 States Rights have taken a back seat to the Federal, or Central Government.

Question: Does every Amendment proposed become a part of the Constitution?

Answer: No. Only a small percentages of those submitted maneuver their way into the Constitution. The Constitution was purposely designed to make it difficult to make unwise changes.

Question: What would America be like today if those three men had not the courage to stand at a critical juncture in the history of America and say – No, we will not sign that document?

Answer: The America my generation was born into would not exist today. Family firearms would have been either registered or confiscated by now. One's freedom to speak against the government would not be allowed, and far more curtailed than it is. And the freedom to peaceably assemble would have gone by the wayside long ago.

Donald S. Conkey

Chapter Eleven

What is Government?

Opening commentary: Government is so pervasive in everyone's life that few take the time to ask what government really is or if there are different forms of governments – the people simply accept the form of government they live in. When one does ask about the different forms of government they learn there are many titles but all governments fall under one of these three forms of government: Rulers Law, People Law, or Anarchy or the law of the jungle.

When Thomas Jefferson declared in the first paragraph of his Declaration that "the Laws of Nature and of Nature's God" were to be the two foundational laws for America he was in effect declaring that God's "perfect law of liberty" (James 1:25) would be the foundational law of America. Today, having removed God from the public square, lawyers refer to this law as the **"Rule of Law," or the peoples law,** not law by the whims of man – or woman. But regardless of what today's progressives would have Americans believe, today the Constitution of the United States of America is a written document of law that was patterned after those laws of liberty the Lord gave to Moses anciently on Mt. Sinai, laws first given to Moses and to the people by the **"thundering voice"** of Jehovah but later written on two stone tables by the finger of Jehovah and placed in their **Ark of the Covenant**. This chapter is a reminder that to be a free people, a few but dedicated people, either as individuals or in groups, must step up and provide the leadership, as did the Founders, needed to preserve those freedoms that are so precious to all Americans today.

The first known form of government was a traditional family government: Adam and Eve. And this cannot be emphasized too often

196

- the traditional family, one man and one woman legally married, raising children, is the very foundation of all civilized society. And built around this stable and solid family government is a stable and solid civil government. While many still believe the Bible is only a religious book for personal living, others now see the Bible as being much more: the Bible is, they believe, **"God's foundational textbook for self-government"**.

As God's textbook for self-government it provides guidelines, very specific guidelines for family and civil government. In reality, beginning with God's covenant with Abraham, the rest of the Bible, including the New Testament, is the story about Jehovah's relationship with Abraham's dysfunctional family. Through Abraham's family the Lord has shared with the world his love for, his patience with, and how, even when being the 'chosen family,' it, the 'chosen family' was not immune to the wrath of God when they failed to live by, which was often, that 'perfect law of liberty' Jehovah gave to his people via Moses. And then, when this dysfunctional family finally abandoned God's laws, statutes and commandments, He sent his 'only begotten Son' to preserve those laws. Then, when Abraham's dysfunctional family rejected His Son, then crucified him, an act so terrible that the Gospel Plan that had been given to Abraham's family was finally given to the gentiles via Paul – the same Gospel Plan that the Pilgrims carried with them to America when they were escaping religious persecution in Europe in the early 1600s. And should America fully abandon or reject God's laws, as seems to be happening today, it can expect God's wrath to come down upon it much as it did on ancient Israel when it abandoned God's laws of liberty anciently.

Question: What is Government?

Answer: Government's simplest definition is: "to be organized." Government, then, is the "art of governing," or "being organized," and "Politics is the Science of Governing." Government is so pervasive and so all-encompassing it becomes second nature to us as we go about our daily living. It's such a part of our lives that we accept it without thinking about it unless we are stopped by the police for running a stop sign, or for speeding, or until we attempt to get our first driver's license, or any of a multitude of situations that will bring us into contact with our local, state, or federal government. Note how tax deductions affect your pay check – you have just come face to face with the government's power to tax. Many think of government as "them," when they should be thinking of government as "us." "We the people" should be the real power of a free government.

Politics are a part of government, but politics are not the government. Government is more than politics, much more. Politics is, as John Adams described it, **"The 'Divine Science of sound government for human happiness."** Where two or more are gathered, someone takes charge, with "understood" rules, formal or informal, that provides direction. When many are involved, there are differences of opinions and debates, often with charges and counter charges following. How, one may ask, can politics be anything akin to science, especially a "divine science?"

Just before the Revolutionary War ended in 1783, John Adams was in Holland and wrote home to explain his understanding of the "divine science of government" with these words:

- "The science of government is my duty to study, more than all other sciences; the arts of legislation and administration and negotiation ought to take place of, indeed to exclude in a manner, all other arts. [Under present war conditions] I must study politics and war, that my sons may have liberty to study mathematics and philosophy...." (From Dr. W. Cleon Skousen's book, *The Making of America*, page 195)

Question: Why should Americans study government?
Answer: Because every human being is governed by some form of government. It is essential that the people comprehend the form of

government he or she is living under, the rules he/she must live by, and how and where these rules and laws originate from – its history.

One should also fully understand that every American is subject to governmental intrusion from the day they are born until the day they die. The newborn baby must be registered by law in its home county, the birth record becoming a permanent record of the child's existence. When older, the birth certificate is a required form of proof to travel abroad, obtain a social security card, etc. The child is subject to the local laws governing school attendance, deportment, etc. A teenager is subject to local laws regarding driving an automobile, riding bicycles, registering in local sports programs, etc.

The descendants of a person who dies are subject to the laws governing burial and reporting the death of their loved one, again as a record to prevent fraud, voting irregularities, etc. Others in between are subject to all the various laws that regulate us in our home town, county, state, and nation. If we travel abroad, we are subject to the rules and laws of those nations we visit, which are often very different than America's laws.

Question: What is man's source of government?
Answer: God. Nature is fully organized with unbending and unbreakable laws. Man is subject to these laws of Nature; but beyond this, man is social. Mankind has been given the gift of agency by God which is the "right to choose" and to accept the responsibility to make "right choices." Following the example of Adam and Eve, mankind organized into family units, and families organized for security reasons into villages. They then hired a "sheriff" to provide greater protection for their village. **Laws of Nature** thus provide a pattern for a government ordained by 'the Laws of Nature's God.'

Question: Where was the first government organized?
Answer: On this earth it was in the Garden of Eden. Afterwards, man was created in the image of God (Genesis 1:26) and given **a "help**

meet" (Genesis 2:18). We are told Adam was to **"cleave unto his wife: and they shall be one flesh."** (Genesis 2:24) This was man's first government. The first commandment to Adam and Eve was to be **"fruitful, and multiply and replenish the earth, and subdue it."** (Genesis 1:28) They obeyed and man's first family government was created. Children came and more families were formed. And as Adam's descendants moved across the land villages were formed, and a **patriarchal or tribal** form of government began. When one looks out into the universe it is obvious that there is law and order there also, governed by the gods of the universe.

Question: When and how are governments organized?

Answer: A new family government begins when one man and one woman marry, with each having his/her "God-given" role to play in this new family government. From the Family Proclamation to the World, published in 1996, we read these defining roles: "By divine design fathers are to preside (govern) over their families in love and righteousness and are responsible to provide the necessities of life and protection for their families. Mothers are primarily responsible for the nurture of their children. In these sacred responsibilities, fathers and mothers are obligated to help one another as equal partners."

The role of each marriage partner is defined, according to this Proclamation, by divine design. A careful reading of the scriptures will provide even greater understanding of these roles, not only as husband and wife, but as parents. Parents are under a divine commandment to:

> ➢ **"teach them (their children) ordinances and laws, and shalt shew them the way wherein they must walk, and the work they must do."** (Exodus 18:20)

These are clear concise words that are difficult to misunderstand. This is family government in operation. Family rules govern the family. The parents are the executive, legislature and judge. The parents rule in the home until the child is of age to leave the home and create his/her own family government. Righteous patterns for governing the family are provided from the scriptures, helping the parents lead their family in righteousness, loving and uplifting them to a higher level. When parents abdicate their parental responsibilities the community often steps in and tries to substitute for parents. This does not work well. There is no substitute for a loving family environment in which to raise children where both the father and the mother are involved in raising the child.

When two families join together to provide needed protection we see the beginning of a village. When two or more villages join together to provide added functions we see a county created, then on up the local governmental ladder until we reach the national government. This is the course of action that was followed when America's thirteen colonies, of their own accord, decided to band together for mutual protection, first under the Articles of Confederation, then later, after they found the Articles wanting, under the banner of the Constitution. Six distinct purposes or goals are found in the Preamble to the Constitution of the United States. These six goals created America's Mission Statement.

Question: What roles do families play in building strong free governments?

Answer: The traditional family is the basic building block of every free government. Though many never associate the traditional family, a father, mother, with children, as a governmental unit, the family is indeed a divine governmental entity, the very foundation of all civilizations, in every sense of the word.

Thomas Jefferson supported this divine premise of the family when he declared, **"the Laws of Nature and of Nature's God,"** as the "two cornerstone laws" of America's self government. Jefferson then defended his words in paragraph two of the Declaration of Independence with these words:

- "We hold these Truths to be self-evident, that all men are endowed by their Creator with certain unalienable Rights, that among them are Life, Liberty, and the Pursuit of Happiness [family] –that to secure these rights Governments are instituted among Men, deriving their just Powers from the Consent of the Governed, ..."

The family, as a divine unit of government, is sustained throughout the writings of Moses. In Moses' books we find the guidelines, laws, statutes and commandments for personal living – the Ten Commandments – and nearly sixty statutes (laws) provided to "govern" the relationships between men, laws, statutes and commandments referred to by the apostle James as God's **"perfect law of liberty."**

The Anglo-Saxons, under King Alfred the Great, provided another pattern to emulate. King Alfred had emulated the patterns used to govern the Israelites (Exodus 18:21-26) – rulers over thousands, hundreds, and tens, with groups of tens forming villages, similar to the pattern practiced by Solomon. These patterns are well documented in the Old Testament books of Judges, Samuel, Kings, and Chronicles. These historical writings tell how Solomon brought together the "princes, and governors," and "leaders of thousands and hundreds." The Bible is a wealth of knowledge dealing with family, village and/or tribal government.

Question: What is the proper role of a free government in the lives of the people?
Answer: In 1835, in the town of Kirkland, Ohio, a small gathering of men, local leaders, defined what many consider to be the clearest definition of what a free government of the people should be. These are their recorded words:

1. "We believe that governments were instituted of God for the benefit of man; and that he holds men accountable for their acts in relation to them, both in making laws and administering them, for the good and safety of society.

2. "We believe that no government can exist in peace, except such laws are framed and held inviolate as will secure to each individual the free exercise of conscience, the right and control of property, and the protection of life.

3. "We believe that all governments necessarily require civil officers and magistrates to enforce the laws of the same; and that such as will administer the law in equity and justice should be sought for and upheld by the voice of the people if a republic, or the will of the sovereign.

4. "We believe that religion is instituted of God; and that men are amenable to him, and to him only, for the exercise of it, unless their religious opinions prompt them to infringe upon the rights and liberties of others; but we do not believe that human law has a right to interfere in prescribing rules of worship to bind the consciences of men, nor dictate forms for public or private devotion; that the civil magistrate should restrain crime, but never control conscience; should punish guilt, but never suppress the freedom of the soul.

5. "We believe that all men are bound to sustain and uphold the respective governments in which they reside, while protected in their inherent and inalienable rights by the laws of such governments; and that sedition and rebellion are unbecoming every citizen thus protected, and should be punished accordingly; and that all governments have a right to enact such laws as in their own judgments are best calculated to secure the public interest; at the same time, however, holding sacred the freedom of conscience." (Doctrine & Covenants 134:1-5)

6. "We believe that the commission of crime should be punished according to the nature of the offense; that murder, treason, robbery, theft, and the breach of the general peace, in all respects, should be punished according to their criminality and their tendency to evil among men, by the laws of that

government in which the offense is committed; and for the public peace and tranquility all men should step forward and use their ability in bringing offenders against good laws to punishment.

7. "We do not believe it just to mingle religious influence with civil government, whereby one religious society is fostered and another proscribed in its spiritual privileges, and the individual rights of its members, as citizens, denied." (Doctrine & Covenants 134:8-9)

These are true principles that proclaim the proper role of government in the domestic affairs of the nation.

Question: What were the two forms of government in use when America was founded?

Answer: The two forms of government at the time America's Constitution was crafted in 1787 were: **Ruler's Law** and **Anarchy or no law.**

The Founders were looking for a better form of government. They knew they were pioneering new territory after realizing that ninety-nine percent of all people who had preceded them had lived out their lives under what is described as **Ruler's Law**. **Ruler's Law** comes in different forms and is known by different names, such as aristocracy, oligarchy, military dictatorship, and emperor or king.

Question: What form of government were the Founding Fathers looking for?

Answer: A "People's Law, or Balanced Center" form of government.

The Founders were searching for a **"Peoples Law,"** or a "Balanced Center" form of government located in between **Ruler's Law** and **No Law** or **Anarchy** on the scales of government. The Founders were then living in America under British rule, a limited form of **Ruler's Law.**

Ruler's Law is a form of government which allows total authority and power to rest with the central government. The ruler or ruling group makes the law, interprets the law, and enforces the law. James Madison called this tyranny.

The chief characteristics of **Ruler's Law** are:

- Government power is exercised by compulsion, force, conquest, or legislative usurpation.
- All power is concentrated in the ruler.
- The people are treated as "subjects" of the ruler.
- The land is treated as the "realm" of the ruler.
- The people have no unalienable rights.
- Government is by the rule of men rather than the rule of law.
- The people are structured into social and economic classes.
- The thrust of government is always from the ruler down, not from the people upward.
- Problems are always solved by issuing new edicts, creating more bureaus, appointing more administrators, and charging the people more taxes to pay for these "services." Under this system taxes and government regulations are always oppressive.
- Freedom is not considered a solution to anything.
- The long history of **Ruler's Law** is one of blood and terror, both anciently and in modern times. Those in power revel in luxury while the lot of the common people is one of perpetual poverty, excessive taxation, stringent regulations, and continuous existence of misery. (*The Making of America*, page 45)

The extreme opposite to Ruler's Law is **No Law**, or **Anarchy**. This form of law exists, even today, but people prefer Ruler's Law to No Law, or Anarchy.

The English, after being captured by the Normans in 1066 AD, never lost their taste for the freedom they had experienced under King

Alfred the Great. Conditions became so bad under the Normans "the people" rose up and forced, with sword in hand, King John to sign the Magna Charta in 1215 AD. Even then they were constantly challenged by the monarchy over issues of their freedoms.

America's Founding Fathers studied many forms of government, including 'Roman Law.' They were well read in both the scriptures and the classics of their day, including the writings of the great thinkers including: Cicero, John Locke, William Blackstone, Adam Smith, and many others. The Founders were like the biblical characters of Joseph, Moses, Daniel and others raised up by God and then "endowed" with "knowledge and skill in all learning and wisdom..." (Daniel 1:17)

The colonists, after winning the war and their freedom, were in many ways like a teenager who buys his first car – not quite sure what to do with their newfound freedom, a freedom from the constraints of their previous strict family home government.

The Founders found two examples, or patterns of government worth further study. Jefferson, a student of ancient Israel, had a great admiration for the Anglo-Saxons' form of government, especially its government under King Alfred. Both the Israelites and Anglo-Saxons were examples of a **"Peoples Law"** or a **"Balanced Center"** form of government.

The similarities the Founders found between themselves and Israel were impressive. Dr. Skousen, in his book, *The Majesty of God's Law*, provided these comparisons. They include:

- Israel was a nation created by a people who had been held in spiritual bondage and physical slavery by Egypt for nearly 400 years, a people that had cried out to their God for "deliverance" from their bondage.
- The colonists of America had been held in spiritual bondage in Europe, and in answer to their prayers to their God, were led to a land much like Moses' desert – a wilderness where they could worship God according to their own conscience, not a

religion or faith dictated by the state, as was their situation in Europe.

- Israel: Twelve tribes, 13, if you include Joseph's two sons, Ephraim and Mannasah, and America's 13 colonies.

- There were approximately three million Israelites when they were "led out" of Egypt. When the Revolutionary War began there were approximately 3.6 million colonists.

- To rescue Israel God sent Moses to lead "His People" out of bondage into the desert. There they were given God's "perfect law of liberty" via Moses to be led into the "promised land" of freedom after forty years of preparation. The colonists had been led by God out of "spiritual bondage" to an unknown land "discovered" by Columbus. Here the colonists could worship God according to their own conscience and create their own governments that were initially patterned after God's revealed law. In 1639, the first written Constitution in America was prepared for Connecticut by Reverend Thomas Hooker and his friends. It, the Connecticut Constitution, was patterned after God laws found in the first chapter of Deuteronomy. Later the settlers of Rhode Island copied Connecticut's Constitution for their own Constitution. (For more details see Dr. W. Cleon Skousen's *The Majesty of God's Law*, page 24)

- Both groups lived in "the wilderness" for long periods of time in order to be prepared for their coming days of trial. Each felt the influence of their God; each depended entirely upon the mercies of their God out in their own "wildernesses," a long way from home.

- Powerful leaders, well prepared, were raised up out of both ranks to lead them into the "promised land of self-rule freedom." For Israel, it was Joshua and the others who had been trained by Moses. For the colonists the men we honor as our Founding Fathers, especially George Washington, were raised up and prepared for the roles that lay ahead of them.

They fought and won a challenging war and wrote and adopted the Declaration of Independence and the Constitution, two documents that would become a "Standard of Liberty and a Beacon and Ensign of Hope" for freedom-loving people worldwide. These documents were patterned after and inspired by the laws and statutes of ancient Israel. The Founding Fathers, like Moses, knew God and believed, as did Moses, they had been "chosen" to restore God's "perfect law of liberty."

- The actions of both Moses and the Founding Fathers were acts of "restoring" freedom to a world dominated by tyrants, with millions being held in the bonds of servitude and slavery worldwide.

Question: There are varieties of "People's Law." What are they, and how do they differ?
Answer: The two main forms of People's Law are those used by the United States, a **"Constitutional Republic"** form of government which provides "Checks and Balances" in authority; and a **"Parliament"** form of government used by Canada, Great Britain, and other nations in Europe and around the world. Parliamentary law is a popular form of government, but does not have the same **"Checks and Balances"** as provided for in the U.S. Constitution.

Question: What are the major differences between these two forms of "People's Law?"
Answer: With a **Parliament** form of government, the political party that wins a majority of "seats" to **Parliament** controls the entire government; that is, the ruling party controls both sides of the aisle, controlling the legislative body while naming the head of government from their members. For instance, in 2003, Tony Blair was the Prime Minister of Great Britain. But he was not elected by the people, as is the President of the United States. He ran, and won a seat to the House

of Commons from "a district" he didn't even have to live in. His party won the election and controlled Parliament. His party members then elected Blair Prime Minister of Great Britain. Blair then chose his Cabinet from the other elected party members of his party in the House of Commons. Many of the parliamentary forms of government continue to honor their "monarchs," as does England, but in reality the power of government is in the Parliament.

In the United States the legislative body, the House of Representatives and Senate, can be from one party, and the President can be from another party (a check). When this happens legislation can be stopped by either the legislative body or by the President with a veto, another check. In Great Britain when the members of Parliament pass a bill, often with only shrill voices from the opposition, there is little chance for a veto, except in rare cases.

There are numerous differences between these two forms of republican government. The following chart shows the location of Ruler's Law, People's Law, and No Law or Anarchy.

Question: What is Anarchy?
Answer: Anarchy is where no law exists. It is often referred to as the "Law of the Jungle," where brute strength and guns prevail, and where fear rules. The world still provides examples of this form of government. In 2004 the recognized government of Haiti, though weak, was destroyed and chaos reigned. Tyranny ruled until the rule of law was restored in America in 1789! In 2014 some areas in Middle East are examples of nations in near anarchy.

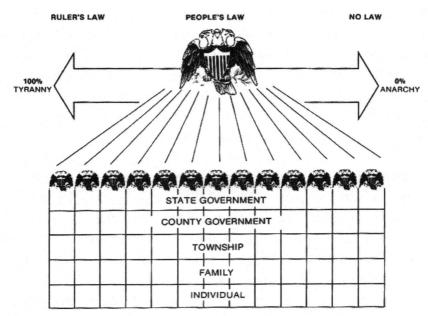

Vertical separation of powers allows the federal government to reach down to the states in specified areas.

This chart is courtesy of the National Center of Constitutional Studies, Malta, Idaho

Chapter Twelve

What is Freedom?
– How is Freedom Achieved?

Opening commentary: It has been said that freedom is a spirit, not a commodity. It has also been said freedom is an essence, a quality of spirit whose blossoms, when oppressed, can wither and die. Freedom, as the Founding Fathers learned, is not bestowed; it is achieved by fighting for it as the Founders did during America's Revolutionary War. And people died – thousands of them, and people still die to retain their freedoms.

And it has been said that freedom is not a gift, that freedom must be wanted and wanted enough to fight and die for it when necessary. Others say freedom is a conquest and that freedom does not abide: that **freedom must be preserved,** as more and more Americans are learning as today's dedicated enemies of freedom – the progressives, socialists and communists - continue in their dedicated and organized efforts to 'fundamentally change' America's Constitution and re-enslave America – and the world.

BUT when government pushes too far or becomes too radical the people will respond by organizing and begin to fight back. Many freedom loving Americans are just beginning to wake up and realize that they must fight to preserve their freedom today just as much as George Washington and his fellow patriots had to fight to win America's freedom during the Revolutionary War.

Following the elation of winning the Revolutionary War, but before the creation of America's Constitution, the challenges of making a free government work caused George Washington to become depressed. On November 5, 1786 Washington wrote to James Madison:

- "No day was ever more clouded than the present.... We are fast verging to anarchy and confusion.... How melancholy is the reflection. What stronger evidence can be given of the want of energy in our government than these disorders? A liberal and energetic constitution, well guarded and closely watched to prevent encroachments, might restore us."

Then, as conditions in the new nation continued to worsen, if that were possible, Washington, on December 26, 1786, wrote to General Henry Knox these words:

- "I feel, my dear General Knox, infinitely more than I can express to you, for the disorders, which have arisen in these states. Good God! Who...could have foreseen, or ... predicted them?"

Conditions did continue to worsen and on February 3, 1787, just months before the beginning of the Constitutional Convention Washington wrote,

- "If ,... any person had told me that at this day I should see such a formidable rebellion ... as now appears, I should have thought him a bedlamite, a fit subject for a madhouse."

The new nation had reached its lowest level of humiliation. Alexander Hamilton listed a number of serious challenges the new nation was facing: The Articles of Confederation gave the Central Government 'No Power to Act;' The Articles lacked fundamental power and authority to govern a nation. Shays' rebellion was taking place in Massachusetts and other states feared similar uprisings. There was no power in the Articles to raise revenue. There was an immediate need for a stronger union, and the United States was too weak to be feared or respected by foreign nations. If a man as revered as George Washington was depressed how must have the other Founding Fathers felt with state fighting state and with the military might of England, France and Spain waiting offshore to move inland

and re-conquer this leaderless nation floundering under a toothless constitution, and not having the power to act on behalf of the newly created thirteen states.

Yes, those were difficult times between 1775 and 1787 but no greater than the struggles America faces today at the beginning of the 21st century. Progressivism began poking its nose under America's freedom tent in the early 1900s and began wreaking havoc on America's freedoms as America **lulled itself into believing no one would want to destroy its precious freedoms**. Wrong! Since that War in Heaven, described elsewhere in this book, Satan has been active in destroying the freedoms of mankind, and frankly he has been quite successful at it, that is until God took an active hand in raising up a few strong well-educated leaders who yearned more for freedom than they did for their own safety.

Many, including me, strongly believe that God raised up and inspired a few very wise and noble men to restore freedom in the deep rich soil of America. **I also believe that He, if asked by a humble body of Americans, will again raise up wise and inspired men and women to preserve America and its Foundational Documents of freedom BECAUSE America has not yet completed its God-given mission.** America's inspired Foundational Documents were inspired to become beacons of freedom, liberty and hope to a world then enslaved by rulers who ruled with "Ruler's Law."

These Founders were men of faith, none more so than George Washington. But his words of doubt remind us that even strong leaders can falter in their faith in their fellow man as well as of their faith in God. It truly was a test of his character. And shortly after his February 3, 1887 depressed mood Washington was contacted by James Madison and soon became involved in the constitutional convention that convened in May 1787 and by September 17, 1787 had created a document that has served America and the world well, and will continue to do so, so long as men and women of character are willing to stand and do "their duty" in the face of oppressive opposition, as

Jefferson declared in the Declaration of Independence.

Bible students understand that God's miracles are most often accomplished through efforts of mortal men and women who are inspired by God in their efforts, as were Adam, Eve, Noah, Abraham, Isaac, Jacob, Moses, Joshua, Samuel, David, Solomon, and even America's Founding Fathers. God, I believe, worked through America's Founding Fathers to create America's Foundational Documents and has preserved them through men such as Abraham Lincoln and Dr. Martin Luther King. I see the inspiration of God in the creation of America because I do not believe any human being, without divine help, could have drafted a document as profound as the Declaration of Independence, where Jefferson boldly declared that the 'cornerstones' of America's freedoms were and are **"the Laws of Nature and of Nature's God,"** and perhaps without knowing it established America as a covenant nation.

This belief leads me to strongly support the belief that those men America reveres as its Founding Fathers were fifty-six men "endowed" by God with "knowledge and skill in all learning and wisdom" to create, adopt and sign, but not without strong disagreements and a few compromises, America's Declaration of Independence, while totally separating themselves from their mother land, and knowing full well they had just signed their own death warrants had their efforts to separate failed. Likewise those fifty-five men who in the summer of 1787 sat in a 'sealed' room, sworn to secrecy, for nearly four months to hammer out, often with heated debate, with some issues requiring as many as sixty votes to create a new document for governing thirteen very independent but connected states as one nation. This was a document that I believe was created to govern not only the United States of America but to become a pattern for all other nations of the world, who in 1787 were all ruled by despotic Ruler's Law.

There are those who contend that America's Constitution is outdated and needs to be modernized to meet the ever-changing needs

214

and mores of the "modern world." **I strongly disagree.** America's Constitution is a Constitution for the ages, as James Madison wrote to Thomas Jefferson, a Constitution that was inspired so that it could adjust to the changing times and needs of an ever-changing society without losing those governing powers inspired by the **"just and holy principles"** embedded in both of America's Foundational Documents by God, Jefferson's 'Creator and Supreme Judge of the World.'

Progressives, to be successful, have to destroy those **'just and holy principles'** that inspired the Founding Fathers who found these principles in their Bibles and then embedded them into America's Foundational Documents. **The first thing any despotic government does, including progressives, is to burn the people's scriptures.** Stalin did it, Hitler did it, and progressives will do it if given full reign of power. But with polls showing that eighty-five percent of American homes have a Bible and believe it be the Word of God, this may be a difficult goal for progressives to achieve, especially in a well-armed America.

But there is another factor involved in preserving America's freedoms that is too often overlooked, often totally ignored. I refer to this factor as the "Satan Factor." Americans, for the most part, understand 'good and evil,' attributing good to God but seldom fully associating evil with Satan. As much as I believe God lives and is real, so too do I believe Satan/the devil is real, and advocates evil. Why do I believe the devil is real? Because, as Moses declared, the devil is:

➢ "the father of all lies, [whose job is] to deceive and to blind men, and to lead them captive at his will, even as many as would not hearken unto my voice." (Moses 4:4)

The prophet Isaiah, in 14:12-17 supports Moses' declaration with these words:

➢ "How art thou fallen from heaven, O Lucifer, son of the morning! How art thou cut down to the ground, which didst weaken the nations! For thou hast said in thine heart, I will ascend into heaven, I will exalt my throne above the stars of God: I will sit also upon the mount of the congregation, in the sides of the north: I will ascend above the heights of the clouds; I will be like the most High. Yet thou shalt be brought down to hell, to the sides of the pit. They that see thee shall narrowly look upon thee, and consider thee, saying, Is this the man that made the earth to tremble, that did shake kingdoms; That made the world as a wilderness, and destroyed the cities thereof; that opened not the house of his prisoners?"

Geneses 3:1-5 declares how the serpent (devil) deceived Eve with words that read:

> "Now the serpent (Satan) was more subtle than any beast of the field which the Lord God had made. And he said unto the woman, Yea, hath God said, Ye shall not eat of every tree of the garden? And the woman said unto the serpent, We may eat of the fruit of the trees of the garden: But of the fruit of the tree which is in the midst of the garden, God hath said, Ye shall not eat of it, neither shall ye touch it, lest ye die. And the serpent said unto the woman, Ye shall not surely die: For God doth know that in the day ye eat thereof, then your eyes shall be opened, and ye shall be as gods, knowing good and evil."

John the Revelator, in Revelation 12:7-9, explains that the devil was cast out of heaven with these words:

> "And there was war in heaven: Michael and his angels fought against the dragon; and the dragon fought and his angels, And prevailed not; neither was their place found any more in heaven. And the great dragon was cast out, that old serpent, called <u>the Devil</u>, and <u>Satan</u>, which deceiveth the whole world: he was cast out into the earth, and his angels were cast out with him." In verse 4 John explains that it was a mighty war and Satan with: "his tail drew the third part of the **stars of heaven, and did cast**

them to the earth…" That must have been a huge war!

As this battle for the soul of man, between God and Satan, continues to play out, those willing to step forward and battle to preserve the precious freedoms of mankind need to be reminded of the words of Edmund Burke, a British philosopher and contemporary of the Founders, words of caution that read:

- "Self-government involves self-control, self-discipline, and acceptance of and the most unremitting obedience to correct principles. Its demands are commensurate with its high privileges. **Duties are the inseparable companions of rights.** No other form of government requires so high a degree of individual responsibility. It is ordained in the eternal constitution of things 'that men of intemperate minds cannot be free'."

Concerned Americans should not be deceived into thinking that this will be an easy battle to preserve America with its **'just and holy principles.'** But if America's freedoms are to be preserved men and women, of the same character as were the Founding Fathers, must step forward and become involved. Hand wringing and depressive declarations will be useless and those negative fears the people have for their children and grandchildren's future will come to pass.

We learned from Alexander Hamilton about a few of those challenging issues that created so much stress with the Founders. Now it's time to identify a few of the challenging issues that plague Americans today, issues, if not resolved, that could lead to the self-destruction of our beloved America, even as the Roman Empire self-destructed. In his famous *The History of the Decline and Fall of the Roman Empire* [1789], Edward Gibbon listed the five steps that led the Roman Empire into self-destructing. These five steps were:

1. "The undermining of the dignity and sanctity of the home, which is the basis of [all] human society."
2. "Higher and higher taxes and the spending of public monies for bread and circuses for the populace."

3. "The mad craze for pleasure, sports becoming every year more and more exciting and brutal."

4. "The building of gigantic armaments when the real enemy was within the decadence of the people."

5. "The decay of religion – faith fading into mere form, losing touch with life, and becoming impotent to warn and guide the people."

When one compares these five steps that led to Rome's self-destruction with the agenda America's current administration is following it is easy to see why so many Americans, especially senior citizens, those of us who have lived through America's 'Golden Years,' are really concerned about the direction America is headed today.

The following list is only a few of the issues now facing America. New challenges keep popping up every day as we see what appears to be a dysfunctional government heaping new abuses on a staggering America. But as much as they seem to be dysfunctional I believe they (this dysfunctional government) have a plan, a plan to dismantle America and make America "just another nation," not the covenant nation the Founders created beginning in 1776.

Ponder these self-destructing issues facing America today:

1. A citizenry generally ignorant of the history of the United States of America and how it was founded, by whom, and equally important – why?

2. A nation so deeply in debt that its debt threatens the very existence of the United States.

3. A nation that is fast becoming a welfare nation.

4. A nation whose tax code is so complicated and heavy that it destroys innovation and expansion.

5. A nation whose mainstream press has badly failed in its mission to investigate wrongdoing of the current administration.

6. A nation that worships environmentalism – not God, the God of America.
7. A federal government that has destroyed the world's greatest health care system with the Affordable Care Act, a law that was passed with lying, bribery and Hitler-like thuggery tactics.
8. A federal government bent on destroying America's second amendment and removing the use of guns by individuals and families for self-protection.
9. A nation, and press, that is using political correctness as a means of destroying the free speech aspect of America's first amendment.
10. An administration that is attempting to trample on the religious freedoms of all Americans.
11. A judicial court system that legislates.
12. A nation that is basically ignoring God's Ten Commandments.
13. A Federal Reserve Bank not accountable to anyone but themselves.
14. A divided Congress unable to exercise its constitutional powers effectively.
15. A government that has refused to balance its budget.

While this list sounds depressing these issues are not insurmountable. My beliefs also include the belief that America was chosen by God as the land where freedom and liberty could be reinstated by America's Founding Fathers. I believe it is also a land whose God-given mission is not yet complete, and that He will yet inspire and uplift those few who are willing to engage in this modern-day fight against the evils that are plaguing America today, even as evils plagued Sodom and Gomorrah anciently before being totally destroyed.

What many people miss in the Bible's story of Sodom and Gomorrah is, I believe, that Abraham, an advocate of the people, as Moses would be later, pleaded with the Lord not to destroy those two evil cities if there were ten righteous people left in the city. Note how Genesis 18:31-32 records this discussion:

> ➤ "And he said, Behold now, I have taken upon me to speak unto the Lord: Peradventure there shall be twenty found there. And he said, I will not destroy it for twenty's sake. And he said, Oh let not the Lord be angry, and I will speak yet but this once: Peradventure ten shall be found there. And he said, I will not destroy it for ten's sake."

The Lord apparently agreed but when His angels went to Sodom the evil was so pervasive they, His angels, told Lot and his family to leave and said, as recorded in Genesis 19:13:

> ➤ "For we will destroy this place, because the cry of them is waxen great before the face of the Lord; and the Lord hath sent us to destroy it."

And destroy it they did.

But how does all this relate to modern America, some will ask? There are those who believe that some elements in America are becoming as evil as were the people of Sodom and Gomorrah and are as ripe for destruction as were Sodom and Gomorrah. Another similar story is how the Lord destroyed his own wayward and disobedient people, the ancient Israelites. This is one of the major themes of the Old Testament. The story begins in 1 Samuel and ends with Malachi. This is the story, where after about 356 years of being led by the Lord via a theocracy with prophets like Samuel, corruption by the leaders became so pervasive that the people wearied of the corruption, much as what Americans are doing today, and the people went to Samuel and said:

> ➤ "now make us a king to judge us like all the nations" (1 Samuel 8:5)

Bible students remember how He gave them a king, but not before warning them of what a king would do to them, first Saul, followed by David and Solomon. However the Lord also told Samuel what a king would do to them. But the people rejected God's counsel and told

Samuel they wanted a king anyway. They got their king and eventually they self-destructed.

The one hundred and twenty years during which those three Israelite kings ruled were considered to be the Golden Years of Israel. Israel was the envy of the surrounding world, much as America has been envied by many other nations. But the good times ended and everything the Lord warned them would happen happened, just as the Lord told Samuel. This is a story Americans should take note of and ponder deeply. The prophecies of Isaiah, Jeremiah and Ezekiel all relate to this downfall of Israel, with the book of Lamentations recording the lamenting of Jeremiah over the total and final destruction of Israel – and of their enslavement and scattering. Americans should read and reread this part of the Old Testament. Its message is a warning to America. The parallels between what happened to ancient Israel and what could happen to modern America are striking and should not be ignored.

However, because there are more than ten people in America who are God-fearing and God- abiding people, God is not about to destroy America in the near future. But that is not to say that the Lord will not **rebuke and chasten** America to cause them to turn around and once again become that beacon of freedom it was for nearly two hundred years. I believe that if at least ten percent of Americans are willing to become involved in the fight to preserve America as God's Promised Land and become an example of a righteous people willing to help other nations bring true freedom to their people, America will survive. But it won't be easy, nor will it be a one night project. It will take time, energy, money, dedication, and above all Faith in God to Preserve America's Foundational Documents for the decades yet to come.

See chapter fourteen for details on how to bring about this Preservation of America and America's way of life when ten percent of its citizens are willing to become involved in Preserving America's freedoms and liberties.

Chapter Thirteen

Are God's Blessings, Curses and Wrath Real?

Opening commentary: The answer to both of these questions is yes. God's blessings, curses and wrath are real and this chapter will show where God's wrath is recorded in the Bible..

The biblical verses that reference God's wrath are many, but only a few of them are used in this book. However to help the reader more fully comprehend that the wrath of God is real several other verses are named as recommended reading.

God's Blessings, Curses and Wrath are Real

Question: What scriptures in the Bible would have caused the Founding Fathers to realize that God's anger and wrath have destroyed other nations for disobedience of his laws?

Answer: The following scriptures are only a few of the many that declare God's wrath:

> ➤ "And God saw that the wickedness of man was great in the earth, and that every imagination of the thoughts of his heart was only evil continually. And it repented the Lord that he had made man on the earth, and it grieved him at his heart. And the Lord said, I will destroy man whom I have created from the face of the earth; both man, and beast, and the creeping thing, and the fowls of the air; for it repenteth me that I have made them. But Noah found grace in the eyes of the Lord." (Genesis 6:5-8)

➢ "The earth also was corrupt before God, and the earth was filled with violence. And God looked upon the earth, and, behold, it was corrupt; for all flesh had corrupted his way upon the earth. And God said unto Noah, The end of all flesh is come before me; for the earth is filled with violence through them; and, behold, **I will destroy them with the earth**." (Genesis 6:11-13)

➢ "And all flesh died that moved upon the earth, both of fowl, and of cattle, and of beast, and of every creeping thing that creepeth upon the earth, and every man: All in whose nostrils was the breath of life …" (Genesis 7:21-22)

➢ "And the children of Israel went away, and did as the Lord had commanded Moses and Aaron, so did they. ¶ And it came to pass, **that at midnight the Lord smote all the firstborn in the land of Egypt,** from the firstborn of Pharaoh that sat on his throne unto the firstborn of the captive that was in the dungeon; and all the firstborn of cattle. … " (Exodus 12:28-31)

➢ "And the Lord said unto Moses, Go, get thee down; for thy people, which thou broughtest out of the land of Egypt, have corrupted themselves: … they have made them a molten calf, and have worshipped it … And the Lord said unto Moses, I have seen this people, and, behold, it is a stiffnecked people: Now therefore let me alone, **that my wrath may wax hot against them, and that I may consume them:** and I will make of thee a great nation." (Exodus 32:7-10)

➢ "**And I will make your cities waste**, and bring your sanctuaries unto desolation, and I will not smell the savour of your sweet odours. **And I will bring the land into desolation:** and your enemies which dwell therein shall be astonished at it. And I will scatter you among the heathen, and will draw out a sword after you: **and your land shall be desolate**, and your cities waste." (Leviticus 26:31-33)

➤ "Because Manasseh king of Judah hath done these abominations, and hath done wickedly above all that the Amorites did, which were before him, and hath made Judah also to sin with his idols: Therefore thus saith the Lord God of Israel, Behold, **I am bringing such evil upon Jerusalem and Judah,** that whosoever heareth of it, both his ears shall tingle. And I will stretch over Jerusalem the line of Samaria, and the plummet of the house of Ahab: and I will wipe Jerusalem as a man wipeth a dish, wiping it, and turning it upside down. And I will forsake the remnant of mine inheritance, and deliver them into the hand of their enemies; and they shall become a prey and a spoil to all their enemies; Because they have done that which was evil in my sight**, and have provoked me to anger**, since the day their fathers came forth out of Egypt, even unto this day." (2 Kings 21:11-15)

➤ "How hath the Lord covered the daughter of Zion **with a cloud in his anger**, and cast down from heaven unto the earth the beauty of Israel, **and remembered not his footstool in the day of his anger**! The Lord hath swallowed up all the habitations of Jacob, and hath not pitied: **he hath thrown down in his wrath the strong holds of the daughter of Judah;** he hath brought them down to the ground: he hath polluted the kingdom and the princes thereof. He hath cut off in his fierce anger all the horn of Israel: he hath drawn back his right hand from before the enemy, and he burned against Jacob like a flaming fire, which devoureth round about. He hath bent his bow like an enemy: he stood with his right hand as an adversary, and slew all that were pleasant to the eye in the tabernacle of the daughter of Zion: he poured out his fury like fire. **The Lord was as an enemy: he hath swallowed up Israel**, he hath swallowed up all her palaces: he hath destroyed his strong holds, and hath increased in the daughter of Judah mourning and lamentation." (Lamentations 2:1-5)

➤ "But when he saw many of the Pharisees and Sadducees come to his baptism, he said unto them, O generation of vipers, **who hath warned you to flee from the wrath to come**?

➤ (Matthew 3:7)

Commentary: Additional scriptures recommended include: Exodus 14:26-28; Deuteronomy 9:5-8; Joshua 6:21-24; 2 Kings 24:8-14. For more scriptures regarding God's wrath consult your Bible's Topical Guide.

Could God's Wrath come to America?

Question: Is God's wrath becoming more pronounced in our modern world?

Answer: Yes. God's curses and wrath are visible to those who have the spiritual eyes to see them - in many ways. America's Civil War is an example of the wrath of God. World War I and II are both examples of the wrath of God where over 100 million people were killed or maimed. The natural disasters that devastate the world from time to time are examples of the wrath of God, reminders to man that He still watching. The following scriptures are reminders of what can happen when a people or nation rejects God's laws and turns to idolatry:

➤ "**And every living substance was destroyed which was upon the face of the ground,** both man, and cattle, and the creeping things, and the fowl of the heaven; and they were destroyed from the earth: and Noah only remained alive, and they that were with him in the ark." (Genesis 7:23)

➤ "And Moses said, Thus saith the Lord, About midnight will I go out into the midst of Egypt: **And all the firstborn in** the land of Egypt shall die, from the firstborn of Pharaoh that sitteth upon his throne, even unto the firstborn of the maidservant that is behind the mill; and all the firstborn of beasts. And there shall be a great cry throughout all the land of Egypt, such as there was none like it, nor shall be like it any more." (Exodus 11:4-6)

➤ "And Nebuchadnezzar king of Babylon came against the city, and his servants did besiege it. And Jehoiachin the king of Judah went out to the king of Babylon, he, and his mother, and his servants, and his princes, and his officers: and the king of Babylon took him in the eighth year of his reign. ... And he carried away all Jerusalem, and all the princes, and all the mighty men of valour, even ten thousand captives, and all the craftsmen and smiths: none remained, save the poorest sort of the people of the land. And he carried away Jehoiachin to Babylon, and the king's mother, and the king's wives, and his officers, and the mighty of the land, those carried he into captivity from Jerusalem to Babylon. And all the men of might, even seven thousand, and craftsmen and smiths a thousand, all that were strong and apt for war, even them the king of Babylon brought captive to Babylon." (2 Kings 24:11-16)

➤ "So the people shouted when the priests blew with the trumpets: and it came to pass, when the people heard the sound of the trumpet, and the people shouted with a great shout, that the wall fell down flat, so that the people went up into the city, every man straight before him, and they took the city. And they utterly destroyed all that was in the city, both man and woman, young and old, and ox, and sheep, and ass, with the edge of the sword." (Joshua 6:20-21)

➢ "The princes of Judah were like them that remove the bound: therefore **I will pour out my wrath upon them like water.**" (Hosea 5:10)

➢ "The great day of the Lord is near, it is near, and hasteth greatly, even the voice of the day of the Lord: the mighty man shall cry there bitterly. **That day is a day of wrath, a day of trouble and distress, a day of wasteness and desolation, a day of darkness and gloominess, a day of clouds and thick darkness,**" (Zephaniah 1:14-15)

➢ "For the wrath of God is revealed from heaven against all ungodliness and unrighteousness of men, who hold the truth in unrighteousness;" (Romans 1:18)

➢ **"Let no man deceive you with vain words: for because of these things cometh the wrath of God upon the children of disobedience."** (Ephesians 5:6)

➢ "When Christ, who is our life, shall appear, then shall ye also appear with him in glory. Mortify therefore your members which are upon the earth; fornication, uncleanness, inordinate affection, evil concupiscence, and covetousness, which is idolatry: For which things' sake **the wrath of God cometh on the children of disobedience**:" (Colossians 3:4-6)

Question: How could God's anger/wrath come down upon America?

Answer: God's anger/wrath could come down on America is a variety of ways, as it has come down on nations all through history. It could come by invasion, as happened with Canaan, it could come as a drought as has happened many times in the history of the world, it could come in a form of hurricanes, tornados, earthquakes and volcanoes, natural events that cause food shortages, flooding, etc.

Matthew 24 is recommended reading in its entirety. It relates the words of Jesus spoke to his disciples regarding a coming disaster, a disaster not unlike what could come to any nation today, including

227

covenant America, if that nation rejects God's basic laws of civility and turn their back of Him. The following verses from Matthew 24 could reflect the world we live in today – in the 21st century.

> "And Jesus said unto them …And ye shall hear of wars and rumours of wars: see that ye be not troubled: for all these things must come to pass, **but the end is not yet. For nation shall rise against nation, and kingdom against kingdom: and there shall be famines, and pestilences, and earthquakes, in divers places.** All these are the beginning of sorrows. Then shall they deliver you up to be afflicted, and shall kill you: **and ye shall be hated of all nations for my name's sake.** And then shall many be offended, and shall betray one another, and shall hate one another. (Matthew 24:6-10) … When ye therefore shall see the abomination of desolation, spoken of by Daniel the prophet, stand in the holy place, **(whoso readeth, let him understand:)** Then let them which be in Judaea flee into the mountains: Let him which is on the housetop not come down to take anything out of his house: Neither let him which is in the field return back to take his clothes. And woe unto them that are with child, and to them that give suck in those days! But pray ye that your flight be not in the winter, neither on the Sabbath day: For then shall be great tribulation, such as was not since the beginning of the world to this time, no, nor ever shall be." (Matthew 24:15-21)

What were God's blessings and curses for ancient Israel

Question: Where does God name the blessings and curses he bestows on peoples and nations?
Answer: In two Old Testament books – first in Leviticus 26, then they are repeated in Deuteronomy 28. And these curses are not pretty.

These are the curses God declared he would put on a disobedient Israel. As a covenant nation, as was Israel, these same curses could well come down upon a wayward America.

The reader is encouraged to read Leviticus 26 and Deuteronomy 28 in their entirety. Both are eye opening. Deuteronomy 28 lists 14 blessings and 54 curses. For the sake of brevity only five blessings and ten of the curses are listed below.

Among the promised 14 blessings were:
> 1. And it shall come to pass, **if thou shalt hearken diligently unto the voice of the Lord thy God**, to observe and to do all his commandments which I command thee this day, that the Lord thy God will set thee on high above all nations of the earth:
> 3. **Blessed shalt thou be** in the city, and blessed shalt thou be in the field.
> 7. The Lord shall cause thine enemies that rise up against thee to be smitten before thy face: they shall come out against thee one way, **and flee before thee seven ways**.
> 10. And all people of the earth **shall see that thou art called by the name of the Lord**; and they shall be afraid of thee.
> 12. **The Lord shall open unto thee his good treasure**, the heaven to give the rain unto thy land in his season, and to bless all the work of thine hand: and thou shalt lend unto many nations, and thou shalt not borrow.

Among the promised 54 curses were:
> 15. But it shall come to pass, if thou wilt not hearken unto the voice of the Lord thy God, to observe to do all his commandments and his statutes which I command thee this day; that **all these curses shall come upon thee, and overtake thee**:
> 18. **Cursed shall be** the fruit of thy body, and the fruit of thy land, the increase of thy kine, and the flocks of thy sheep.

> 20. The Lord shall **send upon thee cursing, vexation, and rebuke**, in all that thou settest thine hand unto for to do, until thou be destroyed, and until thou perish quickly; because of the wickedness of thy doings, **whereby thou hast forsaken me**.

> 32. Thy sons and thy daughters shall be given unto another people, and thine eyes shall look, and fail with longing for them all the daylong: and there shall be no might in thine hand.

> 39. Thou shalt plant vineyards, and dress them, **but shalt neither drink of the wine, nor gather the grapes;** for the worms shall eat them.

> 41. Thou shalt beget sons and daughters, but thou shalt not enjoy them; **for they shall go into captivity.**

> 45. Moreover all these curses shall come upon thee, and shall pursue thee, and overtake thee, till thou be destroyed; **because thou hearkenedst not unto the voice of the Lord thy God, to keep his commandments and his statutes which he commanded thee**:

> 48. **Therefore shalt thou serve thine enemies which the Lord shall send against thee**, in hunger, and in thirst, and in nakedness, and in want of all things: and he shall put a yoke of iron upon thy neck, until he have destroyed thee.

> 58. If thou wilt not observe to do all the words of this law that are written in this book, that thou mayest fear this glorious and fearful name, THE LORD THY GOD;

> 61. Also **every sickness, and every plague**, which is not written in the book of this law, them will the Lord bring upon thee, until thou be destroyed.

Question: Has America ever been blessed since it because a covenant nation in 1776?
Answer: Yes, many times. These blessings would include:
1. Being settled by men and women who came to America to worship God.

2. The raising up of wise and noble men to write and implement the worlds two greatest documents of freedom since the delivery of God's 'perfect law of liberty' to Moses on Mt. Sinai.

3. The winning of the Revolutionary War by a rag tag army led by General George Washington at Yorktown in 1781, with divine interventions on many occasions.

4. The Louisiana Purchase, expanding America westward.

5. The North winning the Civil War and keeping the nation intact.

6. Opening America's doors to the economically and religiously enslaved of the world.

7. The signing of the Emancipation Proclamation by Abraham Lincoln in 1863.

8. The development of America as a capitalist nation where individuals are free to, with study and hard work, attain financial and spiritual independence.

9. A nation where the worship of God can be according to one's own conscience.

10. A nation where the individual can speak out without fear of the law

11. A nation where people can peaceably gather to protest their government without fear of reprisals.

12. A productive well watered land with abundant mineral resources.

13. Defeating evil empires during both World War I and World War II

14. Standing fast against the spread of communism by Stalin and Russia during the Cold War.

Question: Has America been cursed since becoming a covenant nation in 1776?

Answer: Yes. Few at first but in the past 100 years these curses have become more evident.

1. By not resolving the slave issue with the Declaration of Independence or Constitution.

2. The Civil War that cost the lives of hundreds of thousands of Americans on both sides.

3. The assassinations of major political and religious leaders in America. .

4. The great depression accompanied by the great dust bowl of the 1930s.

5. World War I and II accelerated the loss of the biblical principles America was founded upon.

6. By a people who are rejecting America's Founding Father's God, Jefferson's 'Creator and Supreme Judge of the World,' the Founder's God of Abraham, Isaac and Jacob.

7. By a Supreme Court that has weakened those inspired principles of freedom so deeply embedded in its Declaration of Independence and Constitution by America's Founding Fathers.

8. The killing of Abraham Lincoln in 1865, creating hatreds between the north and south that have yet to be fully healed.

9. The assassination of President William McKinley in September 1901.

10. The passage and ratification of the 16th and 17th amendments to the Constitution in 1913.

11. The bombing of Pearl Harbor in Hawaii on December 7, 1941 by the Empire of Japan.

12. The assassination of John F. Kennedy in November 1963.

13. The passage of Lyndon Johnson's Great Society.

14. The assassination of Dr. Martin Luther King on April 4, 1968 in Memphis, Tennessee.

15. The destruction of the Twin Towers in New York City September 11, 2001 by terrorists.

Question: Can America expect more blessings or more curses in the years ahead.

Answer: This answer depends on whether America's Spiritual Quotient rises or falls. If America's SQ rises, blessings will follow; if it falls, curses will follow that likely will include the wrath of God.

Chapter Fourteen

Three Powerful Biblical Tools Available for Preserving America

Opening commentary: Throughout the Bible one reads how fasting and prayer have been used by both individuals and nations to call down the powers of heaven and bring to bear heaven's power and influence to help resolve either personal or national challenges. Leaders of the United States have called on the American citizenry to fast and pray for divine help: George Washington did it during America's Revolutionary War; Abraham Lincoln called for a day of fasting and prayer when the future looked bleak during the Civil War; and President Franklin D. Roosevelt called for a national day of prayer and fasting when Americans feared an imminent invasion by the Empire of Japan at the beginning of World War II. And Americans responded with fasting and prayers and then saw miracles and divine interventions as America and her military Allies beat back and defeated the Axis nations after nearly four long years of killing.

Prayer and fasting are two of the powerful tools available to Americans to preserve America; the third available tool is the fourth of God's Ten Commandments. It reads:

> ➤ "Remember the Sabbath day, to keep it holy. Six days shalt thou labour, and do all thy work: But the seventh day is the Sabbath of the Lord thy God: in it thou shalt not do any work, thou, nor thy son, nor thy daughter, thy manservant, nor thy maidservant, nor thy cattle, nor thy stranger that is within thy gates: For in six days the Lord made heaven and earth, the sea, and all that in them is, and rested the seventh

day: wherefore the Lord blessed the Sabbath day, and hallowed it." (Exodus 20:8-11)

These three powerful biblical tools, when used by millions of Americans, will preserve America's freedoms, liberties and America's unique way of life. Remember E.T. Benson's description of a nation kneeling in prayer… **"The spectacle of a nation praying is more awe-inspiring, more powerful, than the explosion of an atomic bomb. The force of prayer is greater than any possible combination of man-controlled powers, because 'prayer is man's greatest means of tapping the resources of God."** This is an eternal truth. The ancient king Hezekiah understood this eternal truth; America's Founding Fathers understood this eternal truth; Abraham Lincoln understood this eternal truth; and Franklin D. Roosevelt understood this eternal truth. But does modern America understand this eternal truth? We hope it does, but only time will tell.

Hezekiah's story found in 2 Kings 20 is related here to emphasize this eternal truth:

> ➢ **"In those days was Hezekiah sick unto death**. And the prophet Isaiah the son of Amoz came to him, and said unto him, **Thus saith the Lord, Set thine house in order; for thou shalt die, and not live. Then he turned his face to the wall, and prayed unto the Lord, saying, I beseech thee**, O Lord, remember now how I have walked before thee in truth and with a perfect heart, and have done that which is good in thy sight. And Hezekiah wept sore. **And it came to pass, afore Isaiah was gone out into the middle court, that the word of the Lord came to him, saying, Turn again, and tell Hezekiah the captain of my people, Thus saith the Lord, the God of David thy father, I have heard thy prayer, I have seen thy tears: behold, I will heal thee:** on the third day thou shalt go up unto the house of the Lord. And I will add unto thy days fifteen years; **and I will deliver thee and this city out of the hand of the king of Assyria; and I will defend this city for**

mine own sake, and for my servant David's sake." (2 Kings 20:1-6)

Commentary: Few scriptures relate so well the speed with which the Lord will hear and answer prayers.

Regarding God's defending Judah and Jerusalem we need only turn to 2 Kings 19 to understand how quickly the Lord will hear the prayers of a humble America. Pertinent scriptures from this chapter read:

> ➤ "Now therefore, O Lord our God, I beseech thee, save thou us out of his hand, that all the kingdoms of the earth may know that thou art the Lord God, even thou only. ¶ Then Isaiah the son of Amoz sent to Hezekiah, saying, Thus saith the Lord God of Israel, That which thou hast prayed to me against Sennacherib king of Assyria I have heard." (2 Kings 19:19-20)… **And the <u>remnant</u> that is escaped of the house of Judah shall yet again take root downward,** and bear fruit upward. **For out of Jerusalem shall go forth a <u>remnant,</u>** and they that escape out of mount Zion: the zeal of the Lord of hosts shall do this. Therefore thus saith the Lord concerning the king of Assyria, He shall not come into this city, nor shoot an arrow there, nor come before it with shield, nor cast a bank against it. By the way that he came, by the same shall he return, and shall not come into this city, saith the Lord. **For I will defend this city, to save it, for mine own sake, and for my servant David's sake. ¶ And it came to pass that night, that the angel of the Lord went out, and smote in the camp of the Assyrians an hundred fourscore and five thousand: and when they arose early in the morning, behold, they were all dead corpses."** (2 Kings 19:30-35)

Commentary: These six scriptures relate two powerful truths: 1. That God is always concerned about his covenant people; and 2. That God saved a "remnant" of his people and sent them elsewhere (perhaps America) where, as Moses explains, this remnant could take root again and eventually fulfill their role in helping God "bring to pass the immortality and eternal life of man." (Moses 1:39)

When concerned Americans realize that they can play a major role in preserving America's freedoms by praying, fasting and keeping their Sabbath day holy they will then understand that the real solution for healing America's great divide will be a spiritual solution. And if Benson's vision of America on its knees comes to pass God will hear America's prayers and provide another Moses as He did for the Israelites; or a Jefferson, a Washington, a Madison or a Lincoln as he did for America when they prayed when they needed divine help to bring forth the nation God had in mind who would then "proclaim liberty throughout the land" – to the whole world.

Question: Where does America begin to help preserve its freedoms?

Answer: Most everyone is familiar with how human Intelligence (IQ) in measured. But few have ever measured their own Spiritual Quotient (SQ). Below is a Spiritual Quotient Chart designed to measure America's SQ – and yours if you're so inclined? Assuming that the SQ of the Pilgrims and that of America's Founding Fathers was 100, this chart provides you the opportunity to measure America's SQ and compare it to the Founding Fathers SQ. My evaluation of America's SQ today shows that I believe it has fallen to a 61.5 percent level. In my opinion America is dying spiritually and needs immediate attention.

America's Spiritual Quotient (SQ) Chart

No.	The Ten Commandments Biblical source for each commandment!	My personal SQ	America's SQ
1.	**Thou shalt have no other gods before Me.** Exodus 20:2-3; Exodus 34:10-14; Deuteronomy 5:6-7. **Commentary:** It's clear that America has replaced God with its own form of the Golden Calf and scores low on the point.		50
2.	**Thou shalt not make unto thee any graven image.** Exodus 20:4-6; Exodus 34:17; Deuteronomy 4:15-19. **Commentary:** America also scores low on this point because its number of graven images is numberless.		50
3.	**Thou shalt** not take the name **of the Lord thy God in vain.** Exodus 20:7; Leviticus 19:12; Deuteronomy 5:11 **Commentary:** As the use of vulgarity increases in America its ratings on this commandment begin to plummet.		55
4.	**Remember to keep the Sabbath day holy.** Exodus 20:8-11; Exodus 31:12-17; Deuteronomy 5:12-15. **Commentary:** As fewer and fewer Americans keep their Sabbath days		30

	holy, this rating will continue to drop.		
5.	**Honor thy Father and Mother.** Exodus 20:12; Exodus 21:15, 17; Deuteronomy 21:15-21. **Commentary:** Most Americans honor their parents.		85
6.	**Thou shalt not kill.** Exodus 20:13; Exodus 21:12-14; Deuteronomy 5:17. **Commentary:** The numbers who kill for the sake of killing are growing in the larger cities but generally are still low.		80
7.	**Thou shalt not commit adultery.** Exodus 20:14; Exodus 22:16-17; Deuteronomy 5:18. **Commentary:** As more and more Americans think of this commandment as passé this rating continues to decline.		65
8.	**Thou shalt not steal.** Exodus 20:15; Leviticus 19:13; Deuteronomy 5:19. **Commentary**: As social conditions worsen in America those who steal will increase and this number will go lower.		80
9.	**Thou shalt not bear false witness.** Exodus 20:16; Psalm 101:7; Deuteronomy 5:20. **Commentary:** As social conditions continue to worsen the false witnesses increase proportionally.		80

10.	Thou shalt not covet. Exodus 20:17; Proverbs 28:16; Deuteronomy 5:21-22. **Commentary:** As the government promotes income equality the people begin to covet anything and everything.		40

Question: How close is America to being spiritually dead?
Answer: Close. By taking your own SQ you will learn in what areas personal improvements are needed to restore your Spiritual Quotient. America needs help in restoring its SQ to a healthy 90 percent and this is where America's concerned citizens can help, thus helping Americans preserve America as a covenant nation for themselves, their children and their future posterity.

Question: How does this Spiritual Quotient chart help?
Answer: This chart points out America is spiritually vulnerable and strongly suggests that America's spiritual foundation has cracks in it and is vulnerable to those same diseases (curses) that descended on ancient Israel and caused them to be scattered and to eventually be destroyed as a nation.

Question: Are the Ten Commandments as relevant in the 21st Century as they were in the days of the ancient Israelites or in the days of America's Founding Fathers?
Answer: Yes! The following quote from Cecil B. DeMille declares the Ten Commandments are never out of vogue and are as relevant in today's society as they were anciently, perhaps more so. DeMille produced the movie *The Ten Commandments*. His words were spoken during a Commencement address given at Brigham Young University, Provo, Utah in May 1957.

- "Some, who do not know either the Bible or human nature, may see in the orgy of the Golden Calf only a riot of Hollywood's imaginations – but those who have eyes to see will see in it the awful lesson **of how quickly a nation or a man can fall, without God's law**. .. **If man will not be ruled by God, he will certainly be ruled by tyrants** – and there is no tyranny more imperious or more devastating than man's own selfishness – without the law. .. **We cannot break the Ten Commandments. We can only break ourselves against them – or else, by keeping them, rise through them to the fulness of freedom under God.** God means us to be free. With divine daring, He gave us the power of choice."

Commentary: Who amongst us today, especially from Hollywood, would dare speak such clear words to the world about the Ten Commandments? Few indeed, for his words would be considered politically incorrect and/or inflammatory by those who have successfully led the movement to remove God from America's public square, and especially from its public education classrooms. While I believe God is still watching over America he is now waiting to see if America will reconnect with Him after America's courts cut America's umbilical cord by declaring there is a separation between church and state.

But DeMille's words are still truth, and truth brings forth light and beats back darkness. While studying the LDS Institute Manual for Exodus 20 on my Gospel Library app I learned that the Ten Commandments "show us the three great priorities of life. The first four commandments show us our proper relationship to God. The fifth commandment establishes the importance of the family and proper family relationships. The last five commandments regulate our relationships with others. If we are committed to the perfection of our relationships with God, family, and others, we are well on our way to being perfected in all things." And then God will hear America's prayers, as He did the Israelites, and raise up a new Moses.

Question: Did George Washington ever allude to obedience to God's higher laws?
Answer: Yes, many times. Two of his more powerful quotes read:

- "I dwell on this prospect with every satisfaction which an ardent love for my Country can inspire: **since there is no truth more thoroughly established, than that there exists in the economy and course of nature, an indissoluble union between virtue and happiness**, between duty and advantage, between the genuine maxims of an honest and magnanimous policy, and the solid rewards of public prosperity and felicity: **Since we ought to be no less persuaded that the propitious smiles of Heaven, can never be expected on a nation that disregards the eternal rules of order and right, which Heaven itself has ordained:** And since the preservation of the sacred fire of liberty, and the destiny of the Republican model of Government, are justly considered as deeply, perhaps as finally staked, on the experiment entrusted to the hands of the American people." (Paragraph four, Inaugural Address to Congress, 1789)

- "**Of all the dispositions and habits which lead to political prosperity, religion and morality are indispensable supports.** In vain would that man claim the tribute of patriotism, who should labor to subvert these great pillars of human happiness, these firmest props of the duties of men and citizens.... **Let it simply be asked, where is the security for property, for reputation, for life, if the sense of religious obligation desert the oaths which are the instruments of investigation in courts of justice?** And let us with caution indulge the supposition that morality can be maintained without religion. Whatever may be conceded to the influence

241

of refined education…reason and experience both forbid us to expect that national morality can prevail in exclusion of religious principle."

Question: What would be another logical step for Americans to take to preserve America?

Answer: Enter into a personal covenant with America and America's God to better live his commandments, and to keep his Sabbath-day holy; willing to pray daily and fast when needed for America's spiritual, political and cultural health while helping Americans remember that their future depends on their obedience to what Thomas Jefferson declared were America's Foundational Laws of freedom – "the Laws of Nature and of Nature's God" – that is, God's "perfect law of liberty" – His Ten Commandments.

   Such a personal Covenant Contract with God and America might read as follows:

My Personal Covenant Contract with God and with America!

I, _____ covenant, as a citizen of the United States of America, to faithfully accept my responsibility as a citizen of the United States of America, the nation established by wise and noble men, men raised up by America's Founding Fathers "Creator and Supreme Judge of the World" to become a citizen dedicated to the preservation, protection and defense of those principles of freedom and liberty America's Founders embedded deep into America's Foundational Documents by:

1. Offering a daily prayer asking God to help preserve, protect and defend America against its enemies, both those internal and external enemies dedicated to destroying America.

2. Fasting and praying for the wisdom to know what I can do to help preserve, protect and defend America better against its enemies, both from within and from without.

3. Being more aware of God's commandment to keep the Sabbath day holy, and the blessings associated with keeping the Sabbath day holy, and the curses for ignoring this commandment.

4. Better educating myself regarding the source of America's foundational laws, "the Laws of Nature and of Nature's God," and of their importance in preserving America as a free nation.

5. Acknowledging that America's Founding Fathers, those wise and noble men who created and signed America's Declaration of Independence and Constitution created America as a covenant nation, a nation subject to the those same curses that destroyed ancient Israel.

6. Becoming one of America's covenanted citizens and join and associate with, when and where possible, other like-minded Americans in praying, fasting and keeping the Sabbath-day holy to preserve, protect and defend America's freedoms and liberties and work to elect men and women of character who will work to preserve, protect and defend America's just and holy principles of freedom.

Signed this____ day of _____ of the year _____

_____

Signature

Question: What would a 'Spiritual Formula' to preserve America as a Covenant Nation look like?

Answer: Such a Spiritual Formula would likely read: $F = G + B + M + P + F^1 + S$ where...

- **'F'** represents **FREEDOMS,** those potential freedoms available to America, and to the world, when America fully implements and protects all those "pure and holy principles" that were embedded in America's Foundational Documents by America's Founding Fathers when they created America as a Covenant Nation founded on God's 'perfect law of liberty,' or as Jefferson paraphrased God's law as "the Laws of Nature and of Nature's God," America's two cornerstones of freedom and liberty.

Commentary: This idea that America has yet to reach its full potential in creating freedom for its own citizens, while being an example for other nations, came from the opening paragraph in Frank W. Fox's final chapter of his 2000 book, *The American Founding*. It reads: **"America is first and foremost an idea. As such it can never be fully finished and complete – for it is an idea about perfectibility.** As long as people on the planet believe there may be better ways of doing things, the American idea will continue to prove elusive."

This paragraph reminded me of man's continual striving to become better, an opportunity available only when man is free and unfettered by tyrannical restrictions on the individual him/herself or of the businesses that must of necessity be allowed to be created by risk-taking men and women to serve the ever-changing needs of a consuming public, a public that creates with its buying habits the economy that provides for the betterment of all mankind. Two scriptures came to mind while writing this paragraph. Note how similar these two scriptures are. Their message, for me, is that mortality is to be used to work towards personal perfection, which is not attainable until one completes one's sojourn in mortality.

- ➤ "Be ye therefore perfect, even as your Father which is in heaven is perfect." (Matthew 5:48)
- ➤ "Therefore I would that ye should be perfect even as I, or your Father who is in heaven is perfect." (3 Nephi 12:48 – Book of Mormon)
- • **'G'** is for **God,** the source of all freedom. Remember John 8:31-32 – these scriptures read:

> "Then said Jesus to those Jews which believed on him, If ye continue in my word, then are ye my disciples indeed; **And ye shall know the truth, and the truth shall make you free.**"

- '**B**' is for the **Bible**; God's text-book for government and for reaching one's eternal potential.
- '**M**' represents **the millions of God-loving Americans** who also love their America and what it represents – an opportunity for all citizens to reach their God-given potential by using their agency to choose good over evil – and are willing to pray, fast, and keep their Sabbath day holy to help preserve, protect and defend America's freedoms for their posterity.

> "Watch ye therefore, **and pray always**, that ye may be accounted worthy to escape all these things that shall come to pass ..." (Luke 21:36)

> "… **pray** one for another, that ye may be healed. **The effectual fervent prayer of a righteous man availeth much.**" (James 5:16)

- '**P**' represents the **daily prayers** that will be needed to get God's attention. Remember what Jehovah told Moses about the prayers of his people in Egypt coming up to him.

> "And the Lord said, I have surely seen the affliction of my people which are in Egypt, and have heard their cry by reason of their taskmasters; for I know their sorrows; And I am come down to deliver them out of the hand of the Egyptians, and to bring them up out of that land unto a good land and a large, unto a land flowing with milk and honey; unto the place of the Canaanites, and the Hittites, and the Amorites, and the Perizzites, and the Hivites, and the Jebusites." (Exodus 3:7-8)

- '**F¹**' is for **fasting**. To "fast" is to prepare one's mind and body to receive an answer to one's prayers via revelation from the Holy Spirit or by the actions of others whom the Lord will prepare and send to aid the individual, individuals or nations who is or are praying and fasting for help. Moses went without food and water for forty days as he prepared himself to become Jehovah's chosen leader to lead the Israelites out of slavery and into the Promised Land. Christ prayed to His Father for forty days as he prepared for his three-year ministry. The following two scriptures show how fasts were used.

> "Is not this the fast that I have chosen? **to loose the bands of wickedness,** to undo the heavy burdens, and to let the oppressed go free, and that ye break every yoke? Is it not to deal thy bread to the hungry, and that thou bring the poor that are cast out to thy house? when thou seest the naked, that thou cover him; and that thou hide not thyself from thine own flesh?" (Isaiah 58:6-7)

> "And Jehoshaphat feared, and set himself to seek the Lord, and proclaimed a fast throughout all Judah. And Judah gathered themselves together, **to ask help of the Lord: even out of all the cities of Judah they came to seek the Lord.**" (2 Chronicles 20:3-4)

• 'S' represents one's covenant **to keep their Sabbath day holy**. Keeping the Sabbath day holy is God's fourth commandment and was mentioned earlier in this chapter:

Other scriptures that would have likely inspired America's Founding Fathers would include:

> "Yet **I have left me seven thousand in Israel**, all the knees which have not bowed unto Baal, and every mouth which hath not kissed him." (1 Kings 19:18)

Commentary: This scripture is included as a reminder that even with only seven thousand believers left in Israel God was aware of them and sent help when requested by prayers. In America that seven thousand is likely many millions of Americans that are willing to pray, fast and keep the Sabbath day holy to preserve America's freedoms.

➢ **"So the people of Nineveh believed God, and proclaimed a fast,** and put on sackcloth, from the greatest of them even to the least of them. For word came unto the king of Nineveh, and he arose from his throne, and he laid his robe from him, and covered him with sackcloth, and sat in ashes. And he caused it to be proclaimed and published through Nineveh by the decree of the king and his nobles, saying, Let neither man nor beast, herd nor flock, taste any thing: let them not feed, nor drink water: But let man and beast be covered with sackcloth, and cry mightily unto God: yea, let them turn everyone from his evil way, and from the violence that is in their hands." (Jonah 3:5-8)

➢ "Now in the twenty and fourth day of this **month the children of Israel were assembled with fasting,**" (Nehemiah 9:1)

➢ "Jesus answered and said unto them, Verily I say unto you, **If ye have faith, and doubt not**, ye shall not only do this which is done to the fig tree, but also if ye shall say unto this mountain, Be thou removed, and be thou cast into the sea; it shall be done. **And all things, whatsoever ye shall ask in prayer, believing, ye shall receive.**" (Matthew 21:21-22)

➢ "And he said unto them, This kind can come forth by nothing, but **by prayer and fasting**." (Mark 9:29)

➢ **"As many as I love, I rebuke and chasten:** be zealous therefore, and repent. Behold, I stand at the door, and knock: if any man hear my voice, and open the door, I will come in to him, and will sup with him, and he with me." (Revelation 3:19-20)

Ignorance of God can be Expensive – very Expensive

Commentary: Recently I reread a talk given by Hartman Rector Jr. in 1973, as recorded in the May issue of the *Ensign* magazine, a talk he titled "Ignorance is Expensive." While Rector's talk dealt mainly with the spiritual realm of life it came to me clearly, especially in today's challenging 'political correct' culture, that not only is ignorance of God's laws expensive, but that ignorance of the Foundational Laws of the United States of America, its Declaration of Independence and Constitution, is expensive, very expensive. It is so expensive, in fact, that in this one area of ignorance Americans could lose their treasured freedoms and liberties. The words of Rector that caught my full attention were: **"Ignorance is expensive; in fact, it is the most expensive commodity we know anything about."**

This book is written to remind those concerned Americans who are truly concerned about the future of America, not only for themselves but for their children and grandchildren, about God's love for America. We see how expensive ignorance is in every aspect of our lives, especially with government today in Washington D.C. and in the many state capitols where the laws of this nation are being written and implemented. In recent years many of the laws written and implemented are contrary to those **"just and holy principles"** the Lord embedded into America's Foundational Documents via its Founding Fathers. This must change! And only concerned Americans, you, can help bring about this needed change!

To emphasize this subject of ignorance the following scriptures are included that should help readers better understand just how much the Bible emphasized the need for ongoing education and knowledge.

The scriptures regarding ignorance include:

> "For this they willingly are **ignorant** of, that by the word of God the heavens were of old, and the earth standing out of the water and in the water: Whereby the world that then was, being overflowed with water, perished: But the heavens and the earth, which are now, by the same word

are kept in store, **reserved unto fire** against the day of judgment and perdition of ungodly men." (2 Peter 3:5-7)

➢ "Let him that **is ignorant learn wisdom by humbling himself and calling upon the Lord** his God, that his eyes may be opened that he may see, and his ears opened that he may hear; **For my Spirit is sent forth into the world to enlighten the humble and contrite**, and to the condemnation of the ungodly." (Doctrine & Covenant 136:32-33)

The scriptures regarding education include:

➢ "Hearken now unto my voice, I will give thee counsel, and God shall be with thee: Be thou for the people to God-ward, that thou mayest bring the causes unto God: **And thou shalt teach them ordinances and laws, and shalt shew them the way wherein they must walk, and the work that they must do.**" (Exodus 18:19-20)

➢ "Take fast hold of **instruction**; let her not go: keep her; for she is thy life. Enter not into the path of the wicked, **and go not in the way of evil men.**" (Proverbs 4:13-14)

➢ **"Train up a child in the way he should go:** and when he is old, he will not depart from it." (Proverbs 22:6)

➢ **"Search the scriptures;** for in them ye think ye have eternal life: and they are they which testify of me." (John 5:39)

➢ "That ye might walk worthy of the Lord unto all pleasing, being fruitful in every good work, **and increasing in the knowledge of God.**" (Colossians 1:10)

➢ "All scripture is given **by inspiration of God**, and is **profitable for doctrine**, for **reproof,** for correction, for instruction in righteousness: That the man of God may be perfect, thoroughly furnished unto all good works." (2 Timothy 3:16-17)

Donald S. Conkey

> "For the prophecy came not in old time by the will of man: but holy men of God spake as they were moved by the Holy Ghost." (2 Peter 1:21)

The scriptures regarding knowledge include:
> "And out of the ground made the Lord God to grow every tree that is pleasant to the sight, and good for food; the tree of life also in the midst of the garden, and **the tree of knowledge of good and evil**." (Genesis 2:9)
> "And I have filled him with the spirit of God, in wisdom, and in understanding, and in **knowledge, and in all manner of workmanship**." (Exodus 31:3)
> "As for these four children, God gave them knowledge and skill in all **learning and wisdom**: and Daniel had understanding in all visions and dreams." (Daniel 1:17)
> "The Lord is exalted; for he dwelleth on high: he hath filled Zion with judgment and righteousness. And **wisdom and knowledge** shall be the stability of thy times, and strength of salvation: the fear of the Lord is his treasure." (Isaiah 33:5-6)
> "**Ever learning, and never able to come to the knowledge of the truth**." (2 Timothy 3:7)

Commentary: This scripture from 2 Timothy seems to be a perfect fit for our day – **"Ever learning, and never able to come to the knowledge of the truth."**

**Becoming 'A Covenanted American Citizen'
And introducing "Covenant Nation's" web site –
www.donaldconkey.com/covenantnation**

Commentary: To survive as a free nation, led by God, millions of concerned Americans must become more involved, more involved in their local governments, and more involved in seeking God's help by praying for America on a daily basis, fasting when needed, and keeping the Sabbath day holy. And these Americans need to remember why America was created: 1. to be an example of a nation of free people led by God; 2. to assist God in freeing the world's economically and spiritually enslaved; 3. to be subject to those same curses that destroyed ancient Israel; and 4. to remind America that if it is going to return to its Founding Principles it will require America's covenanting citizens **to humbly ask God, America's God, the Founding Fathers' Creator and Supreme Judge of the World,** in daily prayer, fasting as needed, as did America's Founders, and to raise up men and women prepared by Him , as were America's Founding Fathers, to lead America through its coming challenges to remain a free nation led by God, while always remembering **The spectacle of a nation praying is more awe-inspiring, more powerful, than the explosion of an atomic bomb. The force of prayer is greater than any possible combination of man-controlled powers, because 'prayer is man's greatest means of tapping the resources of God.** The Founding Fathers accepted this eternal verity. Will we? Only time will tell.

Question: Who will become a Covenanted American Citizen?
Answer: America's Covenanted Citizens will be those Americans who are willing to become involved in preserving, protecting and defending America's precious freedoms by praying daily for America, by fasting as needed and by striving to keep their Sabbath day holy each week.

Question: Does the Bible provide guidelines on how to pray for God's deliverance?
Answer: Yes, in Matthew 6 Christ provides clear instructions. His words read:
> ➤ "And when thou prayest, thou shalt not be as the hypocrites are: for they love to pray standing in the synagogues and in the corners of the streets, that they may be seen of men.

Verily I say unto you, They have their reward. But thou, when thou prayest, enter into thy closet, and when thou hast shut thy door, pray to thy Father which is in secret; and thy Father which seeth in secret shall reward thee openly. But when ye pray, use not vain repetitions, as the heathen do: for they think that they shall be heard for their much speaking. **Be not ye therefore like unto them: for your Father knoweth what things ye have need of, before ye ask him.** After this manner therefore pray ye: **Our Father which art in heaven, Hallowed be thy name.** Thy kingdom come. Thy will be done in earth, as it is in heaven. Give us this day our daily bread. And forgive us our debts, as we forgive our debtors. And lead us not into temptation, but deliver us from evil: For thine is the kingdom, and the power, and the glory, forever. Amen. For if ye forgive men their trespasses, your heavenly Father will also forgive you: But if ye forgive not men their trespasses, neither will your Father forgive your trespasses. (Matthew 6:5-15)

Question: Can one person ever hope to influence a major political movement?

Answer: We learn from the words of Nehemiah's prayer how one person and his family were effective in the rebuilding of Jerusalem. Every one of America's Covenanted Citizens can become a modern day Nehemiah and be helpful in preserving those freedoms so many Americans fear losing. A personal prayer and fast, while keeping their Sabbath day holy, could be effective in helping restore those pure and holy principles of freedom to America similar to how Nehemiah's prayer and fasting led to the restoration of Jerusalem and its temple. Nehemiah's prayer reads:

> ➤ "The words of Nehemiah the son of Hachaliah. And it came to pass in the month Chisleu, in the twentieth year, as I was in Shushan the palace, That Hanani, one of my

brethren, came, he and certain men of Judah; and I asked them concerning the Jews that had escaped, which were left of the captivity, and concerning Jerusalem. And they said unto me, The **remnant** that are left of the captivity there in the province are in great affliction and reproach: the wall of Jerusalem also is broken down, and the gates thereof are burned with fire. ¶ **And it came to pass, when I heard these words, that I sat down and wept, and mourned certain days, and <u>fasted, and prayed before the God of heaven,</u> And said, I beseech thee, O Lord God of heaven, the great and terrible God, that keepeth covenant and mercy for them that love him and observe his commandments:** Let thine ear now be attentive, and thine eyes open, that thou mayest hear the prayer of thy servant, which I pray before thee now, day and night, for the children of Israel thy servants, **and confess the sins of the children of Israel,** which we have sinned against thee: both I and my father's house have sinned. **We have dealt very corruptly against thee, and have not kept the commandments, nor the statutes, nor the judgments, which thou commandedst thy servant Moses.** Remember, I beseech thee, the word that thou commandedst thy servant Moses, saying, **If ye transgress, I will scatter you abroad among the nations**: But if ye turn unto me, and keep my commandments, and do them; though there were of you cast out unto the uttermost part of the heaven, yet will I gather them from thence, and will bring them unto the place that I have chosen to set my name there. Now these are thy servants and thy people, whom thou hast redeemed by thy great power, and by thy strong hand. O Lord, I beseech thee, let now thine ear be attentive to the prayer of thy servant, and to the prayer of thy servants, who desire to fear thy name: and prosper, I pray thee, thy servant this day, and grant him mercy in the sight of this man. For I was the king's cupbearer." (Nehemiah 1:1-11)

Commentary: Yes, one person, with faith and a strong desire to become involved in preserving America's freedoms can make an impact, a strong positive impact, especially when that one person invites their family and friends to join them in fasting and praying for God's blessings on America, and that individual then becomes involved with a local active organization organized to preserve America's freedoms and liberties. And should tens of millions God-fearing American's join in praying and fasting for America, these tens of millions, with God's help will indeed preserve America's freedoms and liberties for ourselves, our children and our future posterity. Nehemiah's prayer is as relevant for America today as it was for ancient Israel. This is not Pollyanna talk – it is God's program - and it will work.

While writing these words the following scriptures in Matthew came to mind. **These words clearly explain what the power of faith, prayer and fasting will do** – help remove those mountains of corruption, incompetence and greed that now infest our governments, like termites, at most all levels of government. Yes, one person, multiplied by loving family and good friends can help begin the process of changing the direction America's federal government is now going. **It's either we, the God-fearing people of America who will do it, or America could soon be subject to the same treatment God gave to those disobedient Israelites long ago** – first scattering the ten tribes before destroying Judah. The Book of Lamentations tells this sad story in minute detail. It is not a pretty story, as these scriptures tell us.

> ➤ "How doth the city sit solitary, that was full of people! how is she become as a widow! she that was great among the nations, and princess among the provinces, how is she become tributary! She weepeth sore in the night, and her

tears are on her cheeks: among all her lovers she hath none to comfort her: all her friends have dealt treacherously with her, they are become her enemies. Judah is gone into captivity because of affliction, and because of great servitude: she dwelleth among the heathen, she findeth no rest: all her persecutors overtook her between the straits. The ways of Zion do mourn, because none come to the solemn feasts: all her gates are desolate: her priests sigh, her virgins are afflicted, and she is in bitterness. Her adversaries are the chief, her enemies prosper; for the Lord hath afflicted her for the multitude of her transgressions: her children are gone into captivity before the enemy." (Lamentations 1:1-5)

Faith in God, praying, fasting and keeping the Sabbath Day holy will help resolve America's existing challenges and problems:

➤ "And Jesus rebuked the devil; and he departed out of him: and the child was cured from that very hour. Then came the disciples to Jesus apart, and said, Why could not we cast him out? And Jesus said unto them, Because of your unbelief: for verily I say unto you, If ye have faith as a grain of mustard seed, ye shall say unto this mountain, Remove hence to yonder place; and it shall remove; and nothing shall be impossible unto you. **Howbeit this kind goeth not out but by prayer and fasting."** (Matthew 17:18-21)

One final Question: Will America and America's Constitution survive?

Answer: Yes, but not before both America and its Constitution are buffeted to near destruction – and hanging only by a slender thread. This book's mission is to help educate concerned Americans on its history, one person at a time, and then covenant to become involved in the democratic process involving 'we the people' and hopefully bring in ten other concerned Americans, be they family or friends, who will follow the same path and become a part of this growing movement to preserve, protect and defend America from its dedicated enemies - both from without and from within.

Ending Commentary: America is so badly divided, ideologically and politically, that a political solution is highly unlikely. America's enemies from within have been eating away, like termites, at America's foundation for a hundred years and only recently, with the rise of growing numbers of concerned Americans as a political movement have Americans begun to realize just how close to re-enslavement America really is. But few of these new organizations encourage the use of prayer, fasting and keeping the Sabbath day holy. They should!

Still there are millions of Americans who will be reluctant to exercise their rights and responsibilities as American citizens because they know not whom to turn to for help. Covenant Nation's web site, www.donaldconkey.com/covenantnation , along with another web site, **Treasures of Truth**, www.donaldconkey.com ,were designed to help bridge the gap between those who would like to be involved and those who are involved by providing supportive data that will allow them to make that leap of faith and become a part of a growing movement whose goals are to restore those pure and holy principles of freedom and liberty that America's elderly generations, those of us who fought in wars to preserve freedom in a war torn world, have enjoyed for many decades.

To access these two web sites, Google for:
Treasures of Truth @ www.donaldconkey.com
Covenant Nation @ www.donaldconkey.com/covenantnation

Chapter Fifteen

Brief Summaries of America Past & Future

Summarizing America's Past

Opening commentary: This book, Covenant Nation, is a brief overview of the important historical events leading up to April 30, 1789, the day the United States became a nation. This was the day George Washington took the Oath of Office as the first President of the United States and overtly reaffirmed America had entered into a political covenant with God by adding four words, "so help me God," to the prescribed Oath of Office

This book was also written to help Americans become more aware of how America entered into its political covenant with God, thus becoming a covenant nation, and to...

- Remind Americans that as a politically covenanted nation America is subject to those same blessings and curses God pronounced on ancient Israel found in chapter 28 of Deuteronomy- and to remind Americans that if, or when, America ignores "the Laws of Nature and of Nature's God," those laws Jefferson declared America's freedoms depended on, America could face the same fate as Israel?

- Point out the similarities between ancient Israel and modern America: how God prepared Moses and then sent him to free the Israelites from their Egyptian bondage and how America was created to free those being held in spiritual and economic captivity and bondage all around the world.

- Point out that both Israel's Mosaic laws and America's "the laws of Nature and of Nature's God" were founded on God's Ten Commandments, God's "perfect law of liberty" and were preparatory laws designed to lead their people of each covenant nation to economic and spiritual freedom.

- Point out that God made a covenant with Abraham and with Abraham's family, a family similar to most families, dysfunctional at times, and how He patiently worked with this family, continually urging it to become a better example to the world of how a free people led by God brings both spiritual and economic prosperity to the people and their nations.

- Point out how God preserved his 'perfect law of liberty' by having the apostle Paul take it to the gentiles where it, over time, became compromised, and how this compromise led to the Restoration movement, a movement that caused divisions to develop between the common people and their rulers, divisions over gospel doctrines and practices that eventually resulted in deadly religious persecutions, the persecutions that caused the persecuted to flee from Europe to a land prepared for them across the Atlantic where God's gospel message could be preserved.

- Point out how the hearts of America's Native Americans were softened so the influx of immigrants could survive in their new land until the immigrants could grow and organize sufficiently to create their own nation, a new nation where economic and spiritual freedoms could be re-established.

- Point out how Thomas Jefferson first referred to God as 'Nature's God' in the first paragraph of the Declaration of Independence and then, in paragraph two, he referred to God as the "Creator" and "Supreme Judge of the World." And with eight words, "the Laws of Nature and of Nature's God," Jefferson's words for God's "perfect law of liberty," strongly implying that America's future as a free nation depended on America's obedience to these two foundational laws.

- Point out that the Judeo/Christian Bible, God's textbook for life and eternal salvation, was a powerful influence to America's Founding Fathers, those wise and noble men raised up by God to establish America as a free and politically covenanted nation.

- Show the influence of the Bible in the writing of both of America's Foundational Documents by associating a biblical scripture to many of the phrases and/or segments of those two documents.

- Point out that America's freedoms and liberties were purchased with a price, much blood, but by turning to God in prayer George Washington was able, against great odds, to wear down a superior British Army that finally gave up and surrendered at Yorktown following a divine intervention.

- Point out that the major figures involved in the creation of America as a politically covenanted nation testified through their writings about God's involvement in their efforts to create a new nation.

- Remind America that its massive ideological and political divides will only be solved with the help of God if Americans turn to God in prayer, fasting, and keeping their Sabbath-day holy and then getting involved in the selection of men and women of high moral character as their elected leaders.

- Strongly suggest to America that it is more likely America's increasing natural calamities are being caused by America's growing moral decadence and rejection of God than by the warming of the atmosphere, as some would have America believe.

- Point out that Satan/Devil/Lucifer is real and is the epitome of evil whose role is to tempt mankind today even as he tempted Eve in the Garden of Eden anciently.

- Point out God allows, perhaps causes 'curses' to come upon America in the form of wild fires, lightning, tornadoes, hurricanes, volcano eruptions, droughts, flooding, reducing the food supply, or by epidemic-like plagues: diphtheria, flu, polio, Ebola, AIDS, or any number of other social diseases.

- Point out that the world has seen the wrath of God come down on nations on numerous occasions since America's Civil War began in 1861: the destructions of Germany, Italy, Japan and most of Western Europe during World War II are among those curses.
- Point out how that when 'the people' elect wicked or evil leaders they are heading for bondage, even as Hitler led his people to near total devastation – in only twelve years, 1933 to 1945.
- Point out that the Lord is real and does answer prayers – both for individuals and for nations as a whole. One of the more explicit prayers was offered by Nehemiah.
- Remind Americans that the prayers of a nation on its knees are, according to E.T. Benson "**... more awe-inspiring, more powerful, than the explosion of an atomic bomb. The force of prayer is greater than any possible combination of man-controlled powers, because <u>prayer is man's greatest means of tapping the resources of God</u>.**"
- Remind Americans that the quickest way to get God's attention will be through sincere daily prayers, accompanied with appropriate fasts, and by keeping their Sabbath day holy.

Question: Has America ever been blessed by God during its first 225 years?

Answer: Yes, many times. A few of those blessings include:

- Being blessed with wise men raised to create its Declaration of Independence and Constitution.
- Being blessed by its capitalistic monetary system that provides incentives to work and create.
- Being blessed by living in a nation founded upon those pure and holy principles of freedom found in the Bible.
- Few governmental regulations, until recent years, that allowed Americans to build its foundational industries that have hired millions of laborers that helped the poor to rise out of poverty.

- The freedom to worship God according to one's own conscience, not the states' religion.
- The right to organize and work to right wrongs. Examples of this would be the Suffrage Movement, the Labor Movement, the Civil Rights Movement, etc.
- The privilege of living in the world's first true pluralistic society – with people coming from all nations, all races, speaking many tongues, and bringing to America their own religions. This is perhaps God's way of testing His people to see if they will accept and live with God's 'other people' as equals, helping the less advantaged to climb God's ladder of freedom and prosperity.

Commentary: This book points out what most believers do not want to believe – that their freedom to worship God according to their own conscience was won and preserved by the shedding of blood in wars: the Revolutionary War; the war of 1812; America's Civil War; World War I and II; the Korean War and the continuing wars since then. This book also points out that the war for man's soul continues between God and his adversary Lucifer - in that never ending war that has both mortal and eternal consequences.

A Look at America's Future...

Commentary: This summary of America's past reminded the reader of those assignments God gives to those nations that become covenant nations, with those assignments assigned to America being: 1. to re-establish God's 'perfect law of liberty' back into the world; 2. to be an example to the world of a nation led by God; and 3. to assist God in the gathering of His scattered people. Knowing God's assignments for America the question then becomes: has America fulfilled those assignments? The answer: yes and no – a yes because each of these assignments has been partially fulfilled; a no because those assignments can never be completed fulfilled – they are endless assignments ever in progress. Before taking a look at America's future let's see what progress America has made in fulfilling these three assignments during America's first 225 years. This review begins by understanding that…

1. Progress was made **to reestablish God's 'perfect law of liberty' back into the world** when…

    ✓ Thomas Jefferson substituted the words, "the Laws of Nature and of Nature's God" for God's 'perfect law of liberty' in the Declaration of Independence, a document that was then signed by Jefferson and fifty-five other men in July 1776, thus affirming America had entered into a political covenant with God.

    ✓ James Madison and fifty-four other wise men sat in a constitutional convention during the summer of 1787 and crafted a document, America's Constitution, to implement and protect God's 'perfect law of liberty' embedded in America's Declaration of Independence, with thirty-nine of those men signing that Constitution on September 17, 1787, thus reaffirming what Jefferson and his people had affirmed when they entered into a political covenant with God and became a politically covenanted nation.

    ✓ George Washington took the prescribed Oath of Office as the first President of the United States of America and then added four words, "so help me God," to that Oath affirming again that America had entered into a political covenant with God as a politically covenanted nation.

    ✓ America's Foundational Documents became an inspiration for, and a pattern for the constitutions of nearly all the nations of the world in establishing written constitutions for their people.

2. Progress was made on America being **an example of a nation led by God** as it…

✓ Began to implement and put into practice "the Laws of Nature and of Nature's God," Jefferson's inspired words for God's 'perfect law of liberty,' and govern themselves – successfully.

✓ Showed the world how common men could lift themselves out of poverty by the sweat of their own brow, and rise above the level of poverty and more fully enjoy the fruits of their labor. They not only were examples to the world but they were also envied by the worlds enslaved.

3. Progress was made **on America assisting God in gathering his scattered people** when...

✓ America became the melting pot for the persecuted of the world, including the descendants of Judah who immigrated to America, in large numbers, where they prospered.

✓ Orson Hyde was sent to Israel from Kirkland, Ohio, where, on Sunday, October 24, 1841, he climbed the Mount of Olives and offered a dedicatory prayer that focused on three themes: 1. the gathering of Judah [to Israel]; 2. the building up of Jerusalem; and 3. the rearing of a temple in Israel. On October 24, 1979, in commemoration of this 1841 dedication of Israel the Orson Hyde Memorial Garden was dedicated on the Mount of Olives in the presence of Latter-day Saint leaders, Israeli dignitaries, including Jerusalem's mayor, Teddy Kollek, and Arab notables.

✓ With the urging of President Harry Truman the newly created United Nations in San Francisco, California, created a modern day Israel. The day following Israel's creation in May 1948 Harry Truman acknowledged Israel as a separate and equal nation.

✓ With the financial help of American Jews the newly created Israel defended itself and has become a gathering place for Jews from throughout the world, and a staunch defender of freedom and liberty in face of continued opposition by its Arab neighbors.

Commentary: While it has taken America a long time to make a little progress on its assignments we learn from Isaiah that God's ways are not always man's ways and that God has his own time table to accomplish His goals. Isaiah 28:9-10 explains God's time schedule for accomplishing his goals. These scriptures read:

> ➤ "Whom shall he teach knowledge? and whom shall he make to understand doctrine? them that are weaned from the milk, and drawn from the breasts. **For precept must be upon precept, precept upon precept; line upon line, line upon line; here a little, and there a little:"**

Those who combine their study of the Bible with a study of America's early history will clearly see these words of Isaiah in operation. It is difficult to read the words of George Washington and not visualize him as America's modern day Moses and/or Joshua – the prayers of gratitude he offered up, his prayers for help and with God coming to his aid time after time - or seeing King George III as America's Pharaoh, with England finally giving up only after seeing God create a mini hurricane to drive General Cornwallis' troops back to the Yorktown shore after he tried to escape across the York River, and then after surrendering at Yorktown, hearing Cornwallis say "it even looked like God was on his (Washington) side." God was on Washington's side. These words by Cornwallis were in effect comparable to the Pharaoh saying to Moses, after Pharaoh's son died of the plague – "go, take your people and go - go." Those scriptures remind us that God's ways are not always pleasant.

> ➤ "And Pharaoh rose up in the night, he, and all his servants, and all the Egyptians; and there was a great cry in Egypt; **for there was not a house where there was not one dead.** ¶ And he called for Moses and Aaron by night, **and said, Rise up, and get you forth from among my people, both ye and the children of Israel; and go, serve the Lord, as ye have said.** Also take your flocks and your herds, as ye

have said, and be gone; and bless me also." (Exodus 12:30-32)

Question: Is America going down the same path that caused ancient Israel's self-destruction?

Answer: Yes, but to understand how America is following the same path ancient Israel took it is necessary to understand the path the ancient Israelites took, following the death of Joshua, during those years they self-governed themselves and were guided by judges. These scriptures from Judges 2 are telling...

> "And also all that generation were gathered (died) unto their fathers: and **there arose another generation after them, which knew not the Lord, nor yet the works which he had done for Israel.** ¶ And the children of Israel **did evil in the sight of the Lord, and served Baalim:** And they forsook the Lord God of their fathers, which brought them out of the land of Egypt, **and followed other gods, of the gods of the people that were round about them, and bowed themselves unto them, and provoked the Lord to anger. And they forsook the Lord, and served Baal and Ashtaroth.** ¶ And the anger of the Lord was hot against Israel, and he delivered them into the hands of spoilers that spoiled them, and he sold them into the hands of their enemies round about, so that they could not any longer stand before their enemies. Whithersoever they went out, the hand of the Lord was against them for evil, as the Lord had said, and as the Lord had sworn unto them: **and they were greatly distressed**." (Judges 2:10-15)

Commentary: But because God loved his people he did not totally abandon them, which is good news for America, but raised up 'judges' to lead them out of their difficulties. Included among those many 'judges' who came to their rescue were Gideon, Deborah, and Samson.

Then, following their rescue the people would soon return to their old ways as these few verses in Judges 2 remind America:

> "Nevertheless the **Lord raised up judges, which delivered them out of the hand of those that spoiled them.** And yet they would not hearken unto their judges, **but they went a whoring after other gods, and bowed themselves unto them: they turned quickly out of the way which their fathers walked in, obeying the commandments of the Lord;** but they did not so. And when the Lord raised them up judges, then the Lord was with the judge, and delivered them out of the hand of their enemies all the days of the judge: for it repented the Lord because of their groanings by reason of them that oppressed them and vexed them. And it came to pass, **when the judge was dead, that they returned, and corrupted themselves more than their fathers, in following other gods to serve them**, and to bow down unto them; they ceased not from their own doings, nor from their stubborn way. ¶ **And the anger of the Lord was hot against Israel;** and he said, Because that this people hath transgressed my covenant which I commanded their fathers, and have not hearkened unto my voice; I also will not henceforth drive out any from before them of the nations which Joshua left when he died: **That through them I may prove Israel, whether they will keep the way of the Lord to walk therein, as their fathers did keep it, or not.** Therefore the Lord left those nations, without driving them out hastily; neither delivered he them into the hand of Joshua." (Judges 2:16-23)

Commentary: These few scriptures are likely the most important scriptures concerned Americans need to understand today as America is in need of another strong leader to get America back on track as a politically covenanted nation. Yes, these are scriptures about what Israel did but they also reflect to those willing to look at America's

225-year history, that America is moving along that same path that ancient Israel took. A few comparisons will show these parallels:

- Moses led the Israelites in the wilderness for forty years before turning the reins of leadership over to Joshua who was then given the ugly task of cleansing Canaan of those who were totally depraved, both as individuals and as tribes.

- Washington and those that were trained by him ruled America from 1789 to 1829 when Andrew Jackson was elected president. During this 50-year period America was being watched over by the Hand of God as it began to grow while becoming a beacon of hope to the world's economically and spiritually enslaved, a role it continues to play, even in our day,

- After America's Founding Fathers died and new presidents (judges) were elected, America's leaders began to do **"evil in the sight of the Lord, and served Baalim"** and forsook the God of their Founding Fathers, the God of Abraham, Isaac and Jacob. They failed to protect those minority groups whose religious beliefs differed from the more popular religions, driving one religious body, after their leaders were murdered, completely out of the then-existing United States. And they failed to eliminate the racial injustices that plagued America, worshipping power and money more than the God of their Fathers. America was badly divided and on the verge of total dissolution, something God was not going to allow to happen.

- God had prepared another Moses to come to America's rescue, Abraham Lincoln, who was elected president (judge) in 1860 and led the North to victory in what has been America's most costly war in terms of men killed, and families divided. Lincoln, a strong believer in the God of Abraham, Isaac and Jacob, wrote often of the times he had no other place to go except to drop to his knees and plead with God for help – and help came to Lincoln even as it had come to Moses and other believing leaders throughout history.

- And like ancient Israel, following the death of a just Judge, Lincoln, the people reverted to their secular ways, worshipping again power and money and failing to implement fully the just and holy principles of God's 'perfect law of liberty' that had been embedded deep into America's Foundational Documents.

- Other examples of leaders raised up by God to prevent America from being destroyed from without and from within would include:
  - ✓ General Ulysses S. Grant who became Lincoln's war leader and defeated the Confederate Army led by its formidable and honorable general, Robert E. Lee.
  - ✓ President Theodore Roosevelt who took on the 'robber barons' of America, those who bought power with their fortunes earned by building America's capitalistic foundation. Teddy Roosevelt also saw the inequality of the people and initiated steps that would allow individuals to rise up out of poverty through their own efforts and labor.
  - ✓ President Franklin Delano Roosevelt who saw the need to prepare America to fight a war to save America and the free world when America was then an isolationist nation.
  - ✓ President Harry Truman who had the courage to step forth and stop the advancement of communism and initiated both the Cold War and the Korean War.
  - ✓ President Ronald Reagan who saw the danger of creeping socialism and faced down Russia, strengthening America capitalistic monetary system, a

system that has allowed both individuals and nations to rise up out of poverty and live more prosperous and free lives.

Question: Will God raise up another leader to save America from itself, if asked?
Answer: Yes, but American believers must unite and get on their knees and ask. God, as we learn from His textbook, the Bible, does not interfere with man's choices until asked.

Question: Where would such a leader come from?
Answer: From the ranks of the American people. There are any number of qualified people in America that could be the President of the United States and lead America back to its initial path of freedom and prosperity build on that rock solid foundation of the pure and holy principles of freedom God embedded in America's Foundational Documents via Thomas Jefferson and other gifted Americans.

Question: What will happen if Americans choose wrong leaders in the future?
Answer: Two thousand years ago a wise and kindly king provided the answer to this question. Said he:
> "Therefore, choose you by the voice of this people, judges, **that ye may be judged according to the laws which have been given you by our fathers, which are correct, and which were given them by the hand of the Lord.** Now it is not common that the voice of the people desireth anything contrary to that which is right; but it is common for the lesser part of the people to desire that which is not right; therefore this shall ye observe and make it your law—to do your business by the voice of the people. **And if the time comes that the voice of the people doth choose iniquity, then is the time that the judgments of God will come upon you; yea,**

269

then is the time he will visit you with great destruction even as he has hitherto visited this land." (Mosiah 29:25-27 – Book of Mormon)

We close this book by declaring that the future of America is in the hands of its people. If the people choose good leaders, blessings will follow, but if they choose unqualified or unvetted leaders the following words from Deuteronomy will serve as a warning of what can happen to America in the future:

> ➤ "But it shall come to pass, if thou wilt not hearken unto the voice of the Lord thy God, to observe to do all his commandments and his statutes which I command thee this day; that all these curses shall come upon thee, and overtake thee:" (Deuteronomy 28:15)

The reader is encouraged to read Deuteronomy 28 and ponder both the blessings that can brighten America's future or the curses that will surely come if America continues to ignore God's **'perfect law of liberty'** or as Jefferson referenced it as **"the Laws of Nature and of Nature's God,"** those two laws the Founding Fathers signed on to when they signed the Declaration of Independence and the Constitution, and then were reinforced by George Washington when he took the Oath of Office as the first President of the United States and added **"so help me God"** to that Oath.

A closing poem: Because this book was introduced with an appropriate poem by John P. Foote it is only fitting that this book be closed with another appropriate poem by Mr. Foote. This closing poem reminds each of us of our mortality and suggests that the things we write, speak and do are recorded out there in time. When John wrote this poem in 1988, Americans had no idea that in 2014 one of the main political issues would be the Federal Government recording and storing personal phone and e-mail messages. The poem reads:

TIME
By John P. Foote

Last night in dreams, if I may prevail,
I saw the earth with a comet's tail.
But not a tail of icy rime
Just one composed of only time

Time's a dimension, as we all know
Like up and down and to and fro
If we can go back to where we were last
Then just as surely, we can find our past

So as each moment slips us by
It trails behind in a cosmic sky
For everything we have said or done
Is out there somewhere around the sun

Is out there somewhere for all to see
The sum and substance of you and me
An indelible record of all that's been
Of pride and passion and darkest sin

Of love and kindness and good intent
Of everything that our life has meant
The story is told of you and I
Somewhere out there in the starry sky

Born in 1927, Donald S. Conkey has lived through 87 years of America's most unique and fast paced history of the 20th and 21st centuries. He lived through the pain inflicted by the 1930s Great Depression. He witnessed the killing and destruction of World War II. He feared as the Cold War developed with Russia. He served America during the Korean War. He obtained his college degree using the G.I. Bill. He survived the turbulent and rebellious sixties. He lived well during America's Golden Era. And today he watches as America chooses false secular promises over God's promised freedoms, a choice that could take America down the same path that destroyed the Roman Empire and ancient Israel from within - as America abandons that God who gave it life and "who alone is able to protect them (America)." .

Conkey's belief in God, the Bible and America began on the lap of his mother. In 1956 he learned for himself that God lives and answers prayer. In 1980 Conkey began an in-depth study of America's unique history – a study that included a line-by-line study of America's Declaration of Independence and Constitution. Following a medical retirement in 1992 Conkey embarked on a second career – writing award winning op/ed columns with over 900 published to date – with each column posted on his web site – 'Treasures of Truth.'

In 1994 and 1995 Conkey and his wife Joan lived in Toronto Ontario where they were involved in 'Building Bridges of Understanding' amongst forty-five faith groups. These faith groups included all major religious cultures of the world and provided Conkey with first-hand observations of both the Christian and non-Christian cultures in action. While in Toronto he helped stage the largest tribute to the traditional family, the basic unit of society, ever staged in North America? That event, Festival to the Family, was staged at the Royal Ontario Museum in Toronto Ontario in December 1994.

Covenant Nation was written because Conkey believes America needs to better understand God's role in creating America as a 'Special Nation' of freedom and liberty – and as a Covenant Nation it is subject to those same blessings and curses as was ancient Israel.

CPSIA information can be obtained at www.ICGtesting.com
Printed in the USA
LVOW04s0554030315

429052LV00005B/7/P

9 781940 395807